Women, Family, and Class

Classics in Gender Studies

Michael S. Kimmel, Series Editor

PUBLISHED

The Jessie Bernard Reader, edited by Michael S. Kimmel and Yasemin Besen

Women, Family, and Class: The Lillian Rubin Reader, edited by Michael S. Kimmel and Amy E. Traver

Women, Family, and Class:
The Lillian Rubin Reader

EDITED BY
MICHAEL S. KIMMEL
and AMY E. TRAVER

Paradigm Publishers
Boulder • London

The Lillian
W. Mann's Odds of Montreal
W. Mann's Odds, North 23,096

Copyright © 2009 Paradigm Publishers

Published in the United States by Paradigm Publishers, 3360 Mitchell Lane Suite E, Boulder, CO 80301 USA.

Paradigm Publishers is the trade name of Birkenkamp & Company, LLC, Dean Birkenkamp, President and Publisher.

Library of Congress Cataloging-in-Publication Data

Women, family, and class : the Lillian Rubin reader / edited by Michael S. Kimmel and Amy Elizabeth Traver.
   p. cm.
   ISBN 978-1-59451-629-0 (alk. paper)
   1. Man-woman relationships.   2. Women.   3. Family.   4. Social classes.   I. Kimmel, Michael S.   II. Traver, Amy Elizabeth, 1975
   HQ801.W665 2009
   301.092—dc22

                                                                              2009015315

Printed and bound in the United States of America on acid-free paper that meets the standards of the American National Standard for Permanence of Paper for Printed Library Materials.

Designed and Typeset by Straight Creek Bookmakers.

13 12 11 10 09   1 2 3 4 5

Contents

Introduction: From "Worlds of Pain" to a "World of Choice"— Lillian Rubin's Worlds

One of the more striking features of a recent collection of autobiographical essays by well-known sociologists was the reluctance on the part of virtually all the authors to see their lives sociologically—that is, to see the role that structured opportunity as well as chance played in their rise to the pinnacle of their profession.[1] With only a few exceptions, the twenty eminent sociologists actually seem to have believed they were the "authors of their own lives," as the title of the book had it, as though the facts that they had been raised in academic families and had doors opened for them by the famous and famously connected had played no part at all. Justly famous were these scholars, perhaps, but strangely, and sadly, also somewhat myopic when it came to a distinctly sociological understanding of their own lives.

One of the few exceptions (and, in our reading, the only male exception) was John Gagnon, the lone proletarian, who, like one or two of the four female authors, saw his career as the result of chance, of luck and pluck. Gagnon titled his essay "An Unlikely Story."

Lillian Rubin's story is equally "unlikely." She was hardly to the academic manor born. Indeed, had you told her at age twenty-five that she would be the first person in her family to get a B.A.—let alone a Ph.D. in sociology and an advanced degree in psychotherapy—she might not even have known enough to laugh at how preposterous that prospect was.

And just as surely, Lillian Rubin is the author of her own life. Born to a poor Jewish family in the Bronx in 1924, she grew up somewhat religious and very

1

rebellious. Her father died when she was young, and her brother was an unreliable shield against a tyrannically harsh mother. Restless and curious, she was a constant thorn in her mother's side—for which she paid dearly.

She learned early to question authority, whether doctrinal or familial. She recalled in an autobiographical lecture that when she was eight years old, she decided to test God. On Yom Kippur, a day of mandatory fasting, she searched her neighborhood for an open candy store "so I could find out if God would strike me dead if I ate a candy bar." He didn't, "but the beating my mother visited upon me was worse than any of my childish imaginings about God." And then, characteristically, she adds, "Nevertheless, I found out what I wanted to know."[2]

She always felt marginal—whether in her family or in a society that didn't seem willing to embrace or accept her for who she was. That marginality defined her childhood, and she took it as a template for her self-authorship. She originally titled her book *The Transcendent Child* (1996), a group portrait of children who had overcome terrible, violent, or painful childhoods, after the old expression "Fall down seven times, get up eight." She was clearly talking about herself. Hers is a story of transcendence, yes, but one so utterly grounded in the social realities of class, race, and gender that it can also serve as a model for others.

As a young woman, Rubin's rebelliousness and restless curiosity led her, as it would so many of the contemporary founders of U.S. sociology (Daniel Bell, Nathan Glazer, Irving Howe, Norman Podhoretz, and David Riesman, to name but a few), to progressive politics in New York City. (Most, unlike the disgracefully apostate Podhoretz, stayed there.) As Rubin states, it was "a natural home for one who felt marginal and who also hated the racial and economic injustice of our society."

But even here, she felt marginal—or, rather, marginalized. There simply wasn't a place for a woman political organizer who was the equal of any of the dedicated leftist male organizers she met. She moved to Los Angeles in 1951, and struggled to be a good wife in the 1950s mold and mother of a young daughter (Marci was born in 1948). But she soon found herself immersed in local politics. By 1960, she was the campaign manager for Norman Martell's congressional campaign, and she also managed Jerry Pacht's campaign for Congress in 1962. And she felt alive and like she was making a contribution, living and breathing politics for sixteen, eighteen hours a day.

Thus, long before she received her Ph.D. in sociology, she was temperamentally a sociologist—sensing that in her marginality lay the keys to understanding her experience and an angle of vision of social dynamics those in the center could only understand, at best, by projection.

One could argue that Rubin was "premature," or before her time, in several other important ways as well. She was a "premature" feminist—a feminist before there was even a name for it. She entered the 1960s a "premature" divorcee—long before divorce was trendy or, at least, commonplace, at a time when people still expressed dismay and compassion for her daughter growing up in a "broken home." And in 1962, she met and married Hank Rubin, himself a "premature antifascist" who had enlisted with the Abraham Lincoln Brigades to fight for the fragile fledgling Spanish Republic in 1936.

Soon after her move to the Bay Area to join Hank in 1962, Rubin became a most "mature" undergraduate student at the University of California–Berkeley—at the ripe old age of thirty-nine. Such structural marginality—she was the age of most of her undergraduate cohort's mothers (literally: her daughter, Marci, would soon enter Berkeley as an undergrad just as Lillian was graduating)—was heightened as she entered the graduate program in sociology at Berkeley in 1967. At the time, the reigning paradigms of the field were what C. Wright Mills had called "grand theory" (Parsonian functionalism) and "abstracted empiricism" (doctrinaire quantitative research) represented in the department by Neil Smelser and Charles Glock, respectively.

For Rubin, both perspectives seemed too grandiose and too removed from real people's experiences. "What [people] think or feel, how they respond to the social forces that seek to mold them, how they interpret their behavior and attitudes—in essence, what *subjective* meanings they give to their own experiences and how those affect their relationship to both self and society—these are of minor concern to the sociologist," she would later write.

As a result, even before she finished her dissertation, Rubin enrolled in a graduate program in clinical psychology. And although she finished that program and became a licensed therapist, her sociological imagination put her at odds with that field as well. Clinicians seemed "so concerned with the particular and the individual" that they would "lose sight of the social context within which human life takes place" and thus "fail to comprehend the ways in which society and personality live in a continuing and dialectical relationship with each other."

For her entire career she straddled both fields, never completely fitting into either. At times, it's been convenient for psychologists to claim her, especially when her books on male-female relationships (*Intimate Strangers* [1983] and *Just Friends* [1985]) were climbing up the best-seller lists, but in general, as she says, psychologists "complain that I give too much attention to the social forces that frame people's lives and not enough to the internal dynamic ones that may also lock people in."

Sociologists wonder, however, whether all this concern with internal dynamics is really sociology. Rubin is clear, however, about where she truly lives. As she writes of one of her books, *Families on the Fault Line* (1994): "The fact that the central argument of the work is a sociological one—that is, that the family is a social institution whose socially structured internal arrangements have a profound influence on human development—is somehow lost on these critics who complain about its psychological focus."

This effort to balance psychology and sociology, the larger structural forces and the voices of individuals navigating their way through those structures, as well as her continued, even self-nurtured marginality, forms the core of Rubin's innovative, signature methodology. The conventional wisdom in sociology is that quantitative data focus the eyes downward from above, providing the broad outlines in black and white, the patterns that are the essence of social structures. Ethnography and fieldwork, by contrast, put the ear to the ground and hear people's voices, adding nuance, subtleties, texture and color, the lived experience, to the broad patterns of the large-scale dataset.

Rubin's interview technique focuses on both structure and the people who live within it. By interviewing targeted individuals, she not only observes the texture of people's lives but enables the reader to understand the way social structures are inhabited by the very people whose lives are also circumscribed by them. Her subjects are active agents in their own lives, perhaps even "authors" of their own lives, while they simultaneously feel buffeted by forces outside of their control.

Such engaged and empathic interviewing was embraced initially by feminist researchers as a corrective to the misguided efforts at "objectivity" counseled by other qualitative methodologists. This embrace dovetailed with trends in anthropology, championed by James Clifford and others, in which the researcher was beginning to insert him- or herself into the narrative of the "other culture" to make explicit the dialogic relationship between interviewer and subject. In sociological works by Rubin, Arlie Hochschild, and several others, the empathic, focused, and structured "snowball" interview was developed within sociology.

Substantively as well as politically a feminist, Rubin also sensed that her story was not *only* her story—that her own experiences of navigating the world mapped out for her by tradition and male prerogative were shared by many women of her generation. And, like other pioneers such as Betty Friedan, she wrote her own experiences on a much larger canvas. But Rubin has always managed to touch a sore point in the zeitgeist, to bring up an inconvenient truth—her own.

When the second-wave feminist movement had begun to be written entirely by white middle-class women, Rubin's breakthrough book, *Worlds of Pain* (1976), reminded them that their self-congratulatory tone excluded the voices of white working-class women. When younger women were reclaiming their bodies and themselves, Rubin discussed the impact of feminism on older women in *Women of a Certain Age* (1979).

When her feminist friends and colleagues had described male-female relationships—sexual and romantic, and even friendships—as utterly overdetermined by patriarchy and gender inequality, Rubin responded with three works of her own—*Intimate Strangers* (1983), *Just Friends* (1985), and *Erotic Wars* (1990)—that deftly married structural dynamics of gender relations, economic shifts, and family changes to the *pas de deux* (or, perhaps as likely, the *folie à deux*) that often characterized Americans' fumbling attempts to relate to the opposite sex.

And when multicultural feminists' insistence on racial difference seemed to tear apart the fictive unity of the women's movement, Rubin's *Families on the Fault Line* (1994) reminded readers that race and class are so intimately intertwined in U.S. society that one often serves as a proxy for the other (when Americans hear the word "poverty" most of them often conjure up the image of a black person). Moreover, class and race are also inextricably joined to gender (the black person imagined was probably a woman).

In that sense, Lillian Rubin was the first intersectionalist. From *Worlds of Pain* in 1976 to her most recent forays into political journalism with articles such as "Welcome to the World of Choice," she has managed to juggle race and class and gender by neither subsuming one or two under the reductionist rubric of the third nor diluting them so they cease to bear any singular identifying characteristics. It has been Rubin's great achievement as a social scientist to explain the gendered politics of racial and class resentment, the racial politics of class and gender resentment, and the worlds of pain of specifically white working-class women.

And it's obviously struck a nerve. When American Sociological Association president Herbert Gans compiled a list of the best-selling sociology books of the second half of the twentieth century, two of Rubin's books appeared in the top ten (*Worlds of Pain* at no. 8 and *Intimate Strangers* at no. 9; *Just Friends* was no. 33). Equally significant, she was the only sociologist to appear twice in the top ten, and the only woman in the top fifteen.[3]

Her work struck that nerve, we think, in part because her vision was intersectional before feminist social scientists had a word for it. For what is intersectionality other than a constant—and constantly shifting—focus on marginality? No sooner does one angle of vision emerge than it must be interrogated, decentered, and the event seen from other, multiple, perspectives. Lillian Rubin advocated intersectional analysis not because it suited her political or professional ambitions but because for her there was little choice. Intersectionality is the perspective of restless marginality.

Looking back at her work more than a decade ago, Rubin commented that her marginality—class, age, or profession—was among the defining features of her life. It's had its downside, to be sure—there is always an emotional cost, the pain of not feeling like you fit in, especially when you want desperately to fit in. But there are benefits as well, she notes: "Being outside the system has allowed me to do the work I wanted to do without interference or worries about the judgments of its gatekeepers."

NOTES

1. Bennett M. Berger, *Authors of Their Own Lives* (Berkeley: University of California Press, 1990).
2. All quotations from Rubin, except where noted, are taken from a 1992 speech delivered to the faculty at Queens College as she took up the position of distinguished professor on that City University of New York campus.
3. Herbert J. Gans, "Best-Sellers by Sociologists: An Exploratory Study," *Contemporary Sociology* 26, no. 2 (1997): 131–135.

PART I

ASKING LIKE A THERAPIST, LISTENING AS A SOCIOLOGIST

Up from the Immigrant Ghetto

I started out to do a paper entitled "Family Values and the Invisible Middle Class," which argues that the national discourse on family life that has so engaged this nation in recent years is a discussion in a vacuum. For as family values advocates frame it, the family itself *becomes* the context, as if families were atoms afloat in space, unconnected to the social and institutional life in which they're embedded.

Class plays no part in this discourse. Yet it's obvious to anyone willing to stop and think about it for even a moment that the class status of a family is the single most important element in determining where and how it fits into the social and institutional life of the community. Which means that it determines the experiences of every family member—from the schools children attend, to the kind of work parents do, to the financial and social resources available to them, to the issues that preoccupy and engage them.

But since I've just finished a memoir in which my own background as an immigrant working-class girl figures very largely, I thought I'd rather do a more personal kind of telling here because it's so perfectly reflective of the often invisible ways immigration, class, and gender affect the course of a life. And also how hard it is to put those experiences behind us—even when, in adulthood, our lives are very far removed from them.

Not, mind you, that I knew the words *working class* when I was growing up. I knew we were poor, of course, and that my mother worked in a factory—and I very early on learned to be ashamed of that. And I knew, too, that my teachers saw me and my immigrant family as some kind of savages that had to be civilized as quickly as possible. But in all the years I went to the NYC schools—from first grade through twelfth—I never heard the word *class*.

I was born in 1924, just ten months after my parents and brother (then six months old) arrived from Russia and settled in Philadelphia, where my father had family. My father died when I was five years old, leaving my mother, a twenty-seven-year-old illiterate immigrant who spoke only the most rudimentary English, with two

9

small children to support and no way to do it. She looked for work cleaning other people's houses, but in 1929, the beginning of the Great Depression, there wasn't much call for her services. As she cast about desperately for alternatives, one of my father's brothers urged her to come to New York and try her luck there. Within a year after my father's death, we moved away from the family and community I'd known all my life. By then I was nearly six years old; time to go to school.

Yiddish was the language of the home I grew up in as well as the tongue of most of the Philadelphia community in which we had lived. It was in my first grade classroom, therefore, that I had my first serious brush with English. But none of the programs that so commonly ease the way for immigrant children today were available then. Our teachers—often young women just a generation away from their own immigrant experiences—helped us with a word when we got stuck, but turned a deaf ear when, in frustration, a child broke into a foreign language, whether Yiddish or Italian—the other large language group in the schools I attended. The rules were clear and unrelenting: We were to speak only English while our teachers inducted us into American ways with a fervor that suggested we were embarrassing reminders of a past they wanted to leave behind.

But giving up the language that frames our world from infancy through early childhood isn't easy. I don't just mean that it's hard to learn a second language. That's true, but far easier than the psychological feat necessary to abandon our mother tongue. For a language is more than its words and syntax; it's a way of thinking about the world, of meeting it, of being in it. When we learn a language, we absorb its aura—its rhythms, its color, its emotion, its lightness and darkness, its subtleties of expression and meaning, To give it up means relinquishing a part of ourselves, the part that experienced the world through that language.

A word learned in early childhood carries with it an accumulation of associations that give it its emotional power. The same word translated later into the new language is stripped of its internal resonance. So, for example, even after I could understand the meaning of the word *tree,* the word had no evocative power. It was a word without pictures, a word sundered from the thing it was meant to represent. It took a long time before I could associate it internally with the vibrant, changing, living *boim* (the Yiddish word) whose leafy branches shaded me on a hot summer day.

Children in non-English-speaking immigrant families also often have difficulty with English because of the split between their private and public worlds—between the family language, with its familiar, welcoming warmth, and the public language, with its cold, unfeeling words that are so strange on the tongue.

For me, learning English was easier partly because I had so little to hold on to from the past. Whatever safety and comfort existed in my family life were shattered by the death of my father and our move from the familiar neighborhood in Philadelphia to the Bronx in New York. My mother and I had a difficult relationship even before my father's death; afterward she became more embittered and rejecting. In defense against the anger she acted out on both my body and my soul, I did what I could to distance myself from her. If she embodied the old ways, I would reach for the new. If she spoke Yiddish, I would speak only English.

As both the internal and external pressures toward Americanization increased, I became more and more shamed by our foreignness and more alienated from my family. True, my troubled relationship with my mother escalated that, but even in families where parents and children live more harmoniously, some level of alienation is one of the uncounted costs of the prejudice immigrants meet when they come to this land of their dreams. As their children endeavor to become *real* Americans, to be accepted by the world around them, they adopt the public attitudes as their own and try to protect themselves from the barbs and jeers by distancing themselves from their heritage and shrinking from any public expression of their difference.

By the time my first year at school was over, I was well on my way to fluency in my new language. My mother knew some English by then, but not enough to make her way easily in the world. So my brother and I became her teachers.

This reversal of roles—children as teachers—is one of the more agonizing issues in immigrant family life. Talk about a generation gap! In immigrant families it's more like a canyon. As children become increasingly comfortable in the public world, they not only distance themselves from the family culture, they become their parents' guides through the social and institutional maze of the new land.

But a child's help comes at a price. For the child who is also a parent's teacher is less likely to give unreflective assent to parental knowledge and authority—a shift in the dynamics of the family that's rarely spoken about but that's felt, even if not openly acknowledged, by all.

It's easy to see why and how this reversal of roles between parents and their children is so hard for the adults. But it's equally fraught for the children. Until I became her guide in the public world, my mother seemed huge to me, a powerful woman whose word was law, even when I violated it; the woman who controlled my world, even when I fought her so tenaciously and won an occasional battle.

When it became clear that there were important ways in which she couldn't navigate the larger world as well as I could, that changed. She seemed smaller, diminished—a vision that, given the difficulty of our relationship, was at once relieving and frightening. There was something satisfying in seeing her cut down to size while, at the same time, it was anxiety-provoking, since it shook my belief in her strength and power—a belief a child needs if she's to feel safe in the world.

It was common in those years for poor immigrant families to take in lodgers or boarders, or for one poor family to rent space to another. So for the first year or so after we arrived in the Bronx, we moved into a series of apartments that were already too small for the family that lived there. Sometimes there was a bathroom in the apartment; sometimes it was in the hall outside. My mother, brother, and I lived and slept in one of the rooms and had what were called *kitchen privileges*. Which meant my mother was allowed some space in the ice box and could cook our meals at specified times.

It wasn't until my mother found her way into New York's garment industry that we were able to move into an apartment of our own. The building we moved into—one of the many dreary, red brick, six-story walkup buildings that lined the neighborhoods we lived in—was no different than the one we left when we lived with others. Our apartment was on the fourth floor—a tiny one-room studio with a bed in one wall, a cramped little kitchenette along another, our very own bathroom, and a window that faced a brick wall so close you could almost reach out and touch it. It was dark and cold in the winter, dark and hot in the summer, but it was ours. My mother and I slept in the bed; my brother was on a cot. I was seven years old.

Later, when I was eleven and my brother nearly thirteen, my mother decided we should no longer be sleeping in the same room, and we moved to a one-bedroom apartment—the only one of the many moves we made throughout my childhood that I ever appreciated. After years in a single room, an apartment with a real kitchen, a living room, and a bedroom felt nearly palatial to me. I still shared a bed with my mother at night, but for the first time it was possible—during waking hours at least— to find a corner where I could retreat behind my book without being in sight and sound of her, without having to listen to her complain, "You think you're smarter than everybody else with your nose always stuck in a book."

At work, my mother took her place among the dozens of women who sat hunched over their sewing machines in a large, noisy, dank, and airless room. Eight hours a day on Monday through Friday and four on Saturday they sat there, their hands and feet flying, an occasional shrill scream punctuating the air when, in their haste, they didn't get a thumb or forefinger out of the way of the machine's needle. They were piece workers, these women, paid a few cents for every garment they sewed. No benefits, no overtime, just the privilege of working long hours in abominable conditions for subsistence wages.

Although my mother worked in several different places over the years, those I saw all looked alike to me—the same dirt, the same noise, the same lint-clogged air, the same foul smell, the same cold in the winter, the same oppressive heat in the summer, and the same row upon row of women doing the same repetitive task, hour after hour, day after day, year after year.

I hated the look, feel, smell, and noise of those places. I hated the women in the office who treated the factory workers with such disdain—women who themselves were no more than a few years away from the factory yet who, when they had to come onto the factory floor, sniffed and picked their way through, holding their skirts tightly to their sides so as not to be sullied by contact with anything or anyone there.

For those of us whose lives revolved around the garment industry, there were five seasons of the year instead of the usual four: winter, spring, summer, fall, and the dreaded *slack season*—as real a part of our lives as the winter snow and the summer sun. As each regular season waned, so did the work, and the workers were sent home to wait for the next season and worry about how their families would make it until then.

The anxiety of those times still lives in my bones. My mother, one of the world's most frugal women, usually managed to have some savings to help tide us over the slack season, a feat she accomplished by foregoing most small comforts during the months when she was bringing home a paycheck. We still had no radio; we wouldn't see a telephone in our house for years; leaving an electric light on beyond what was absolutely necessary was a crime of high order; even a subway ride, then only a nickel, was taken only when it was impossible to walk.

As the weeks of unemployment piled up, we hunkered down into a real subsistence level. But even this stripped-down life usually didn't keep us from running out of money before it was over.

We were saved from disaster by a $2,000 life insurance policy my father bought a few years before his death. It was common then for such insurance policies to be sold door-to-door, especially in poor neighborhoods. There, where people knew firsthand about all kinds of hardships and calamities, including early deaths, it wasn't hard for a salesman to convince a man that his family needed the security a life insurance policy offered. The terms were easy—ten or fifteen cents a week. And they didn't even have to go anywhere to pay their money; the salesman came around regularly to collect.

My mother tapped that insurance money carefully and only when she had no choice—when she ran out of money for food, when we were threatened with eviction. But even that small cushion would soon be lost in the bank failures of 1932.

For my mother—and for the millions of others whose life savings were swept away with a turn of a key in a lock—the unthinkable happened. Hundreds of banks all over the country simply closed their doors. I don't remember how she heard the news, only that she flew out of the house in a panic, with me following closely behind, as we raced the few blocks to the bank.

Hundreds of people were already congregated there by the time we arrived. Some were so shocked they could only stand there silently, not believing what they saw. Others were shouting and pounding on the locked doors while the few bank employees who were still inside peeked out helplessly. Like a wild woman, my mother pushed through the crowd and joined those who were demanding entry. I can still see her, her fists beating furiously on the closed doors, her eyes wild with terror, her lips calling down the wrath of God with every Jewish curse and invective at her command.

I stood at the edge of the crowd—a frightened and bewildered eight-year-old child. I wanted to go home, to run from the terror and rage that filled the air. But I was afraid to move, afraid to leave my mother, afraid I'd never see her again if I did.

Finally, the police came and, threatening the crowd with their night sticks, quickly broke it up. Defeated, my mother turned and walked slowly home, all the while talking as much to herself as to me. How could a bank simply close its doors? This was America; such things didn't happen here. The bank, she had been told, was the one safe place for her money. Now it was gone. What could she ever believe in again? For a woman who already looked so suspiciously at the world, the bank closings confirmed for her that she could trust nothing or no one.

Every autobiography is a construction built on our need to develop a life story that's not only coherent but that reflects who we are—or at least who we want to believe we are—as well as our unique way of filtering and internalizing experience. That's why it's so common to find members of a family who, having lived through the same events, record and narrate them differently.

In my own narrative of the events that stand out as crucial turning points in the life of my family, the year 1932—with its bank failures and the election of Franklin

Delano Roosevelt—is high on the list, although I certainly didn't understand it that way when it was happening. FDR's famous National Industrial Recovery Act (NRA), which became law in 1933, included a clause that gave renewed life and energy to the trade union movement. For the first time, the United States government guaranteed the right of unions to organize. Which also meant that workers couldn't be fired for joining a union.

When the law went into effect, only a small fraction of New York's garment workers were members of the ILGWU. Now, with the law on their side, the union called a general strike of garment workers in New York City. Seventy thousand workers shut down the entire industry.

The strike was a triumph that solidified the union's power over the industry and changed the working conditions—hence the lives—of garment workers forever. By the time the Supreme Court declared the NRA unconstitutional in 1935, the union's power was firmly entrenched and the garment factories of New York were closed shops, meaning that a worker had to be a union member to get a job.

For me, living through the organization of New York's garment workers, experiencing firsthand how the union movement touched and changed my family's life, was the beginning of my political understanding, providing an education in the power of collective action I would never forget. Many years later, when I became a political activist and organizer, it was the lessons I learned as a child about the importance of collective action in bringing about social change that fueled the energy and conviction I brought to my work.

But even with the gains made by the union, the life of a garment worker didn't become a walk on the sunny side of the street. True, wages and working conditions improved dramatically, extra hours meant overtime pay, grievance procedures were set in place. But the really big difference in our lives came when—partly due to union agitation and partly because of the extensive suffering wrought by the depression—the Roosevelt administration cobbled together the New Deal legislation that provided a safety net for families in need.

It was then that what we now know as the modern welfare state came into being, first with the Federal Emergency Relief Administration (FERA), later with Aid to Dependent Children (ADC), the first national program designed to assist widows with young children. Until then there had been poor relief, meaning subsidies administered capriciously by local jurisdictions to people they defined as "the deserving poor." Now, for the first time, the federal government joined the cities and states in assuming some share of the responsibility for poor families who couldn't make it on their own.

For my mother these new federal programs provided the first small bit of security she had ever known. Later there would be unemployment insurance to tide her over the worst effects of being out of work. But in the first years of the New Deal there were only these public assistance programs to which my mother could turn when slack season rolled around.

When I listen to the mean-spirited discussions about welfare now, to the endless talk about the value of self-reliance by people who will never know the shame of being in need no matter how reliable you have been, I want to shout, *How dare you? What do you know about being relegated to the lowest paid work this society has to offer? What do you know about working to the point of exhaustion and still not earning enough to feed and clothe a family? What do you know about being called out of your fifth grade class by a social worker who has come to check on the story your mother has told?*

It's unforgettable for me—the agony of that walk to the front of the room with all eyes upon me, the humiliation when I saw my teacher's obvious concern, the tears that stung the back of my eyes as I struggled for control, the fear that everyone would know my shame. School, which had been my haven, my place of retreat, became, in that moment, my hell.

My mother had warned me that this might happen—warned me and coached me to be sure I was ready with the right answers. Like so many poor women seeking welfare, she sometimes did some sewing on the side to supplement the inadequate dole. My job, if I was asked, was to know nothing of these activities, to say only that she was unemployed.

Lying, however, has never been my strong point, and I did it even less well as a child. So I was frightened by the whole idea and pleaded with her not to make me do it. But she was determined to collect her due, even if she had to bend the rules to get it. There was no way out for me.

Later I came to understand how poor people who feel abused and victimized by society can find it hard to play by its rules. I understand, too, that for my mother, there was an element of retribution every time she foiled the system in some way. When she lost the money from my father's life insurance policy in the bank failures of 1932, she was left with a deep-seated sense of injury, a conviction that the system had failed her and that, therefore, she was entitled to wrest from it what she could.

I don't know what image I'd conjured in my mind as I walked to meet the social worker in the principal's office, but when I finally sat down before her, I was surprised by her soft, gentle voice and the warmth and kindness she displayed. But the questions! "Is your mother working?" "When was the last time she worked?" "What does she do all day?" "What did you eat for dinner last night?" They left me squirming with guilt and dread.

What were the right answers? Nobody told me she'd ask what I ate for dinner. Or what my mother did all day. I didn't know exactly when she last worked. What if I made a mistake? What if I slipped and told that my mother earned some extra money by sewing things for other people? What would happen to us? What would my mother do to me?

I must have gotten the answers right because we were approved for relief. But it took quite awhile before I was comfortable in school again, before I could stop wondering what the other kids knew, what my teacher was thinking. And I was well into adulthood before I was able to put behind me the stigma of those years when we would fall out of the working poor and onto the welfare rolls.

Partly because of my immigrant family, partly because I felt like such a misfit in that family, and partly because most of my classmates were either in or heading toward the middle class while we were always one short step away from poverty (that is, when we weren't in it), I was a lonely and isolated child. The fact that I was a very accomplished student didn't help much either at home, at school, or on the street.

At home, my mother and brother complained endlessly that my head was, in their words, "always stuck in a book." And no matter how good my grades, my mother's response was always, "Your brother's really the smart one; you just get good grades because you study hard." A claim I believed for many years despite all the evidence to the contrary.

As an adult, their response to my accomplishments became something of a joke, although one that carried its own edge of pain. My brother's only comment about any of my books was, "At least the sex part's not so boring." My mother sniffed dismissively when I got my doctorate, "You can't give me a prescription, so what kind of doctor are you?" and shrugged indifferently at each new book I published, "Other daughters take their mother to lunch every week; you write books." But she retained bragging rights in public and boasted to neighbors about her "daughter, the doctor." Not, mind you, without adding the lament, "Some people are lucky, they have a son a doctor, I have a daughter."

It would be easy to write such behavior off to a personal vendetta, unique to my family. And certainly there was some of that. But the hostility was at least partly related to the fact that the difference between us was threatening to them—a common theme in working-class families where parents fear they'll lose their children to a life they don't understand. And where, also, they suffer a sense of inadequacy in the face of a child's accomplishment that so far surpasses their own.

I've heard the same story often in my research, my clinical work, and from students who are the first in their families to go to college: fathers who humiliate and brutalize their sons out of fear that they're slipping from their grasp; mothers who find all kinds of creative ways to subvert a daughter's attempts to move out of their narrow working-class confines. Parents who, like my mother, brag publicly to whoever will listen while privately treating their children and their achievements with contempt and hostility.

Hard as my family situation was for me, it was at least as bad, if not worse, among my peers. At school, where I was nearly always the best student in the class, my teachers showered me with approval while my classmates taunted me with the words *teacher's pet.*

The street was no kinder, since my mother's habit of moving house every year meant that I was always the new kid on the block, trying to find my way into a street world that had been doing just fine without me. Even now the lives and friendships of working-class children are largely neighborhood-bound. In the Bronx of that era, it was the block that determined social life, and moving even a few blocks meant the end of a friendship. Not surprisingly, therefore, my brother and I hated those moves. But our pleas to stay put fell on deaf ears.

It wasn't until many years later that I came to understand that, while my mother's restless searching for something I'm sure she couldn't have named played a central part in the peripatetic life we led, there was another piece to the story. Depression-strapped landlords, hungry for tenants to fill their vacant apartments, offered one month's free rent to anyone willing to sign a year's lease. By moving every year, therefore, she not only momentarily assuaged her restlessness but saved a full month's rent.

Adding to my problems in making friends was the fact that, in those days, the only thing the New York City schools could think to do with very bright children was to let them skip grades. By the time I entered high school in the ninth grade, therefore, I was only 11 years old, three years younger than most of my classmates—a gap so wide that it would have been a tough challenge for a child far more socially skilled than I was. For me, it was an unbridgeable chasm. No matter which way I turned, I couldn't find a place where I fit. Intellectually I was too far ahead of children my own age; socially and emotionally I was too far behind the classmates who should also have been my peers.

So I remained apart, a child who was in the world but not of it, the one who was the observer of life rather than a participant in it. After a while, I was so accustomed to being left out that it was hard for me to come in even when I was invited.

Although I graduated from high school at fifteen, college wasn't an option for a girl of my class. My task was to get a job as quickly as I could so that I could help my brother go to college when his turn came. Never mind that my brother, who was a year-and-a-half older than I, was a semester behind me in school. Never mind either that he didn't have much interest in going to college. He was a boy; I was a girl. That said it all; no other explanation was needed. "You don't have to go to college; you'll get married and your husband will take care of you," my mother declared each time the subject arose.

It seems wholly improbable now that, given my mother's own experience, she made such an assumption. But so powerful was the ideology about gender roles that she took for granted that for me work would be temporary, only until my real life as a wife and mother would begin. Or at most, it would be discretionary, something I would do to keep busy or "help out" should, God forbid, the need arise.

In truth, however, my mother's plan for me wasn't so different from my own. I had no objection to her expectation that I would marry well, which meant a man who would provide me with all she never could. The difference between us was that I wanted to go to college until that happy day arrived, while for her it was enough that I worked in an office at a nice, "clean" job.

It would be many years before women would make it to my list of the oppressed. I knew that women had a hard road to walk; I had only to look at my mother's life to understand just how cruel the path could be. And even as a small child, I had already noticed that men always had the better jobs in the factories where my mother worked. Just as they did in the offices I worked in later.

I didn't have words like *gender discrimination* to describe what I observed, but in the inchoate and inarticulate way in which we often know such things, I understood that it existed and knew it was unfair. But it didn't seriously occur to me to protest, partly because at the immediate level—that is, the level of my daily life and feelings about it—I was pleased to be working in an office. It was the "clean" work my mother had raised me for, and I was proud that I could do it well.

At the deeper psychological level I could ignore my own experience of discrimination in the workplace because it wasn't my gender that seemed so suffocating during the difficult early years of my life. It was the grinding poverty and the struggle to survive; it was knowing that I couldn't evade my mother's rage and rejection no matter how hard I tried; it was the three of us stuck together in one small room; it was sleeping in the same bed with my mother until I was nineteen and got married—the only way a girl of my class and culture could get out of the parental house; it was being a misfit and the deep and abiding sense of isolation that gnawed at my soul.

A misfit! The word no longer carries the sting it used to, but, as a description, it still isn't so far off—at least not in my internal world. I'm aware, of course, that the life I live today looks perfectly well integrated into the larger world. And in some of the more superficial ways it is. But in my internal life that child's sense of marginality, the belief that I can never fully fit anywhere, remains.

It's true that in adulthood I've developed a finely honed capacity for friendship and have had intimate and long-lasting friendships. But I've never experienced myself as an insider, never comfortably belonged to a group, whether in my personal or professional life. In the professional world, I span two disciplines—sociology and psychology—and don't feel wholly at home in either one. And although I complain about that from time to time, I don't jump at the chance to belong when it's offered to me.

When, for example, I was offered a professorship at Harvard, I was pleased and gratified to know that my work had been noticed and appreciated. But I was also anxious, because being "in" was not only an alien experience but an unsettling one. Just contemplating the possibility took me back to my childhood, to the moments when it seemed to me that to be a real part of my family I had to give up my soul. I knew once again the visceral fear of not fitting in that lives alongside the powerful sense that to belong would be to lose myself.

I refused the invitation. To accept it was too profoundly at odds with my sense of myself, with my conviction that my autonomy, as well as my intellectual and creative capacities, is deeply linked to being an outsider.

I tell this story easily, as if I take my present life and all its offerings for granted. But, in fact, the cultured, intellectually driven, upper-middle-class life I live today still seems impossible to me, still fills me with disbelief and wonder, still finds me uncomfortable in places that should by now seem natural. Hardly a day goes by when I don't ask: How did I get from New York's immigrant ghetto to San Francisco's Nob Hill? How did I make it out of that suffocatingly narrow world when my brother could not? How did I, who didn't go to college until I was thirty-nine years old, get invited to teach at Harvard? How did I, who got a "C" in freshman English, become a writer?

Such questions—and the guilt that accompanies the kind of mobility I've experienced—have preoccupied me both personally and intellectually for many years. It's why I keep turning to the study of working-class families, why I choose to teach (when I do) in a working-class school. It's not just a way of paying my dues to my past but a continuing need to understand that past and the ways in which—except for the few—working-class status generally is transmitted from generation to generation as surely as wealth is passed in the upper class.

It's time to wind up these remarks now, and I suppose, after all I've said, I should have some kind of ending that ties everything up in a neat package. But frankly, I'm not much one for that kind of intellectual or emotional neatness. Life is simply too sloppy for that. What I can say only is that my own story has, by most standards (including my own), a happy ending—as does the mobility narrative of those of you who are also up from the working class. But the cost we pay for the upward mobility we sought so eagerly—and that's so widely celebrated in our society—is a continuing sense of alienation and isolation, and the often pained realization that we'll never fully shake the sense of marginality, the feeling that we still have our nose pressed hungrily to the window, looking into a world we want but can't quite fit into, even when we're actually living on the other side of the glass.

NOTE

"Up from the Immigrant Ghetto" is previously unpublished.

Integrating Society into Psychology

The title of our conference today, "Integrating Society and Spirituality into Psychotherapy," presents us with a very large order—one I doubt we'll be able to fill.[1] Indeed, I'm afraid the very idea of attempting such an integration overwhelms me. So if you've come thinking you're going to get some quick and easy tips on how to do it, I'm afraid that I, at least, will be a disappointment to you.

I expect others here have thought about the spiritual aspects more deeply than I have, so I'll leave it to them to do that piece—or, if they dare, to attempt the Herculean task of bringing them all together. And I'll stick to talking about what I know best—the integration of the social and the psychological or, to put it more precisely, the ways in which social institutions can be the birthplace of our psychological needs and desires. But first, a brief professional autobiography.

My whole professional life has been engaged in the attempt to bring together the social and the psychological in both my intellectual and clinical work. My "home" discipline (the one I got my doctorate in) is sociology—a discipline whose primary concern is with the "large" questions of social life. A degree in sociology teaches you about such things as institutions, roles, norms, and the interplay between the economy, the polity, and the society—indeed, all you ever wanted to know, and a lot more, about what Peter Berger and Thomas Luckmann have called "the social construction of reality." But people get lost in the process. What they think or feel, how they respond to the social forces that seek to mold them, how they interpret their behavior and attitudes—in essence, what *subjective* meanings they give to their own experiences and how those affect their relationships to both self and society—these are of small concern.

My adopted discipline (clinical psychology) is equally myopic, but in the opposite direction—so concerned with the particular and the individual that it loses sight of the social context within which human life takes place and, therefore, fails to comprehend the ways in which society and personality live in a continuing and dialectical relationship with each other.

Neither discipline has been a comfortable resting place for me since both have little tolerance for the kind of synthesis that has concerned me through the years. Nor am I a comfort to them. About my earlier work, psychologists have complained that I've given too much attention to the social forces that frame people's lives and not enough to the internal dynamic ones that may also lock people in. But there I've been forgiven; I'm not, after all, one of their own. Among sociologists, however, where I'm counted as one of them, it's different—more akin to the feelings in a family when one of the children strays from the accepted path. So they look at my most recent book, *Intimate Strangers: Men and Women Together,* with its focus on internal developmental issues and—sometimes with glee, sometimes with regret—write me out of the tribe. This, they insist, is not sociology. The fact that the central argument of the book is a sociological one—that is, that the family is a *social* institution whose *socially structured* internal arrangements have a profound influence on human development—is somehow lost on these critics who complain about its psychological focus.

Yet I must admit that their complaints are not *wholly* off the mark. Human life is extraordinarily complex, and any analysis—whether clinical or intellectual—must take some issues as matters of central concern and leave others on the periphery. So it's undoubtedly true that, given the task I set for myself then, the analysis in my earlier work fell more heavily onto the sociological side, while *Intimate Strangers* leans more clearly toward the psychological. For while one may *integrate* these two modes of thought, *balancing* them—giving each, with all their complexity, equal time—is another matter.

Since I've just written a book about the problems and prospects of intimate relationships between men and women in this era, let me now give a context to these general remarks by talking a bit about the ways in which the changing social world has affected not just the external ways in which we live our personal lives, but our inner psychological needs and desires as well.

Much has happened to change our world and the way we live in it over the last two decades. The sixties started with a movement to humanize the work environment. That, in some important way, was what the famous Free Speech Movement was all about—a movement to bring bureaucratic structures within human control. It ended with a well-established counterculture and the beginnings of the modern feminist movement whose major commitment was (and still is) to reorder the rules of love and work in the interest of a more human and humane society for all.

Once, not so long ago, we heard the words "I love you" and thought about forever. Once, those words held the promise that loneliness would be stilled, that we'd marry and live happily ever after. Now we're not so sure.

Who really knows how "happy" ever after was? What we do know is that the dream of that earlier time seemed a simpler one. Women and men each had a place—a clearly defined, highly specific set of roles and responsibilities that each would fulfill. She'd take care of home and hearth; he'd provide it. She'd raise the children; he'd support them. She'd subordinate her life to his, and wouldn't even notice it; her needs for achievement and mastery would be met vicariously through his accomplishments or those of the children.

As time tested it and the world changed, it became clear that the old dream didn't work so well for most people most of the time. Marriages staggered under the burden of these role definitions; the dream began to look like a nightmare. Most women couldn't simply give themselves and their needs away so readily, at least not without some covert rebellion—rebellion that took the form of depression, of overcontrolling and demanding behavior, of nagging, or of any of the other ways in which women have sought to reclaim some parts of themselves and some power in their relationships with their men.

The men faced an equally difficult set of tasks. The tough, fearless, unemotional hero of folklore was a hard act to keep up in real life, the attempt carrying with it enormous emotional stress. In an economy that's almost always short on jobs, and in which most men who are lucky enough to have one simply can't earn enough to meet the idealized notions of male responsibility, making it in the world of work is no less problematic—especially when a man's accomplishments are supposed to do for two, when his successes are expected to serve for hers as well. Like hers, his rebellions, too, have come under the cover of behaviors not easily recognized as rebellious: hostile withdrawals; critical, perfectionist demands of wife and children, escapes into work, television, drinking, sometimes even violence.

More and more we've come to see we made a bad bargain—if not an impossible one. But cultural ideals are powerful forces, shaping not only our ways of thinking and doing but our ways of being as well, giving form to both the conscious and unconscious content of our inner lives. Change, therefore, comes slowly, meeting enormous resistance both inside us and in the system of social institutions that supports our society's mandates about femininity and masculinity—about how a good woman lives, how a good man behaves.

Still, however haltingly, however incompletely, change does come. The ideal visions of one age eventually are seen as its excesses by the next. Thus, for example, the corseted repression that constrained the Victorian era was the yoke against which the succeeding generation strained. And the taut bonds of togetherness that were the mark of the 1950s became the target of rebellion by the youth of the 1960s. It was not just an obscene war, not just some abstraction called "society" that came under attack, but the very structure of the family itself and the relationships inside it. Togetherness was out; foreverness was called into question; commitment to another was edged aside by the search for self. Talk about the generation gap became part of our public dialogue and private agony as parents and children were separated by a shifting value system that opened up a huge chasm between them.

But change generally outruns consciousness, and, for most of us, change in consciousness lags well behind the changing social norms, sometimes even behind changing personal behaviors. Indeed, always, no matter how revolutionary a period of change may seem on the surface, the old myths continue to whisper to us. Consciously derogated, unconsciously avoided and denied, they continue to speak with a power and persistence that will not be dismissed. Consequently, two contradictory systems of ideals lie within us—the emerging one vying for dominance with the old one, new behaviors creating internal conflicts as they rub against obsolete but still living rules. Thus, even the children who initiated the change haven't wholly given up the happily-ever-after dream. They have instead made it time-limited. Each new relationship raises again the fantasy of eternal love and endless joy—the difference being that, when disappointment sets in, they feel freer now to move on to continue the search.

No small change, it's true. And the divorce and remarriage rates give testimony to the depth and breadth of the shift. But it isn't, as some critics have charged, simply selfishness, immaturity, narcissism, or some other newly discovered and widespread character flaw that makes binding commitments so difficult in the present era. To write such major social changes off with an analysis that focuses on personal psychopathology is to trivialize the impact of the social world on the lives of the people who live in it and to elevate psychology to a cause of our social malaise rather than an effect of it.

In fact, the recent changes in family life are related to a complicated set of social forces, not least of them the coming together of changes in the economy with important demographic shifts in the society. The burgeoning number of women in the work force, for example—which is surely a central, if not always conscious, contributor to the shifting relations inside the family—is itself related both to economic factors and social ones. The increasing emphasis on consumer goods and the continuing inflationary spiral are two good reasons why so many women have flocked into the labor force over the last two decades. But without the medical advances that have dramatically increased longevity, and without the development of modern birth control methods which make it possible to regulate with some certainty the number and spacing of children, such a shift would not have been possible. Altogether, however, such changes in the world outside the family have profound effects on what happens inside it. This, in turn, affects the family's relationship to both the society and the economy. And, ultimately, all these changes interact to set in motion transformations in the whole meaning and vision of masculinity, femininity, marriage, and adulthood.

This is the situation we find ourselves in today. Advances in health and medical technology have brought striking advances in longevity. From 1920 to 1978, the life expectancy for women jumped almost 23 years, from 54.6 to 77.2. For men, the rise is somewhat less dramatic but still impressive: from 53.6 years to 69.5. Not many years ago, fertility control was a matter of chance and a product of luck. The Pill and the IUD changed all that. And the birth rate dropped from 24.1 per thousand population in 1950 to 15.3 in 1978, while the average number of children per woman fell sharply—from 3.5 in 1950 to 1.9 in 1980.

The increase in longevity means that, for the first time in our history, if we marry at twenty-five, we'll have before us, on the average, forty-five years to live together. The decline in the birth rate means that, also for the first time, a substantial portion of those years will be free of childrearing responsibilities.

Such facts have important consequences for the conduct of both marriage and adulthood. They color how we think about our lives, how we plan to live them, what we come to expect in our interactions with each other. Indeed, it's out of such changes that we might say that adulthood has been "discovered" in this age in the same way that childhood was the discovery of the seventeenth century and adolescence of the late nineteenth. Adolescence as a distinct stage of life became possible when the transformation in production wrought by the Industrial Revolution was complete and children no longer were needed in the factories. And adulthood, as we conceive it today, becomes possible as we have fewer children, live longer, and shift from a production to a service economy in this postindustrial age.

Philippe Ariès, the French historian who documented the discovery of childhood so brilliantly, noted, for example, that in sixteenth-century France there was no concept of a stage in life between youth and old age. Youth was the prime time; after that came old age and death. It seems strange to us now, but, in an era when forty was very old, it made sense. Today, when forty is still young, adulthood becomes a stage of life that brings with it extraordinary new possibilities for living—and a whole new set of problems. Personal change, growth, development, identity formation—these tasks that once were thought to belong to childhood and adolescence alone now are recognized as part of adult life as well. Gone is the belief that adulthood is, or ought to be, a time of internal peace and comfort, that growing pains belong only to the young; gone the belief that there are marker events—a job, a mate, a child—through which we'll pass into a life of relative ease.

Thus, just as marriage is not necessarily an enduring commitment anymore, adulthood is no longer an event, something we achieve at a given moment in our lives—when we reach a certain age, when we pass through a particular stage, when we assume what have, in other times, been called "adult responsibilities." Even the language we use tells the difference. For we don't speak, as we used to, of *stepping into adulthood,* we talk instead of *becoming adult*—the one connoting a crossing of a line, a static achievement; the other implying a dynamic process that includes change, growth, and development as continuing aspects of adult life.

But there's uncertainty abroad—a trembling uncertainty that makes us anxious, fearful, ill at ease. If falling in love gives no guarantee of eternal happiness, what will? If peace, quiet, and contentment are not the rewards of adult life, what can we look for? If dependability, commitment, conformity, and sacrifice are out, what's in? If change, not stability, becomes the watchword of these years, how do we come to know and to define ourselves; how do we learn to live with ourselves, let alone with each other?

These are difficult questions and trying times; contradictions plague us wherever we turn. At one level, for example, we talk about happiness, often look as though we're in a frantic search for it. At another level, "struggle" is the injunction most commonly heard these days. Happiness, in this context, is seen as some kind of mindless stagnation rather than a valued prize. No pain, no gain, we're told. Living is hard, whether alone or together; relationships don't just happen; love is not something we find or fall into. It all requires work—hard work—without guarantee of reward, often without even understanding what the reward might be.

Interesting ideas, aren't they, for what has been called a narcissistic and hedonistic age? And puzzling, too, because intuitively we think: Both are true. We *have* refused to accept the old definitions of adult life, the old ways of relating to each other. Even those of us who don't believe our sole responsibility is to "look out for number one" now insist upon our right not to relinquish self to the interest of others. But our Puritan heritage and frontier mentality still haunt us. And our personal quest is culturally acceptable only in the context of painful struggle—the heroic conquest of yet another frontier, only this time not a geographic one. Perhaps never in history have we expected so much and so little at the same time; never before have we seen such an odd conjunction of heightened expectations about the possibilities in human relationships and disillusion, if not despair.

It's precisely this paradox that gives this era its unique and provocative flavor. Indeed, this is the paradox that has eluded some of our most distinguished social commentators, and that accounts for the common experience among us of reading or hearing an analysis of the ills of present-day society that leaves us with the uncomfortable sense that it is both right and wrong at the same time. It's not our perceptions that are off, but an analysis that has failed to come to grips with these contradictory impulses, which, from one view, make this look like the age of hedonism and, from another, give it a distinctly ascetic stamp.

Altogether, these changes give rise to a new dream about how we can live with ourselves and what we can expect from each other. But because it's so new, it's often not yet coherent or clearly understood by most of us who are trying to live it. We know that the old ways are not for us, but have no clear picture yet of what the new ones will be. We know there's a new vision of masculinity and femininity, but can't figure out how it fits each of us. Men ask themselves: If we're no longer supposed to be the strong, silent, masterful ones, what are we to be; how are we to act? And women want to know: If femininity is no longer to be defined by passivity, helplessness, cuteness, and coyness, what will take their place? If masochism is out of fashion, what's in?

We talk about equality between women and men, then ask ourselves: "What does it mean?" We say we want intimacy, companionship, sharing, but don't always know just what we're looking for. We tell each other we must communicate better, but often have no idea where or how to start the process. We're told that one problem is our inability to express anger, so we read books and take lessons in how to do it, but none of it seems to work. We go to therapists to work on our relationships, but can't say what we really want from each other.

This is the struggle in which women and men are engaged today, both with each other and within themselves. We talk about our relationships, think about them, worry about them, ask ourselves why it is that they seem so difficult. Yet we have no answers that make sense to us. *Intimacy, companionship, sharing, communication, equality*—these are the qualities of relationships we value most highly, we say. We work for them, struggle for them, analyze ourselves and our loved ones, seemingly without end. Still they elude us. We tell ourselves it's the way we were raised, that we'll do better with our children. Then we stand back in pained and weary amazement as we watch our little boys behave in typical "boy" fashion, and our little girls behave in characteristic "girl" style. "So young," we say to ourselves despairingly, "how does it happen so young?" "Maybe we have been wrong," we think silently, even guiltily, not daring to say the words aloud. "Could it really be that these qualities we call 'masculine' and 'feminine' are built into the genes?"

Could it? For over a decade now, feminist scholars of both genders have labored to put before us a new vision of the nature of men and women and of the sources of the differences between us. At one level, the words persuade us; at another, the old questions bedevil us with haunting persistence. We argue with ourselves and with each other, unable to understand why what we believe doesn't always match what we see; why, despite our best efforts at nonsexist childrearing, our daughters are still preoccupied with dolls, our sons with trucks. And we ask ourselves quietly, "Could it really be ... ?"

Our own experiences add to the confusion. For even when we're quite clear about the direction of the change we're aiming for—even when men know they want more contact with what we call the "feminine" side and women look for stronger connections to their "masculine" half—getting there can be so fraught with conflict that we begin to wonder, "Could it really be ... ?"

Over the last fifteen years, I've watched as men and women (my husband and I among them) struggle to change, noting with wonder the intransigence with which old ways hang on even when good intentions oppose them vigorously. As a social scientist, I've studied many hundreds of relationships intensively—examining the kinds of conflicts that preoccupy couples in our time, looking at how the issues that divide them are made manifest, how they're resolved. As a psychotherapist, I've worked with a very large number of women and men, singly and in couples, as they try to deal with the conflicts their attempts to change stir within and between them. As a woman, I have lived in a relationship with a man for most of my adult life—experiencing my fair share of the pain and pleasure to be found there, struggling to reduce the dissonance when the changing vision is at odds with inner experience. And always the questions loom: Why is it so hard? Does it have to be this way?

Of one thing I'm convinced: The social world in which we live is the breeding ground for our internal psychological states. As we move toward new ways of being, we come up against social constraints that give way only very slowly. If and when we finally succeed in pushing past them, we meet psychological barriers that must be overcome. Therefore, to think about mass psychological changes without fundamental changes in the social institutions within which we live and grow is to give in to fantasy. Of those institutions, none influences the experience of adult life more profoundly than the family. For it's there that the very structure of male and female personality is formed—not by accident, not by biology, but by the nature of the traditional roles and relationships that have, until now, existed unquestioned there. But, once that psychology is rooted inside us, it develops a reality of its own. And it is an equally impossible dream to think that psychological change will follow immediately on the heels of social change.

Yet this is the contest that engages us so intensely today—a contest in which so many of us are struggling to rescue at least some part of self from society. It excites us, drains us, and bewilders us as we waver between triumph and despair—telling of our victories one moment, of our defeats the next.

It's just this shifting and changing reality—both in the external world and in our inner one—that makes a book about relations between men and women so difficult an undertaking. For writing is a logical and linear enterprise while living is an interactive and dialectical one—a continuous process of action and reaction within which we are constantly, if not always consciously, contending with our contradictory needs for change and stability. We learn, grow, change, and cling to the past all at the same time—one of life's predicaments that can be at once frustrating and exciting and which none of us escapes, not even a writer who takes upon herself the task of illuminating both change and stability in a historical moment when those forces are in a heady contention.

It must be clear to those of you who are therapists that much of what I've just said about writing is true also of the difficulties we experience in our clinical efforts. And, as in the clinical setting, in writing a book I'm concerned not just to spotlight the present realities but to understand and explain them as well.

The central task I set for myself in *Intimate Strangers* was to show how certain characteristics of male and female personality come into being, why they persist, and how they affect the most basic issues of our relations with each other—from the way we play out our social roles to the deep-seated internal differences between us on such issues as intimacy, sexuality, dependency, work, and parenting. My analysis departs from traditional socialization theorists in that I believe we must look beyond learning theories or theories of role modeling to understand the pervasiveness and persistence of these characteristic differences between us. And I depart also from classical psychological theory in that I do not see a single line in child development—with one, the male, being defined as normal and the other, the female, characterized as a deviation from that norm. Instead I insist that while certain developmental imperatives exist for children of both genders—for example, the establishment of a continuing and coherent sense of self and gender identity—the tasks that confront a girl and a boy are quite different, resulting in different patterns of personality for each of them.

Finally, following the work of such theorists as Nancy Chodorow and Dorothy Dinnerstein, I insist also that those different tasks, and the psychological differences that stem from them, are not inherent in the nature of human development, but are a response to the social situation—in particular to the structure of roles and relationships inside the family—into which girls and boys are born and will grow. From birth onward psyche and society engage in a complex and dynamic interaction. Our earliest experiences in the family lay the basis for our characteristic ways of being, and the cultural commandments about masculinity and femininity reinforce and solidify them.

Listening to these remarks, those of you with a sociological turn of mind will find yourself with a question that asks: Are there no differences across class, race, ethnic groups? The answer: Of course there are. Whether a family is rich or poor, sick or well, black or white, where they live and how, what work they do—all these are crucial to understanding what issues of living become problems for them and how those problems are attended to. Thus, for example, in a family where a mate is seriously ill, the quality of intimacy in the relationship may not, for the moment, be a central concern. Similarly, if children are hungry, a husband and wife are likely to be more concerned about how to find food than whether they can talk about it.

Even when survival issues are not at stake, class makes a difference in how people live, what they value, what they wish for themselves and for their children—all of which I've written about at length in *Worlds of Pain,* a book that's probably familiar to many of you. In that work, I was interested in examining these differences with a view to understanding the experiences of working-class life that lead to the development of a class culture—ways of being and living that enable people to cope and to survive. And, while such differences are not to be dismissed as irrelevant or unimportant in understanding life in these United States, neither are the similarities that exist across all the boundaries of group and class—similarities born of being part of the same society, living in the same historical moment, facing the universal issues of family life: work, leisure, childrearing, interpersonal relations. It's certainly true that class, race, and ethnic differences give a special cast to the shared experience. But that only means that there will be variations among the groups—some which may be culturally unique, others which may simply be subcultural variations on the themes of the dominant culture.

My argument, then, is that the large social changes of our times affect us all. The advances in medical technology which have given us more years to live are met with technological changes in the work world—whether in the factory, the office, or the home—which almost require that we find new ways to live them. Our class situation will define the ways in which we approach these changes and, all too often, it will limit the solutions that are possible for us. But the effects of the changes themselves, and the new aspirations that come on the heels of them, are felt across class and ethnic groups.

In the research for *Intimate Strangers,* I didn't have to look far or probe deeply to find that the hunger for something different in our relationships is profound and widespread. It's there, all across the country, to be seen by anyone who would look—from the eagerness with which men and women from all walks of life are ready to talk of these issues, to the tens of thousands of couples who have attended the various marriage enrichment programs whose appeal across class and ethnic groups, in this country and abroad, has been both astonishing and revealing.

But the style with which we express our concerns—and even what we consider acceptable to express—will differ from one class to another. So a woman who grew up in a family with a father who was drunk, violent, and only intermittently employed tells me that she prizes her husband because "he's a steady worker; he doesn't drink; and he doesn't hit me." But that doesn't mean she doesn't yearn for companionship with him as well. She may remind herself that she's better off than her mother was, may reprove herself because she's not unambivalently grateful. But, with all that, there remains a part of her that feels cheated, as if something is missing. Just so, her husband may tell himself he should be content with a life in which he has a steady job, a wife who's constant, who takes good care of the house and children, who doesn't nag too much. But he's restless—feeling that some promise in life remains unfulfilled, looking for something without knowing what. And, when such feelings surface, wife and husband turn to each other—wanting something else in this marriage but unable to say what it is, blaming each other but not really knowing why.

It seems clear to me then (and I hope by now it is for you as well) that the issues inside a family are not simply private ones. Rather the *source* of the strains with which we live often lies outside the household, in the public institutions of our time that are beyond individual control. Yet too often the emotional struggles that go on between us are negotiated without much immediate interaction with or under-standing of the world outside—which means an added dimension of psychological confusion and conflict.

Thus, for example, those of us who are clinicians working in settings where unemployment is a new condition of life (among middle-class white-collar profession-als, for instance) are beginning to notice that its emotional costs are not so different here than they have been historically in the working class. The increase in depression among men who are unemployed, and the increase in family violence as wife and/ or children become the target of a man's helpless rage, are two of the most obvious ones which now cut across class boundaries.

Less immediately apparent are other connections between the social world and our psychological states. How do our fears of being out on the streets affect our lives and our interactions inside the family? What does it mean to our inner life to know that we live in a society where inequality is so firmly rooted that we have developed a permanent, almost hereditary, underclass of whom we now live in angry terror? How does the heedless depletion of the earth's resources by rapacious multinational corporations and the nations they control affect our internal sense of security? What does it mean to a child to grow up in a world where he keeps hearing there won't be enough left for him? And how does the specter of a nuclear war that hovers always in the background of our consciousness affect our personal lives and development?

One of the profoundly important lessons of the sixties and seventies was that "the personal is political." I'd like to leave you now with the equally urgent reminder that "the political is also personal." And the reciprocal connections between the politi-cal and the personal are nowhere seen more clearly than in the current struggle for change in our intimate relationships. For, as Russell Jacoby puts it so pithily, "The social does not 'influence' the private, it dwells within it."

NOTE

1. This chapter was originally prepared for a conference, "Integrating Society and Spirituality into Psychotherapy," University of California, Berkeley, October 22, 1983.

Sociological Research: The Subjective Dimension

Just as I was beginning to think about what I would be saying here this afternoon, two things came to my attention that colored my vision and set the tone for these remarks. The first is an essay by Spector and Faulkner (1980: 477–482) that offers a survey and critical appraisal of five new journals devoted to publishing the research of sociologists working in the qualitative mode. In trying to understand what's behind this appearance of so many journals whose focus is on work using qualitative research methods and which share a humanistic and interactionist orientation to the task of "doing" sociology, Spector and Faulkner looked at five volumes of *ASR, AJS,* and *Sociological Quarterly* to determine how much and what type of qualitative sociology they publish. Their findings, while not surprising, are worth noting.

Less than 10 percent, 38 out of the total of 494 articles in *ASR* and *AJS,* "draw on or criticize qualitative, interactionist sociology" (Spector and Faulkner, 1980: 478). And of that small number, over half are theoretical essays or critical think pieces. Only 17 are empirical research reports, and of those, just 11 are based *primarily* on qualitative methods.

The *Sociological Quarterly,* with its roots in the Chicago School and a more favorable historical stance toward the interactionist perspective, did a little better: 39 out of 190 articles, or 21 percent. In the balance between theoretical and empirical, *SQ* also held up: two-thirds of the articles were based on empirical research. Still, the dominant fact is that this journal—the one we consider more favorable to our perspective—shows 80 percent of its published articles coming from the mainstream of sociological method and theory. And of the total of 684 articles published in all three journals over the five-year period, only 77—a fraction over 11 percent—were concerned with the interactionist perspective, whether theoretical, critical, or empirical.

On the same day that I read the Spector and Faulkner article, I received from my publisher a packet of reviews of my latest book (Rubin, 1979)—a study of midlife women and their "search for self" based on the data from 160 in-depth, focused interviews. The first of the professional reviews was now in, written by Janet Spence for *Contemporary Psychology.*

Before you groan in fear that you're about to be treated to yet another author's pained and defensive diatribe against reviews and reviewers, let me reassure you. It's not that I'm above being angered or hurt by reviews of my work. But I've learned the hard way that if I'm to survive this game and remain true to myself and to the integrity of the work I set out to do, I had better get some distance between me and "it"—that is, some separation between work and self so that I'll remember what is me and what is a book.

So if I don't mean to use this meeting as a forum to complain about the *Contemporary Psychology* review, why bring it up? Because it's a fine illustration of the perspective that dominates the social sciences—the perfect counterpoint to the Spector and Faulker discussion about the mainstream journals and their publications. For the substance of the work is never dealt with and the method is dismissed as one which left the reviewer in the dark about "what is fact and what is fiction." Her objections are summed up clearly in one line. "The hard work of wrestling the qualitative data into quantitative form remains," she writes, "and this reader, at least, is still haunted by the question of representativeness" (Spence, 1980: 273).

And why is it almost axiomatic that we must "wrestle qualitative data into quantitative form?" How is it that this is defined as the "hard task" while all else is dismissed as indistinguishable from fiction or fantasy? Is it reasonable or possible to speak in quantitative terms of the struggle for the formation of a socially and psychologically valued identity? Are the method and language of quantification best suited for research that seeks to understand a people's hopes, fears, values, conflicts, struggles, and above all, their complex and often contradictory sense of themselves?

These are not questions Spence addresses, nor will they concern most of her readers. Indeed, it is generally accepted that if questions seeking to understand the *meanings* people attribute to the events in their lives or the *process* through which those meanings come to be internalized are not amenable to quantification, then we will ask questions that are. Small matter that these may be trivial questions that tell us nothing about the quality of social life and human interactions; they can be measured and quantified.

And about representativeness? It's true that we have the technical know-how to say with some certainty that a particular sample is representative of a particular population. But whether the data drawn from that sample by the social sciences' most widely used and accepted methods "represent" that population in any way but the demographic is quite another matter—one that many quantifiers close their eyes to all too tightly. Thus, we have plenty of studies that are statistically representative of, for example, black families or women. But precisely because of the quantitative methods employed, they often render portraits of the people in these groups that range from highly oversimplified to downright misleading.

I remember raising such questions with my methods professors when I was a graduate student. And the answer was always the same: "Yes, maybe it's true, but that's only because it's bad research." I hear the same thing now among clinicians as they respond to the feminist challenge about the traditional male biases in psychology. "Yes," they say, "but that's bad clinical work." Somehow these answers are never quite responsive to the challenge. For if there's so much "bad" research and so much "bad" clinical work, maybe there's something inherently wrong with the structure of thought and method that underlies it; indeed, maybe that very structure generates it.

I don't mean for these comments to be taken as an argument against quantitative research. Nor do I mean to dismiss questions of methodological adequacy as unimportant or irrelevant. But I do insist that methodological adequacy is far from enough to give legitimacy to any work. And for too long now, concern with the method of research has obscured attention to its substance, with the result that the credibility of the social sciences has been called into question and public support has been eroded.

Our quarrels about the value of hard versus soft data are irrelevant to the world and its problems, and unnecessary and distracting for us. Different research methods need not compete with each other; we need only understand that they tell us different kinds of things. Large-scale studies based on statistically representative samples have a place in the social sciences. But it isn't the *only* place. Such studies add to our knowledge. But they can't tap all the knowledge that is potentially available.

It would make us all feel good, I'm sure, to spend the next hour talking about the problems in quantitative research. But it's not what I'm about today. I started with some discussion about quantitative sociology because it's the mainstream of the discipline and thereby profoundly affects our lives and our careers.

For example, I recently reviewed a book by a young psychologist about the interface between work and family life in which she insists upon the dialectical relationship between the two and presents powerful data to document the thesis. The research on which the book is based is in the interactionist perspective, relying on in-depth interviews and observations both in the home and on the job. So far so good! But in her presentation and analysis she abandons that perspective and retreats to the traditional linear form—review of the literature, conceptual framework, presentation of data, analysis, summary, and conclusions.

The result is a rather unclear and unfocused product that's not as good as some of its parts. The data of interviews and observations are superb, but data and analysis are rarely brought together in a dynamic interaction that would allow the reader to experience that interplay and understand the impact of work on family life in some new and deeper way. The conceptual frame is weak precisely because it was imposed on the data from without rather than emerging from within as the method of grounded theory requires. There are some fifty pages of detailed observations of a day in the life of one family which give a fine flavor of life in the household, especially for the woman of the family whose work it is to stay at home to care for house, husband, and three young children. But we must wait for the "appropriate" chapter for any explication or analysis of these data.

What I'm describing here is a presentation style itself that wrenches the data out of the interactional context and forces them into a set of discrete segments and static categories that are no match for the dynamic quality of life the author tries to describe and analyze. Thus, for example, a husband's insistence that he does not bring the problems of his work day home with him is made much of in the early conceptual chapters and is left to stand without supporting or, more likely in this case, contradictory data from his wife. As one reads further, the data to call his easy assertion into question are there—usually both in the wife's words and his own deeds. But since the contradictions are not brought face-to-face with each other, the full force of their meaning escapes both analyst and reader and they are left unremarked and unanalyzed.

Even when this is not the case, however, the analysis often is less than compelling precisely because we hear the different sides of the experience only in their "proper" place. Indeed, throughout the book, the impact of the husband's work life on the family is treated separately from the wife's work life—as if the two were not intimately connected. Reading these separate chapters, it was hard to remember that the purpose of the research was to demonstrate just such interconnections. I had to remind myself that the author *must* know that husband's and wife's work lives are each a product of the other, both part of the reciprocal system of gender roles that are part and parcel of the work and family systems she was analyzing.

Part of the problem for this author, as for others of us who work in the interactionist model, is that the canons of social science reporting generally require this formal, linear presentation—stylized and ritualized. Yet the life we would describe and analyze is complex and disorderly, each part interacting with and upon the other in a dynamic and dialectical set of relationships which do not lend themselves to this mode of presentation.

The author of the book in question knows this, of course, as is evident from the avowed purpose of the work—that is, to heal the split of what she calls the "myth of separate worlds" of work and family. Yet she retreated from this knowledge by relying on the traditional model of presentation and interpretation and, in the process, did violence both to her data and to her own wish to portray these interconnections in some coherent form. Worst of all, she perpetuated the very split she set out to heal by her failure to grasp and credit the essential truth that form is no more separable from content than is work from family life.

So why does it happen that way? Why is it that so often those who are strong enough and bright enough to question the established order, those who struggle so diligently to break the bonds of their professional socialization, can't or don't go the whole way? Partly, of course, that's because their careers are at stake. Whether submitting for journal review or to an editor in a publishing house, the safest approach is the standard form.

I was reminded recently of the cold chill some establishment sociologists can put on our minds and hearts. I was at dinner at the home of good friends where another guest was one of the more eminent members of our profession. Throughout the evening conversation with him was difficult because each time I reached for my own experience as a way of trying to understand the issue under discussion—why a particular book achieved its popularity, what meaning friends have in people's lives—he demurred. Finally, in exasperation, he remonstrated: "Come now, Lillian. This discussion cannot proceed if you persist in using yourself as a sample of one, as if that could tell us anything about the rest of the world."

I said nothing because I couldn't. It seemed impossible to continue a conversation where the basic assumptions were so deeply incompatible. But I remember feeling like a chastised child made to wonder about whether I was smart enough to keep this "grownup" company. And I remember, too, how grateful I was that I didn't have to depend on him for a tenure or promotion decision or, more important, for my sense of my self and my worth.

THE INTERACTIONIST METHOD:
DIFFICULTIES AND COMPLEXITIES

But there's something perhaps more important than such considerations—something that lies in the interactionist method itself and the kinds of data it generates. For the very complexity and disorderliness of the data—let alone the sheer volume—can be bewildering, indeed overwhelming. And the model we all learned in our training at least gives some semblance of order.

Anyone who has ever done research in the field knows about the anxiety of that period, and the struggle—too often lost—against premature closure just in order to gain some control, to put some punctuation around what seems like a boundless and limitless enterprise. Even after more than a decade of doing this kind of work, that anxiety haunts me from the day I enter the field until the day I leave it—some days worse than others, but never wholly absent. My own way of handling it is to rush through the fieldwork at breakneck speed, pushing myself almost beyond the limits of endurance because even exhaustion is better than anxiety. But pushing myself so mercilessly is not simply a way to cope with anxiety. For, in truth, I know all too well my need for control and order, and if I move at a slower pace, I don't quite trust myself not to make conceptual order where there is yet none.

Some people, among them those who have less problem with the issue of control—a personality type not terribly common among those of us drawn to the academic life—may be more comfortable in the field but less so at the data analysis stage. If the data haven't been controlled properly from the first day of the research, the volume alone can be so staggering that any ordering device seems like a lifeline to one who is about to drown.

That's not an issue in my own work because I control and code the data so carefully—compulsively, some might say—from the first moment in the field. That ordering system, however, generally reflects a set of descriptive categories rather than analytic ones—deliberately so at that stage of the research because the purpose is, quite simply, to ensure that the data will be accessible for analysis when and as I use them.

Still, the issue of how and where to start can be perplexing indeed. My own way is to pick some piece of the data that is at once discrete enough to be manageable while at the same time so intertwined with the whole that I cannot possibly lose sight of the interconnection in my analysis and presentation. In the case of *Worlds of Pain* (Rubin, 1976), for example, the first data set I tackled was the material on sexual interaction in the families—discrete yet clearly enmeshed in all the issues of marital interaction and communication I was studying. In *Women of a Certain Age* (Rubin, 1979) it was the issue of motherhood that I took on first—one that would serve the same function as sex had in the earlier work.

But for the interactionist researcher, there are few models in the literature that teach how to present the data in context and also to manage the interplay between data and analysis so that they are part of a dynamic presentation; fewer still that give any clues at all to the problems of presenting an array of data that are the product of a series of interviews. Consequently, there is a small vogue now among sociologists of this persuasion to present edited versions of their tape-recorded interviews as a way of managing the volume of data and of not distorting the context. Such work has the advantage of respecting and preserving the richness and complexity of human life and of the individuals who live it. The best of it manages also to convey process as well as content so that we may have a fuller understanding of the issues under study.

But—and in my view, this is a big "but"—most of these researchers have all but abandoned analysis altogether. It's true that their editing sometimes can be quite creative—highlighting common themes, pointing to conceptual possibilities. But the reader too often has only these hints of direction and possibilities to go on, each person left to fill in the blanks, as it were, according to personal or theoretical predilections.

If, however, we think of ourselves as analysts of social life rather than just reporters, this mode simply is not enough. It's not good enough to say that we will let people "speak for themselves." For, in fact, while they will often give us telling and poignant words, they rarely "speak for themselves." It's our task, it seems to me, to try to understand what lies behind those words without violating their spirit and intent, to bring to the surface the latent meanings that may lie outside the immediate awareness of the person who speaks them. And it's our task, too, to develop some system of ordering those words into a conceptual frame that permits a broader and deeper understanding than already exists.

This doesn't mean imposing a theory on the data from without. But our unwillingness to violate the data by such an imposition should not disable us from the search for order from within.

But these are difficult issues, not to be dismissed with a few easy sentences. For that search is an almost infinitely complex and difficult one, made especially so for those of us who take seriously the search for symbolic meanings; who believe in the need to develop a reflexive sociology that respects process as much as product; and perhaps most important of all, who recognize that such order is not a fixed and immutable single truth, but one that is both partial and also is filtered through the subjective experience of the researcher.

Let it be clear that I don't mean by those words to disparage such truths when compared to the kind of truth our quantitative colleagues insist they find. Rather it seems clear to me that there is no other kind of truth, whether in the social sciences or the physical ones. Each bit of knowledge is partial, each great discovery subject to modification when the next comes in. For in any given personal and historical moment, there is a limited store of knowledge accessible to us. We can, as it were, only know what we know. And from the questions we think to ask to the analysis and theory we develop, we are constrained by that limitation.

SUBJECTIVITY AND OBJECTIVITY: THE UTILITY OF CLINICAL TRAINING

The quest then should not be for the fool's gold of objectivity but for the real gold of self-awareness. For it is not our subjectivity that entraps us, but our belief that somehow we can be free of it. Indeed, the danger to sociology lies not in the fact that we who do it are sentient beings, but in our denial of the importance of that reality to the research process and its product. That denial too often leaves us lacking in awareness of both past and immediate experience, therefore, unable to control and use that experience in the search for knowledge and order. Moreover, the failure of awareness of our own inner processes inhibits our capacity for empathy with others and, thereby, deprives us of a rich source of understanding.

Two things are implied in all this. First, the only way we can be trapped by our subjectivity is for it to be out of awareness—a fact that Freud taught us long ago but which we manage so often to forget. And second, that the beginning of all knowledge lies inside the individual—in the subjective experiences of a lifetime and the meanings imputed to them. This position emphatically does not deny the importance of objective, material conditions in shaping both individual behavior and human social life. It insists only that knowledge is subjectively acquired in the sense that each of us gives meaning to our experience. The fact that these meanings often are not singular or unique, but that particular experiences will have common meanings among people who live in a shared sociocultural setting, is a testament to the power of group life in shaping the consciousness of the individual—the singular phenomenon that makes sociology possible as a discipline. For sociologists, therefore, to claim freedom from that consciousness, or to argue that they can stand apart from it without first coming to terms with it, stands in profound contradiction to the discipline's most basic assumption: that is, that their social environment shapes people in countless ways—ways that are sometimes so subtle that they can be brought into awareness only with a difficult struggle.

In that struggle for awareness, training in clinical psychology can be an invaluable aid. For it is precisely in developing awareness of self and other, and in the use of that awareness to facilitate understanding of the interactional field, that clinical training can make its strongest contribution to our research capabilities. The skills gained there not only direct attention to latent meanings, but teach how to interpret them. They can show us where to look for the unspoken message and how to make it articulate. Those also are the skills that facilitate the use of subjective responses and experience in a disciplined way so that they don't degenerate into a kind of confused identification.

In my own case, it took my first major research project—a study of a community in political struggle over its schools that rested on two years of observation and many interviews—to show me the limitations of the skills I brought to the task. In the interviews I was both elated and frustrated—elated, because I learned so much by careful questioning and even more careful listening; frustrated, because I knew intuitively there was more to know and I didn't yet know how to go about getting it. By the time I had been in the field for six months, I was convinced I needed clinical training to find those ways. I spent the next two years in that endeavor while I also finished the research that had started me on that path.

While I started the training as an aid to doing sociological research, today I spend about half my professional time doing clinical work. Partly that's because it's one of the ways I can remain independent of the institutional constraints of academic life, and partly because it remains an invaluable adjunct to my research—a reminder always that there is no meaning without context, constant practice in hearing what isn't said as well as what is, and in using my own reactions to understand and interpret what I see and hear.

Some examples here will help, I think. It is an accepted "finding" of sociological research that most American parents want their children to go to college. Yet in my study of working-class families something else emerged—at the very least a strong ambivalence, sometimes an outright rejection of the idea of college for their children. The method makes the difference.

In a survey, people often say what they know is the socially accepted and expected response. It isn't that they mean to lie or to confound the research; it's that it's in the nature of survey questions to ask for a definite answer, which means that people can speak only to one side of their feelings. Indeed, it's one of the great problems of large-scale surveys that they can neither tap our ambivalence nor leave room for shades of meaning. Thus, when such research asks working-class parents if they want their children to go to college, they respond with a ready "yes." Perhaps they don't precisely mean "yes" to that particular question. But they surely mean they want their children to have a good life, and they know that's at least one meaning of the question as well. So "yes" stands for a lot, even though not exactly a response to the question asked.

In fact, if one knows how to ask the question and to listen carefully to the answers, there's plenty of ambivalence to be heard among working-class parents about higher education for their children—an ambivalence that makes sense in the context of working-class life. For fathers, there's the derogation of what they call "pencil pushers"—work that seems boring done by men who seem unmanly. Not something to aspire to for your own son. For both parents, there are the fears that children will be lost to the family if they climb too high, go too far—fears expressed with superb sensitivity in the interaction between father and son in the film *Breaking Away*. For such uncertain rewards, many working-class parents are unwilling to make yet another sacrifice.

But it's hard to talk about such fears and feelings in a society where it's assumed that the best and the brightest will be college educated, where it's a mark of parental devotion to aspire to that for your child. One way I was able to get to that side of the ambivalence was through a discussion of just what sacrifice college attendance entails.

When people told me that they wanted their children to go to college, I asked if they had any idea of the cost. Almost always they said, yes, they knew it was expensive. How expensive? I asked. Most didn't know. Asked to guess, they generally reckoned it to be about "$500, maybe a little more," and were staggered to hear that their estimates would have to be revised upward by considerable amounts. At that news, most people quickly moved to expressing their negative feelings about college and college students, wondering aloud whether it was worth it, or saying unequivocally that their children would just have to do it on their own. Once that side of their ambivalence was articulated, it was a much shorter step—and now one that was possible for them to take—to open up their deeper-lying fears and feelings about the meaning of college attendance for family relationships. But even then, much of this cannot be said directly, and an investigator must know how to hear the many-sided message in the words that are spoken.

In this case, I was aided by three things. The first is my personal experience in a working-class family where the cost to family relations of my own social and geographic mobility is patently and painfully clear to all of us. The second is my clinical background which has taught me how to use that personal experience to its best advantage in establishing rapport, in eliciting the data, in hearing and crediting ambivalence, in sensitivity to nuance in both what is spoken and what isn't. And the third, of course, is a method that allows me to use *all* my skills and knowledge in my search for understanding.

The formal data collection method of this research was the in-depth, focused interview during which I talked with people for several hours.[1] But I also "hung out" with many of the people I met, often for a long while, after I had packed up my tape recorder and pencil—drinking coffee, a beer, or a glass of wine; chatting informally about many of the matters we had just finished discussing in the interview; sharing my life story with them as they had shared theirs with me; using my clinical experience and expertise to help with a marriage problem, or one with a child.

It was then—when the structure of the interaction bespoke some kind of rough equality—that often they were able to be more open about many things, including whatever criticisms they may have had about my conduct of the research. The changed atmosphere called for more spontaneity of expression and people responded accordingly. In addition, there was time then to reflect on what had been said earlier—to add some things, to modify others. But there was something else as well. We were no longer the researcher and the researched. Instead I was a guest in their home. Those altered identities permitted a different kind of interaction which, quite naturally, tapped a set of responses that were not available during the formal part of the interview.

Out of all this emerged the evidence for findings that contradict the received sociological wisdom—a contradiction that has important implications for both the method and substance of our discipline. For what becomes clear in the course of such face-to-face interactions with our research subjects is how much misunderstanding is attributable to the very methods of our research. In this example, both middle-class and working-class parents may say "yes" to a survey question that asks whether they want their children to go to college. But that seemingly simple "yes" has very different meanings to both populations. For the middle class, it comes out of a set of shared understandings with the framer of the question, and is most likely a statement of intention that is grounded in solid information and understanding about certain realities, such as cost. Therefore, it's a "yes" that has a high probability of being followed by behavior. For the working class, however, it's a response based partly on wish, partly on fantasy, partly on social expectations—all of this muddied by unexpressed, perhaps dimly understood, fears and ambivalence. Without a research method that credits those differences and a strategy that seeks to understand meanings, such answers tell us very little; indeed, may mislead us altogether.

But my purpose here is to point to the utility of clinical skills in the research setting, and it's to that that I want to return more specifically. The sensitivity to timing, the awareness of the meaning and importance of sequencing, the understanding of layering of emotional material, and the care necessary to get from one layer to the next without shutting a person down entirely—these are the skills that clinical training helps to develop, skills that are crucial to getting the maximum amount of data from any interview.

My current work—a cross-class, cross-sex study of adult friendship—recently taught me this lesson anew, but this time by reminding me of the importance of recognizing, understanding, and managing transference and countertransference issues so that they become a source of data rather than a barrier to it.[2]

Anyone who has ever looked at the sociological literature on friendship knows how impoverished it is. And anyone who has ever thought to study the issue will understand why. It's a slippery subject at best—without institutional form, without a clearly defined set of norms for behavior or an agreed-upon set of reciprocal rights and obligations, without even any widely shared agreement about what is a friend. What to me may be just an acquaintance, for example, to you may be a close friend. How then can I know who's who and what's what? If I'm not content simply to count people and encounters (although, of course, I will do that as well), but am concerned primarily with the meaning of these relationships in people's lives, then it becomes particularly important for me to be able to sort out the answer to such a question. But how? A series of experiences in the field gave me my first clue.

I was interviewing a thirty-two-year-old man who spoke with ease and authority about his "fifteen or twenty" intimate friends. No matter how much I pushed, probed, and prodded, he had all the "right" answers. Yes, he could talk to them about anything that was troubling him. Yes, he turned to them in times of trial. "Trust," he said, "and joint helpfulness"—these were the central and defining features of friendship for him. And could he count on all these fifteen or twenty people of whom he spoke to be trusting and helpful in any situation? Yes, he assured me, he could.

As the interview progressed, I became aware that I was feeling empty, restless, bored—feelings I had encountered with some frequency in the study but never before in all my previous research. I wondered then as I had wondered before why I was feeling this way. Was it the subject matter? Was I discovering that I didn't want to be doing this study? Was it too hard? It all seemed muddled and impossible. The only thing I knew with certainty was that these responses were very uncharacteristic of me in the field stage of a project. Anxiety, yes. Boredom, restlessness? Never!

I continued the interview and listened with mounting irritation as he told me about his best friend—a man who lives in the east. How often did they see each other? I asked. Well, in fact, they hadn't seen each other since he moved east 10 years ago. Did they talk on the telephone? Not really; maybe a couple of times in the 10 years. What makes him a best friend, then? "Trust, that's what it is," he asserted stoutly. "I know I can absolutely trust him." Trust him with what? I asked. "With anything," he replied. "With anything I need. I could land on his doorstep in the cold of winter and the dead of night, and I know he'd be right there." Flippantly, and without really expecting any surprises in the answer, I wisecracked, "And just where is that doorstep on which you'd always be welcome to land?" A moment of silence, and then the answer. "I'm not sure. You see, he moved a while back and I don't know exactly where he lives now." How far back? "I don't remember exactly—a couple of years maybe."

Two hours of this and I could hardly wait to get out, which I did at the first reasonable moment. I went back to my office, processed the interview, and prepared it for transcription—all the while feeling both perplexed and depressed, trying unsuccessfully to figure out what was the common denominator in those interviews that stirred these uncomfortable and unaccustomed feelings. It wasn't simply that the data were not making sense. I fully expect that I'll have to sift beneath the surface of people's words to find understanding. I know, too, that each interview probably will contain contradiction—evidence of the many-sided nature of the questions I ask and the people of whom I ask them. Oftentimes I can confront those contradictions in the field and ask for help in their resolution. But it was precisely my inability to do that in some of these friendship interviews that puzzled me so. For I hadn't yet come to realize what was going on. I only knew that I was in the presence of unspoken pain and sensed a certain fragility that warned against the risk of such confrontation. The rest would await my next day of clinical work when I was with a patient who seemed to be speaking earnestly about an issue yet I found myself struggling against the same set of feelings—emptiness, boredom, restlessness.

It was a dramatic moment—another lesson in the power of the social setting to influence perception. As a clinician, there wasn't a moment lost in understanding the meaning of those feelings. It was as if a neon sign lit inside me emblazoned with the word *countertransference*—a complicated phenomenon which is an inevitable part of the therapeutic encounter and that can take many forms (see note 2 for elaboration). In this case, it was quite simply a signal that the patient and I were sharing the same emotional state, an unconscious mirroring on my part of his inner experience, that told me that the words he spoke were not connected to the feelings inside him.

In the same instant, I understood the meaning of my feelings in the interview two days earlier—and all those that went before as well. Like my patient, the words my informant used to speak about his friendships didn't match his inner reality. The result—whether in patient or other—is a disconnectedness from self that is reflected in just such a state of empty, bored restlessness, a state that serves to sustain the denial and repression of emotionally loaded material. Such states often are communicated to us in all kinds of interpersonal interactions. But we can't always bring the message into awareness. Instead, all we know is that we have to move, that we feel somehow at loose ends, bored, maybe even depressed. Leave the setting and we'll usually leave the feelings as well.

What was surprising to me was that I didn't recognize the meaning of my feelings for so long—partly, I'm now certain, out of my own anxiety about the subject matter and whether I could or would ever make sense of it; and partly, and perhaps more important, because of my mental set about what I was looking for—about what can reasonably be called "data." It's an interesting example of the dissociation of which the human mind and psyche is capable when, despite the fact that the two roles are filtered through one person, the researcher couldn't grasp what was instantly clear to the clinician.

But what about the validity of such data? In the clinical setting I can check out whether my reaction is indeed a countertransference phenomenon with an appropriate interpretation. If it works—that is, if the atmosphere in the room visibly changes; if my patient suddenly becomes conscious of the discrepancy and can make the words and the music match, so to speak—then I know I'm on the mark. But how do we affirm such an interpretation in the field of research? It's more difficult, partly because we don't have a therapeutic contract with our research subjects, therefore no right to strip away defenses which may be serving them well. Still, it's not impossible.

For example, once I understood what was going on, I was virtually certain that I had left the man I have been talking about as depressed as I felt after that interview. And having spent those hours with him, I also knew that his defenses would not be easily breached so it would be safe to risk a small confrontation. We had already arranged for me to telephone him to get the names of some of his friends so that I could interview them. In the course of that conversation, I asked him how he had felt after I left his house. "It's funny you should ask," he said, "because I felt kind of low for the rest of the afternoon." Any idea why? I said. "Nope, do you?" he retorted. "Perhaps," I replied. "Maybe you didn't feel quite comfortable with everything you told me about your friendships. Maybe they're not as solid as you'd like to think." Silence at the other end of the line for what seemed like a long while, then a sigh, "Maybe you're right."

In fact, once one learns to read and credit the data of experience, it's not so difficult to find diverse ways to affirm or deny it. In this instance, I interviewed several of the people this man called intimates in order to check out the stories he told. None of them claimed him among their close circle of friends.

All of this, of course, has simply opened up the next set of questions. Why, I now ask myself, is there so much denial and dissimulation about this subject? It never occurred to me before I went into the field that this would be the case—that, in fact, it's harder to get straight answers to questions about friends than it is about family life, including even such intimate matters as sexual relations.

I don't have answers yet—only questions, and some speculations, most of which are beyond the scope of this talk. But let me share a little of that process with you because it certainly touches on the methodological issues with which we're concerned.

It seems clear to me now that one of the problems lies in the very definition of the research. When I approach people about being interviewed, I tell them I'm studying friendship and would like to talk to them about their experiences. People, therefore, are prepared to talk about friends. It's as if the definition of the project predetermines the answers I'll get; people will find friendships even where they don't exist.

That may be true about any subject, of course. If I'm researching marriage, people will talk to me about their marriages. But there's an important difference there. For we all know what is a marriage and what is not. Indeed, even in those relationships—becoming more common today—where people live together without a legal marriage but maintain similarly serious commitments, there's a broad consensus about what is and what is not such a relationship. Perhaps we would not always agree on a formal definition, but there certainly are a set of shared understandings and a shared language that allow us to talk about those relationships with some certainty that we are, in fact, talking about the same thing.

What I'm saying is that, as a general rule, the other side of marriage is "not marriage." So if I want to know about marriage, I find people who are married and rule out those who are not. Similarly, if I want to know about marriage failures, I talk to people who have lived through them. But what's the other side of friendship? Isolation? Loneliness? Alienation? Or is it not so clear and sharp a break? We all know there's a continuum of relationships ranging from casual to intimate. Then why is it that so many people claim intimacy and persist in using the language of intimacy even where it clearly doesn't exist, even where I give plenty of clues and opportunity for talking about their friendship relationships in other terms?

It's interesting, too, that I haven't yet encountered the first serious resistance to being interviewed on the subject; indeed, quite the contrary. A few people have said doubtfully: "I don't know if I have anything to say on the subject, but I'd be glad to talk to you about it." But most comment excitedly about their interest in the matter and look forward eagerly to talking about it. Some people—those who do in fact have committed and intimate friendships; or at the other end, the few who can acknowledge that they feel troubled about those relationships and their capacity to make or sustain them—do speak convincingly. But most expose the contradictions I've been speaking of, often leaving me with the same uncomfortable feelings I described earlier. And I wonder: Are they eager to do the interview because they're trying to learn something about themselves and their friendship history, perhaps trying to work through some unresolved problems and conflicts around this issue?

The same questions, of course, apply to me. For it is surely no accident that I chose to study this subject at this time in my life.

The surprising reality, however, is that people generally seem more able to talk openly about the problems in or failures of their love relationships than their friendships. That might be because we know better what to expect in a love relationship, because the rules and boundaries—however imperfectly articulated or realized, however much in flux in this historical moment—are, for most of us, more clearly understood. I'm not suggesting here that the expectations in love are any more realistic or grounded in self-awareness than are those of friendship. It's only that—whatever they are—the rules of acceptable and unacceptable behavior, of reciprocal rights and obligations, are clearer and experienced with a greater sense of entitlement.

Still, the question haunts me. Why is it easier for people to talk about failure in love than failure in friendship? Is it simply because everyone knows about and accepts failures in love these days, because for most of us that's no longer a stigma? Perhaps because that's true, friends become even more important in both the conduct and quality of our daily lives; therefore we conjure fantasies of them in the same way we have always before done about love relationships.

But whatever it all means, one thing is certain. The eager response to a request for an interview, the contradictions, the emotional tone of the interaction, what isn't said as much as what is—all these are part of the data of the study and must be understood if I'm to know anything more than I did when I started about the meaning of friendship in the lives of adult women and men.

I have talked at length about the usefulness of clinical skills in assessing and understanding the unspoken and the subjective, in penetrating beneath the surface to get at deeper layers of meaning. Am I suggesting then that without clinical training all is lost? Of course not! People have done and will continue to do exciting and outstanding work in the interactionist tradition without that training. But I suspect that many of those people are "natural" clinicians—sensitive to their own feelings and those of others, introspective, intuitive, and psychologically minded; and perhaps have learned much about themselves and their responses to the world from their own psychotherapy. The important point in all this is that, given the complex nature of human social life and the stubbornness—even intransigence—with which it defies our attempts at understanding, we need every bit of ingenuity we can muster and every tool we can beg, borrow, or steal to aid in the task we have set for ourselves.

MARGINALITY AND INGENUITY

Interestingly enough, in that quest for ingenuity—for new tools and new ways—marginality has advantages, painful though it may also be. For given the mainstream of sociology today, it's very nearly impossible for young people to remain true to the interactionist tradition and build a career in a first-line university and first-line department. Recall where I started today—with the fact that in a five-year period, only 11 percent of the articles published in three major journals were in the interactionist perspective, whether theoretical or empirical. With the job market and tenure race what they are today, who can afford to be an interactionist?

In my own case, I finished my graduate work at Berkeley in 1971—already in my mid-forties, married, committed to living in the San Francisco Bay Area. There were no job possibilities for me then, no fantasies about a big-time academic career. So it was easy not to sell out to an establishment that wasn't offering me anything. I had no choice but to set about making an alternative career for myself.

Paradoxically, marginality became opportunity—an important contributor to whatever success I have had, including your invitation to give this lecture today. Because it was precisely that marginal status that permitted me to risk the unorthodox as I searched for a way of doing sociology that seemed to me grounded in reality, and a voice with which to express what I was doing that was authentically mine.

NOTES

This chapter was originally given as the distinguished lecture to the Annual Meeting of the Society for the Study of Symbolic Interactions, August 9, 1980, New York City.

1. In style, the interviews I do lie somewhere between a research instrument and a clinical hour—a technique that serves the goals of flexibility and adaptability, and that facilitates the emergence of unanticipated data. At the same time, the fact that the interview is focused prevents aimless wandering, ensures that all interviews will cover the same basic ground, and gives the interviewer the structure with which to remain in control of the interview situation.

Such interviews are best done by people who have had some training in clinical psychology. Clinical skills are invaluable for extracting the maximum data because (1) they enable the interviewer to establish quickly a facilitative, nonthreatening, neutral atmosphere that frees respondents to share their thoughts, feelings, and perceptions; (2) the interviewer is capable of sorting out and grasping the dynamic underlying the responses she gets; (3) the interviewer is trained to make grounded judgments about when she is meeting resistance or denial, when to push for more data, and when to back off because she runs the risk of threatening or alienating the respondent; and (4) clinically trained persons are not only attuned to the dynamic processes of the other, but have learned to attend to their own in order to minimize countertransference effects. That means that they are more capable of controlling their own tendencies to projection, thus more able than most to "hear" and perceive the pespective of the other, even when dealing with highly emotion-laden material.

2. The psychoanalytic concepts of transference and countertransference have generated a large literature with much controversy. It would be presumptuous to believe that this debate could be explicated, let alone untangled, in a brief footnote. Still, some broad definitions are in order so that the reader outside the field will have some guides to the meanings of these technical terms.

Transference refers to the fact that, as Janet Malcolm (1980) says in her excellent series of articles in *The New Yorker* magazine: "We all invent each other according to early blueprints." That means that in any relationship, we project or "transfer" onto the other the repressed wishes, deprivations, and unconscious fantasies of a lifetime. Then we behave toward that other as if this were an undistorted reality. Thus, for example, in the therapeutic setting, a patient who had a sadistic parent will transfer the expectation of such punishing behavior onto the analyst irrespective of the actual personality or behavior of the therapist.

The defining feature of psychoanalytic psychotherapy (as opposed to some other treatment modes—most notably gestalt therapy and the behavior therapies) is the analysis of the transference. By making conscious the unconscious sources of the transference, the patient gains the ability to relate to the therapist as a real person rather than transforming her/him into the feared parent of childhood.

According to psychoanalytic theory, transference is a universal phenomenon in the clinical setting. Indeed, the clinical enterprise derives its power precisely because it provides a setting within which the patient actually reexperiences the early trauma through its repetition in the transference. The healing is effected through the analysis of the transference which brings the repressed material into memory, therefore under conscious control.

Countertransference, as the word implies, refers to the unconscious emotional responses of the therapist to the patient. The classical psychoanalytic view holds that these countertransference responses are a hindrance to effective analytic therapy. Therefore, when they occur it is suggested that the therapist is in need of further analysis in order to resolve the conflicts that underly these unconscious responses. The notion, then, is that it is both possible and desirable to control the countertransference.

More recent psychoanalytic thinking suggests quite the opposite. In this new view, the emotional responses of the therapist are taken to be an integral and important part of the therapeutic encounter. Countertransference is seen as a continuous and inevitable phenomenon in which the therapist's reactions are a response both to the actual situation and the patient's transference.

Understood and read this way, these responses become part of the therapist's packet of tools in the conduct of therapy. When carefully scrutinized and properly understood, the countertransference becomes the therapist's most reliable guide to knowing what is most salient in the patient's communication and behavior, thus what requires the most immediate response. In sum, countertransference is an important source of information not only about the patient, but about the ongoing therapeutic process as well.

REFERENCES

Malcolm, Janet. 1980. "The Impossible Profession." *The New Yorker* (November 24; December 1).

Rubin, Lillian B. 1979. *Women of a Certain Age.* New York: Harper & Row.

———. 1976. *Worlds of Pain.* New York: Basic Books/Harper Colophon.

Spector, Malcolm, and Robert Faulkner. 1980. "Thoughts on Five New Journals and Some Old Ones." *Contemporary Sociology* 9, no. 4 (July): 477–482.

Spence, Janet. 1980. *Contemporary Psychology* 25: 273–274.

PART II

DISCOVERING DIFFERENCE, CONSTANTLY CLASS-CONSCIOUS

Family Values and the Invisible Working Class

We Americans have a long history of using words to obscure unpleasant realities. We spin, we twist, we label. Sometimes a new label makes sense. The shift from *cripple,* with the ugly associations it has for so long evoked in both literature and life, to the more neutral *handicapped* has enabled us to look the disabled in the face with greater ease. But whether for good or ill, the words we choose, *downsizing,* for example—and those we *don't* choose to use, like *working class*—have social and political consequences that too often go unnoticed.

In the last several years hardly a week has gone by when some corporate giant hasn't announced the firing of more workers. Only we never use that word anymore. We talk instead about *layoffs,* a word that implies that these workers are caught in some temporary company downturn, something like what my mother used to experience during what's known as the "slack season" in the garment industry. But for today's worker, the "regular" season never comes around again.

Not only don't we fire people anymore, but we have a whole new corporate language, words designed to make the process seem harmless, as if we were doing nothing more than tinkering with the corporate structure. So we *downsize, restructure, reengineer,* or, most bizarre of all, *rightsize.*

Rightsize! It's a word coined by IBM's CEO Louis Gerstner and designed to shield companies from criticism by obscuring the human consequences of these greedy moves to increase corporate profits—not to mention their CEOs' earnings. After all, if a company is right-sized—the implication being that something wrong is now being righted—how can anyone complain? For each company that right-sizes or restructures itself, however, thousands of women and men lose their jobs, and with them their hold on the American dream.

But why worry about this now? Government officials and the press keep citing various economic indicators to show that the recession of the early 1990s is over:

unemployment is down; despite the recent gyrations on Wall Street, the economy is growing; we've added an impressive 10 million new jobs since 1993.

So why are so many American families in such pain? Perhaps because the experts forgot to say that nearly 8.5 million people—one out of every fourteen workers, most of them women and men in working-class families—were fired in the two years between 1993 and 1995. That's on top of the 9 million workers who were rendered jobless in the first three years of this decade. Nor do they explain that the official unemployment rate is different from the *real* one, since the Labor Department figures include only those who have been looking for work in the week of the count. Which leaves out the millions of workers who, after months of looking, have given up hope and abandoned the search.

The experts don't tell us either that, while the official unemployment rate may have declined, the number of workers who are downsized out of their jobs continues to climb. Nor do they bother to add that most of the newly created jobs are low-level service jobs that pay a fraction of what these millions of men and women were earning before they got rightsized and downsized out of work. And they ignore the fact that a very large number of these same new jobs are temporary, which means that they offer no benefits and pay less than permanent full-time work.

Characteristically, we now have a new name for these "temps" as well. "Contingent workers," the Labor Department calls them, a name that allows us to look away from the fact that these are, in the words of some labor economists, "throwaway workers." Tens of millions of women and men live with that grim reality every day—with the knowledge that, for their employers, they're interchangeable and, like objects that are no longer useful, just as easily disposable. Emotionally, it corrodes their inner sense of themselves and their value; economically, they live with fear and uncertainty, worrying when they wake each day that by nightfall they'll be out of even the inadequate job they cling to so desperately.

In my recent study of working-class families, *Families on the Fault Line*— those whose voices are seldom heard in the cacophony of noise and demand that make up our public life—I interviewed 162 families who live in cities across the country.[1] The sample consisted of ninety-two white ethnic families, thirty African Americans, twenty Latinos, and twenty Asians. The median age of the women was thirty-two; of the men, thirty-seven. Sixteen percent of the families were headed by a woman—three-fourths because they were divorced; the rest, except for one who was widowed, because they had never married. Roughly a third were second marriages for at least one of the partners. The husband-wife families had been married at least five years; the range was five to thirty years. Whenever possible, I interviewed wives, husbands, and teenage children, for a total of 388 separate in-depth, face-to-face, focused interviews.

Over the course of the last decade about a quarter of the men and women I met learned firsthand about the pain and uncertainty of being disposable workers. And all spoke bitterly of the experience. "It's like they don't see you like a person," complained a thirty-two-year-old father of three children; "like you don't have bills and kids. They don't need you anymore, so they toss you out like you're not a real human being. I've been looking for steady work for eight or nine months, but there ain't none, least none I can get. So me and my wife, we live scared. I've got to depend on these temporary jobs, where the pay's lousy and you don't get any benefits. But at least with both of us working, we can pay the rent. What happens when I can't even get one of these rotten jobs? We'll be out on the street."

The *Wall Street Journal* and others like it keep telling us that the changes in corporate America are good for the country. I don't know whose country they're talking about, but it's certainly not the one in which most working-class families struggle to feed, clothe, and educate their children. In reality, whatever the gains of the lean corporate culture of the 1990s, they come at the expense of both the workers and the nation. For when a person cannot count on a permanent job, a critical element binding him or her to society is lost, and the consequence to both family and national life is devastating.

With millions of poor and working-class American families in just this situation, the current cant about family values, which displays no understanding of the social and economic bases necessary to sustain those values, becomes a shameful kind of political sophistry. Certainly some of the changes in family and social life in recent decades are cause for concern. Old rules have given way in every facet of family life, from the public world of work to the private arena of sex, while a new order is not yet fully in place. As we continue to move into uncertain social and emotional territory, anxieties rise and breed nostalgia for a past when, in retrospect, life seemed simpler, safer, and saner.

From this perspective, it's easy to understand the appeal of the family-values discourse. But it's a discussion in a vacuum. For as the values advocates frame it, the family itself *becomes* the context, as if families were atoms afloat in space, unconnected to the social and institutional life in which they are embedded.

If we're going to preach the politics of virtue, then we need to promote the social conditions that dispose people to be virtuous. The family-values champions, for example, complain endlessly that two working parents don't spend enough time with their children. But when the choice is between time and the money to pay the rent, time loses. If the values partisans care so much about time for family life, they would serve their cause better by, among other things, joining a movement to restructure the world of work and decrease the standard forty-hour work week to thirty-two hours.

Visionary? Yes. But that's what people said a century ago when the reformers of that era engaged the struggle for the forty-hour week that we now take as given in nature.

A job that pays a living wage and affords decent, safe housing—these are the fundamental needs, the twin girders on which family stability rests. Yet now, after two decades of rising rents and falling wages, millions of poor and working-class families have neither. Our national response to this reality? The president signs into law new housing legislation that puts an end to the decades-long promise to subsidize decent housing for low-income families. And the family-values band plays on.

In the real world, IBM rightsizes and families tremble as uncounted numbers of men who have supported their families for twenty years sit home and watch their wives go off to work. Or a single mother finds herself on welfare—that is, in the good old days when there was still a welfare program in place. Or a family that prided itself on its self-sufficiency suddenly finds itself buying groceries with food stamps instead of dollars. Or a child's illness goes untreated because the medical benefits that went with the job are gone and her parents can't afford the care that could help. Or the family loses their home and with it whatever stability they had managed to achieve.

In such circumstances, rates of depression rise markedly and alcohol abuse increases as people—usually men—seek some respite from the voices of shame and blame inside them. Among the families in my study, a fifth of the men were serious drinkers, a problem usually exacerbated by unemployment and underemployment. "My husband drinks a lot more now; I mean, he always drank some, but not like now," said a twenty-eight-year-old nurse's aide and mother of three children. "I guess he tries to drink away his troubles, but it only makes more trouble. I tell him, but he doesn't listen: He has a fiery temper, always has. But since he lost his job, it's real bad, and his drinking doesn't help it none."

As tensions heighten, so does family violence, leaving already fragile families even more at risk. "I worry a lot when he drinks, because he treats my little boy so terrible, punches him around," the same woman continued.

But it's not just the child who gets "punched around." When I asked if she, too, had felt the pain of her husband's violence, she looked away while her fingers plucked agitatedly at her jeans. Finally, as if in an unconscious wish to deny the reality, she shook her head no, but the words she spoke said something else. "Yeah, but only when he has too many beers. He doesn't mean it. It's just that he's so upset about being out of work."

Some kind of violence—sometimes against children only, more often against both women and children—is the admitted reality in about 14 percent of the families in this study. I say "admitted reality," because this remains one of the most closely guarded secrets in family life, a hidden shame that both women and men deny, even when the evidence is clearly visible. It's reasonable to assume, therefore, that the proportion of families victimized by violence is considerably higher.

Alcoholism, family violence, depression—these are old news, problems of family living that always escalate in times of stress. But now there's a new one to add to family tensions—the fear of homelessness. Over and over, people in this study talked about their terror that they might soon find themselves "on the street"—a fear that clutches at the heart and gnaws at the soul as unemployment and underemployment become a way of life in so many families.

Nothing exemplifies the change in the twenty years since I last studied working-class families, in *Worlds of Pain,* than the fear of being on the street.[2] Then, not a single person worried about being homeless. For them, homelessness was something that happened somewhere else, in India or some other far-off and alien land. Then, we wept when we read about the poor people who lived on the streets in those other places. *What kind of society doesn't provide this most basic of life's needs?* we asked ourselves. Now, the steadily growing numbers of homeless in our own land have become an ever-present and frightening reminder of just how precarious life in this society can be. Now, they're in our face, on our streets, an accepted category of American social life—"the homeless."

Just how readily accepted they are was brought home to me recently when my husband, who volunteers some time in the San Francisco schools, reported his experience with a sixth-grade class. He had been invited to talk to the children about career opportunities and, in doing so, talked about his own past as a restaurateur. The students listened, engrossed. But instead of the questions he had expected when he finished, they were preoccupied with how he managed the problem of the homeless. Did he feed homeless people when they asked for food? He explained that at the time he had restaurants in the Bay Area, there were no homeless on the streets. Undaunted, they wanted to know what he did when he found a homeless person sleeping in the doorway of the restaurant. He reminded them that he had just told them that homelessness wasn't an issue when he was in business. They listened, he said, but they couldn't really grasp the idea of a world without the homeless. How could it be otherwise? At their age, homelessness is so much a part of their daily world that they take it for granted, a phenomenon not of their time but of all times.

Obviously, all these family problems aren't with us only because IBM and a host of other companies have downsized, rightsized, and restructured. But these structural changes in the corporate economy have human consequences, and the words we have devised to speak of these events mask that reality and enable us to look away from the anguish they cause.

It's true, too, about the words we choose *not* to speak. Take the words *working class*—perfectly good words elsewhere in the world, but ones that have been written out of the American lexicon. It's another example of our American ingenuity, especially when it comes to using language to cloud reality. We call something by another name and behave as if we've made it so. Except that it doesn't work that way.

Everyone who has ever asked the question knows that most Americans, whether they're rich or poor, identify themselves as middle-class. Occasionally, a working-class man in one of my studies will say, "I'm a working man"—a statement made sometimes with pride, sometimes with anger, but rarely with any consciousness of class and its meaning in his life.

Not a surprise in a country where the media and the experts join in defining the middle class by the car in the driveway, the TV and VCR in the living room, the brand-name sneakers, the designer jeans, and all the other symbols that are the marks of status in our consumer-driven society. Or where the Congressional Budget Office lumps together as middle-class all families of four with annual incomes between $19,000 and $78,000—a range so wide as to be nonsensical to anyone but a politician.

Some progressive writers also now argue that we must cast aside the distinctions between the working and middle classes. In a recent article in *The Nation* (October 7, 1996), for example, Richard Parker insists that we must redefine *"progressive politics— clearly, bluntly and without compromise—as being about the permanent enlargement of the middle class"* (emphasis in original). I have no quarrel with his goal of improving the lot of all Americans, only with his argument that the idea of a working class no longer has any real meaning; only with his insistence that it's "antiquated and out of touch" to talk about the differences between the working and middle classes; only with his belief that progressive politics is best served by an enlarged middle class.

I agree that the old Marxist notion of class no longer applies to the American experience—that is, if it ever did. But that doesn't mean the divisions in this society should be blurred into irrelevancy. Rather, it suggests that we must find new ways to conceive and speak of them. Until we do, the language of class is all we have, and, its problems notwithstanding, it explains more than it obscures.

Even a cursory look at the statistics of the 1996 election reveals that, excepting those with postgraduate training, Americans vote more conservatively as they move up the education and income ladder, which means also the class ladder. In the congressional races, 55 percent of high school graduates—almost certainly working-class men and women—cast their vote for Democrats, while 57 percent of college graduates voted Republican. Voters with annual family incomes under $50,000 fell heavily in the Democratic column—the lower the income, the wider the margin. As income increased, so did support for the Republicans, rising from 53 percent to 63 percent as earnings climbed from $50,000 to $100,000 a year. And a convincing 63 percent of union households threw their support to Democratic contenders.

Certainly, as Mr. Parker points out, the middle class is larger today than it has ever been. Certainly, too, the weekly earnings of some workers at the top tier of the blue-collar pyramid may match those of middle-level white-collar managers. But these are the rare working-class jobs, the dream jobs of a world in which most workers have to settle for very much less. Equally important, even those in the most desirable blue-collar jobs are paid by the hour, while the middle manager earns a weekly wage. Since hourly work isn't as steady, the *annual* income of blue-collar workers is likely to be substantially less than the earnings of their white-collar counterparts, even when the hourly wage is higher.

Still, it's reasonable to ask what difference it makes if we distinguish between working-class and middle-class families. The label we affix doesn't change their lives, does it? The answer is both yes and no. In the immediate sense, no matter what we call people, their daily lives remain the same. But in the larger scheme, it makes a difference.

For one thing, despite all the media attention to the middle-class professionals who have been downsized out of their jobs, it is the blue-collar workers who were hit first and hardest in the new corporate culture. For another, the idea of the middle class is not just a handy social category, a shorthand way to describe a segment of the population. It has broad political and policy implications as well. For the way we conceive of our people determines how we think of their needs and, therefore, how government policy is made.

Someone benefits, someone loses each time a policy is promulgated. If the popular political language denies the very existence of a sector of the population, its needs aren't likely to be taken into account. Take housing, for example. While the federal government says it can no longer afford to subsidize rents for working-class families who have been priced out of the market, the mortgage-interest and property-tax deductions it grants to homeowners—benefits that accrue most heavily to the middle and upper-middle classes—cost the public treasury billions every year.

At a more basic level, it makes a difference in how people define themselves, because they can't see their own self-interest if they don't have the language to affirm it. For words are more than just words; they embody ideas, *our* ideas. Words are the symbols that frame our thoughts and guide our actions. Without the words, ideas are hard to come by—if they come at all. And without an idea that binds people together in some common cause—the idea of a working class that transcends race, ethnicity, and religion, for example—it's virtually impossible for people to organize in their own behalf.

The language of "working families" that dominated the recent presidential campaign—and that was adopted by the unions and other progressives—may serve the political need to appear inclusive. But the very breadth of the idea makes it problematic, since it encompasses the families of the Fortune 500 CEOs along with the families of the janitors, the machine operators, the truck drivers, and the shipping clerks who work for them. Without the language of class—and the *idea* it embodies—these most elementary class realities are obscured, and ordinary working-class families become invisible, swallowed up in the large, amorphous category of "working families." In this setting, the "working" part of the "working families" rhetoric too easily falls away, and we're left with a discourse about families and family values that is disconnected from the social and economic realities that determine the quality of family life.

Psychologically, too, the blurring of class issues makes a difference. In the short run, given the stigma attached to being working-class in this country, calling themselves middle-class may make people feel better about their social situation and enhance their self-esteem. Over the long haul, however, the denial of their class position leads to a confused and contradictory social identity that leaves working-class people riven with status anxiety and impairs their ability to join together to act in their own behalf.

The fact is that class inequalities not only exist in our society, they're handed down from parents to children in the same way that wealth is passed along in the upper class. True, American society has always had a less rigid and clearly defined class structure than many other nations. Poor people climb up; wealthy ones fall. These often well-publicized figures help to support the myth about equality of opportunity. But they're not the norm. Nor is the perpetuation of our class structure accidental. The economy, the polity, and the educational system all play their part in ensuring the continuity and stability of our social classes.

Look at public education. Myth tells us that it's the great equalizer, the one institution in our society that promises every child the same education and, therefore, an equal chance at the good life. Yet educational researchers have known for years that a school's achievement record is closely correlated with its students' socioeconomic status. It's no secret either that schools in poor and working-class neighborhoods have fewer resources and worse physical plants than those in the wealthier ones. The best teachers, the cleanest books, the most supplies seem to find their way more often into the schools that serve white middle-class children than into those attended by the poor and working class.

The problem is not only that schools for middle-class children are more pleasant, better-equipped places, although surely the environment has something to do with how well children learn. These differences also count because they send a message about who and what this society values—a message that working-class children hear very clearly.

Despite their social and political invisibility and the disparity in the resources allocated to their schools and communities (just look at the difference in the maintenance of the streets in urban working-class and middle-class neighborhoods), working-class families are the single biggest group of families in the country. These are the men and women who provide our services and who make our goods in what's left of the manufacturing sector—workers whose education is limited, whose mobility options are restricted, and who work for an hourly rather than a weekly wage. They don't tap public resources; they reap no benefit from either the pitiful handouts to the poor or from huge subsidies to the rich.

But all too often they live on the edge. Any unexpected event threatens to throw them into the abyss. Credit, if they're able to get it at all, is stretched to the limit. The machine spits out the plastic card that helped them deal with the steady erosion of income in recent years; the clerk hands it back to them with an embarrassed "Sorry, the machine won't take it. Do you have another card?" They probably do, but it won't make any difference; the machine will know that one, too, is "maxed out."

For large numbers of working-class families, then, their much vaunted middle-class lifestyle has turned out to be a house of cards built on debt. The American dream—a life filled with goods and comforts bought on credit; goods that in our consumption-driven society are the symbols of worth, the emblems of success—has become a nightmare of uncertainty, if not despair. But even the bankruptcy court—the last refuge of the middle class—is too often closed to the working class.

It takes a certain amount of knowledge, sophistication, and access to legal advice to plan for a bankruptcy—commodities in short supply among most working-class families. In my recent research into the lives of these families, I heard story after story about people who lost everything they had—including their children's beds—because they didn't understand that they could have declared bankruptcy. As a thirty-eight-year-old father of two teenage children remarked bitterly, "After the finance people came, I found out I could have gone bankrupt. Maybe if I'd known about it before, we could have saved some things from those damn vultures. But I never found out about it until it was too late. I mean, I heard of people going bankrupt, but I always thought it was only businesses did that, not plain people. How would I know? Nobody tells you stuff like that; then, when you find it out, it's too late, and you're stuck."

But even if he had known, he might have discovered that he couldn't afford the luxury of having himself declared officially broke. For bankruptcy isn't for the poor and the near-poor, since they rarely have the $1,000 or more it takes in court costs and legal fees. Instead, they lose the possessions that a bankruptcy filing would have protected and remain buried under debts that the bankruptcy court would have canceled. One of the men who found himself in just this position explained angrily,

"I read in the paper about people declaring bankruptcy, and I figured I had to do something or we'd drown in those goddamn bills. So I went to see this lawyer, and he said, yeah, sure, I could go bankrupt and all my bills would be wiped out. Only problem was, it would cost about a thousand dollars. Christ, if I had a thousand, I wouldn't be bankrupt, would I?"

These are not just the sad stories of an unlucky few. Every person in this study had either suffered the loss of a job or had friends, neighbors, or family members who suddenly found themselves on the unemployment line. Some found other jobs, but almost always they were earning substantially less than they had before they were fired.

It's true, of course, that many of the issues confronting families today know no class boundaries. Middle-class families also feel the credit crunch; they too have had to strain their resources nearly to the breaking point to maintain their lifestyle; they too know the anxiety of not being able to spend enough time with their children. Even families at the high end of middle-class incomes are feeling strapped by the cost of housing, feeding, clothing, and educating a family today. But what turns those issues into problems, as well as how families attend to them, is related to the resources at their disposal, which, of course, means their class position.

Middle-class families may be unable to afford the house of their dreams, may find it a strain to pay for their children's private school, may have to go into debt to buy a new car or take a vacation. But will anyone argue that these problems are as wrenching as those of the working-class family earning $35,000 and struggling to come up with the money for the rent, a doctor's bill, or a winter coat for a growing child? The subjective experience of deprivation in both instances may be real, but there's an objective difference that should not be dismissed.

It is precisely these differences that are eclipsed by the language we use. When corporations downsize, they fire people, most of them working-class. As the gap between those who do the firing and those who get fired grows obscenely wide, we do a disservice both to the people who are suffering the cost of this economic dislocation and to the nation at large when we accept uncritically language that befogs this reality.

Just so, there *is* a working class in America, and its families have suffered the economic shifts of recent decades most acutely. To perpetuate the long-held American fiction that this is a society without class distinctions, that we all have an equal chance at the promise of this bountiful land, helps to keep the working class from a sustained and organized effort on its own behalf. And no agency in the nation has more reason to encourage that effort, nor is there any better equipped to aid and abet it, than a revitalized labor movement.

NOTES

1. *Families on the Fault Line* (New York: HarperPerennial, 1995).
2. *Worlds of Pain* (New York: Basic Books, 1976).

Worlds of Pain *Revisited:*
1972 to 1992

In the closing pages of *Worlds of Pain,* I wrote: "What I have drawn here is a portrait—a still picture, a frame abstracted from a movie that continues to run long after the viewer leaves the theater."[1] Twenty years have passed since I began the research for this book; the film is still running. It's time to stop it once again, to lift another frame from the ongoing lives of working-class families in America.

A QUESTION OF CLASS

In the two decades between 1972 and 1992, enormous social, political, and economic changes have been at work, defining and redefining family and social life, relations between women and men, between parents and children, and between the various ethnic and racial groups that make up the tapestry of American life. But our inability to deal realistically with the question of class has remained relatively unchanged.

In some ways class distinctions are more apparent in 1992 than they were twenty years ago. The frenzied corporate spending of the 1980s and the Reagan and Bush administrations' policies that lined the pockets of the rich have been of no benefit to ordinary working people.[2] Quite the opposite! The gap between the working class and the professional middle class—the two groups I compare in this book—is wider than ever. Even with the economic contribution of women, median family income has remained virtually flat when measured in constant (1989) dollars—$33,656 in 1973 and $34,213 in 1989[3]—which, given the increase in two-earner families, means that men's wages actually declined.[4] Only among the top one-fifth of American families has income climbed steadily—rising from $73,764 to $92,663 in the single decade between 1980 and 1990.[5]

But that's the *objective* reality. At the *subjective* level something else has been going on. There, it seems to me, we have been witness to the *declining significance of class in favor of the increasing salience of race.* If the strength of organized labor is one measure of class consciousness, then there's clearly less of it in 1992 than there was twenty years earlier. Among white workers, membership in labor unions, once their hedge against exploitation, dropped from just under 20 percent at the beginning of the 1980s to a little more than 15 percent by the end of the decade[6]—a fall aided and abetted by a hostile government.

The protections that unions once offered have become less available at precisely the time when the fortunes of the working class have been falling so sharply, leaving them with an acute sense of vulnerability to fates beyond their control. This would seem to be an ideal situation for the mobilization of class anger. Instead we have seen an escalation of racial anger beyond anything we have known in the recent past.

In 1972 David Duke, an ex-Nazi and former Grand Wizard of the Ku Klux Klan, would have been laughed off the podium. Twenty years later he could run for governor in Louisiana and win 55 percent of the white vote. Two decades ago Patrick Buchanan, a wealthy, right-wing Republican newspaperman who had never held public office, would hardly have made a dent in the vote of a sitting president. In those 1992 presidential primaries in which he ran, he was taken seriously enough to win between a quarter and a third of the vote. It's true that economic discontent was the bedrock on which these votes were cast. But it's also true that for a considerable number of American voters this discontent found expression in the racist and xenophobic campaigns of these candidates.

The class issue has become especially muddled in the presidential electoral politics of 1992. With the economy stalled in its longest recession in more than half a century, Democratic and Republican hopefuls court what they call the "middle class" with the persistence of a penitent, love-smitten suitor. They speak soothing words of compassion about the "middle-class squeeze" and promise help in a variety of ways. But whom are they wooing? The Republicans are trying to hold on to the white, working-class urban voters who have defected from the Democratic party in recent presidential elections; the Democrats are out to recapture them. Which suggests that, for some at least, the words "middle class" may be the election-year code words for "white people." Meanwhile, both parties seem ready to give the store away to the more affluent. As Gwen Ifill, writing in the *New York Times,* noted acidly: "Take the word 'needy.' It sometimes seem to have been effectively redefined to mean those who are considered to be otherwise capable of earning $50,000 or more a year."[7]

In fact, all the talk about the middle class serves to obscure class realities rather than to clarify them, since this "middle class" is usually defined so broadly that it encompasses everyone but the rich and the poor. The head of the Congressional Budget Office, for example, holds that any family of four with an annual income somewhere between $19,000 and $78,000 falls into the middle class[8]—a range so wide as to be nonsensical to anyone but a politician. Could a family with an income of $19,000 conceivably experience itself or its life choices in the same way as a family earning over four times as much? Do they really share the same problems in finding housing, providing health care, buying shoes for the children, or putting food on the table?

The political director of the Democratic National Committee has offered a narrower, but equally flawed, definition. The typical middle-class family whose vote the Democrats seek, he said, consists of two full-time working parents under forty-five, who live in the suburbs and have two children and a combined income of $35,000.[9] Notice that in 1992 it requires the full-time labor of both wife and husband to reach the $35,000 figure he cited[10]—a major change from the past, which he glossed over as if it were insignificant. More important, however, in 1989 the median income in a family with two earners was $45,266.[11] Since income is one important determinant of class standing, the Democrats' "typical middle-class family" doesn't qualify for the label. But to acknowledge the existence of a working class challenges the long-held American fiction that this nation has conquered the invidious distinctions of class. Instead, the political rhetoric supports and strengthens the myth that we are a classless society—a myth that plays an important part in the racial polarization that has become increasingly common over these past two decades.

Finally, in defining the middle class, neither of these politicians has taken into account the kind of work people do and how they are compensated. It makes a difference whether one is a blue-collar or service worker paid an hourly rate or a white-collar worker paid a weekly wage. It is the hourly workers who are always more vulnerable in times of economic stress.

Even in the recession that began in the spring of 1990, when, for the first time since the Great Depression of the 1930s, unemployment struck at white-collar workers and professionals, their job losses have been about two-thirds of those in the blue-collar sector.[12] And despite media headlines about stock brokers, lawyers, executives, and Harvard graduates who haven't been able to find jobs, it's the low-level sales and office workers in the white-collar work force who have taken the biggest hit. In November 1991, for example, the unemployment figures for managers and professionals stood at 2.9 percent, while the lower-level white-collar unemployment rates hovered around 6 percent.[13]

I don't mean to deny the suffering of the unemployed no matter where they stand in the work hierarchy. To the woman or man who's out of a job, it doesn't make much difference whether the rate is 2.9 or 6 percent. Nevertheless, those jobless rates are mild compared to the numbers of blue-collar workers who were on the unemployment lines during the same period—9.8 percent for operators and laborers, 7.3 percent for those in manufacturing, and a stunning 16 percent for workers in the construction industry.[14]

WOMEN IN THE LABOR FORCE

If the myth about the nature of America's class structure lives on relatively unchanged, life inside the working-class family has seen some profound transformations since 1972. Then, what one writer called the "workadaddy-housewife family" already had suffered several dramatic challenges.[15] But the full realization of the impact of those challenges and the magnitude of the changes they would generate wasn't yet evident. Now it's clear: Trends that were emerging in 1972 have become fixed realities in 1992.

The 1970s saw the beginning of the economic roller coaster on which working-class families would travel over the next twenty years. During this decade the economic growth that had marked the period from the end of World War II slowed markedly. Hundreds of thousands of manufacturing jobs, which had provided the basis for whatever working-class affluence existed then, disappeared as we continued the move from a manufacturing to a service economy. Before the decade hit midpoint, the nation was mired in a recession that was felt most deeply among blue-collar workers. Men who lost jobs in manufacturing, construction, and other relatively high-paying occupations were forced to settle for lower wages in one of the service industries—that is, if they were lucky enough to find work. Those who continued to work in the same fields found that their paychecks bought less and less as wages failed to keep pace with inflation. And women flooded into the labor market to make up the deficit.

Today, therefore, it's hard to pick up a newspaper without finding an article about the extraordinary numbers of married women with young children in the labor force. Social scientists study the situation; politicians wring their hands in alarm and worry about the impact on the family. But poor women have always held paid jobs outside the home. In fact, 58 percent of the women in this book were in the labor force in the early 1970s, most of them in part-time jobs. So why the flurry of public attention and concern in 1992, when there was barely a murmur in 1972?

In part it has to do with numbers, which, starting in the 1960s, have increased dramatically with each succeeding decade. At the beginning of the 1960s, 18.6 percent of married women with children under six worked outside of the home; by the end of the decade the figure had jumped to 30.3 percent—an increase of 62.9 percent. The 1970s saw another steep rise, to 45.1 percent. By the time the 1980s were over, 58.4 percent of these women were in the labor force—more than triple the 1960 figures.[16]

At least equally striking is the fact that very few married women with infants were in the work force two decades ago. Now about half the mothers with babies under a year are working at least part-time. The older the children, the greater the number of women who work outside the home as well as inside. Just over 49 percent of married women with children aged six to seventeen were in the labor force in 1970, climbing to 61.7 percent in 1980, and to a whopping 73.2 percent by 1989.[17]

Add to all this the fact that women who worked part-time in 1972 are likely to be full-time workers in 1992, and it becomes obvious that these numbers are more than simple descriptive statistics. They represent a major transformation in family life, which, in turn, has had a profound impact on public life. Among other things, this enormous increase in full-time working women has strengthened the effort to reorder gender roles in the private realm as well as in the public one—a struggle that was once the province of the educated elite and that by now has become part of the consciousness of women at all class levels.

But these vast changes are not the only reason for the rise in public alarm about women, work, and the family. Class also plays its part. In 1972 it was poor and working-class families who needed a working wife to pay the bills. Twenty years later, it's nearly everyone but the rich. When the pinch was felt by people at the lower end of the class spectrum, it was easy for public officials and politicians not to notice. Or if they did, they could explain it as part of the "natural" order of things, a fact of life that the less fortunate had to endure. When it touches those who are, in fact, middle-class—families of relatives, friends, and neighbors who are no different from their own and who, in addition, have the social, political, and financial resources to make their discontent felt—then the politicians take note and the state of the family becomes a matter of public concern.

CHANGE AND CONTINUITY IN FAMILY LIFE

Despite the fact that so many women who appear on the pages of this book held paid jobs outside the home, they defined themselves as wives and mothers, not as workers. Work was something they *did,* an instrumental activity that served the economic needs of the family. They may also have felt good to be out of the house for a few hours each day, to have their competence acknowledged there. But housewifery and mothering remained at the core of their definition of self; these defined who they *were.*

They wanted some help from their husbands from time to time, of course, but the traditional division of household labor generally seemed just to them. They shared with their husbands the view that a man who works hard all day has the right to come home, put his feet up, and expect his wife to see to his comfort. And they were grateful for small favors: the husband who helped clear the table, who dried the dishes once in a while, who knew how to push a vacuum cleaner, who "baby-sat" his children from time to time.

Not surprisingly, then, when asked about their response to the Women's Liberation Movement, their talk was dominated largely by the negative stereotypes that were the fashion of the day. They complained that "women's libbers" held them in contempt because they chose marriage and motherhood instead of a career; or they insisted simply that the issues the movement spoke to were irrelevant to their lives. Even on the question of equal pay for equal work, most were ambivalent—on the one hand, agreeing that it was only fair; on the other, saying that if a man had a family to support and a woman didn't, then he ought to earn more than she.

By 1992 changed circumstances created changed expectations. As I write, I have just finished a new study of working-class family life. The women I interviewed for this research are the class and status counterparts of those I spoke with twenty years ago. But the differences between them are stark. Most working-class women today no longer think the aims of the women's movement are so distant from their lives. They may still disavow any connection to feminism, may cringe at the idea of applying that label to themselves, but it's form over substance, habit over reality. This is their sop to the current disfavor of the word "feminist." In reality, their economic situation, coupled with the feminist ferment of the preceding decades, has transformed their view of family life and their role in it.

In 1972 most of the women who worked outside of the home spoke guiltily of the gratifications they found in their jobs, as if they were betraying their families by admitting that something else could hold their interest and bring them satisfaction. Two decades later most of the women I interviewed freely acknowledge that, although they may have entered the paid work force because of economic need, they enjoy the benefits they have found there and would not leave willingly. They talk easily of an enhanced sense of competence that they cherish, of heightened self-esteem born of their ability to negotiate and master the complex world of work, and, not least, of a measure of financial independence that allows them to feel more adult and more in control of their lives.

Twenty years ago both husband and wife usually claimed that her income was discretionary, just so they could buy some luxury they couldn't otherwise afford—a new car, a camper, a family vacation, new furniture for the living room. Sometimes it was true. More often it was a myth constructed to protect the husband from the knowledge that he didn't earn enough to meet the family's needs. By 1992 such fictions no longer work; everyone now agrees that a woman must work if a family is to maintain its lifestyle. This difference—the shared understanding that, like her husband, a wife works because she has to—frees her to own a formerly unrecognized side of herself. She may continue to define herself primarily through her roles as wife and mother, but a secondary definition as worker is no longer alien to her sense of self.

Therefore, most of the women in my recent research endorse the principle of equal pay without the equivocation and ambivalence with which their counterparts greeted the idea two decades earlier. Similarly, they no longer believe that a man has a right to come home and relax while his wife rushes about picking up toys and dirty clothes, fixing the evening meal, cleaning up afterward, and trying to give the children some "quality time." Instead, like their professional middle-class sisters, they wish their husbands would share the tasks of housekeeping and childrearing. When this wish is transformed into a demand, it often becomes a wrenching source of conflict in these families.[18]

True, men whose wives work full-time outside the home are much more likely now than they were twenty years ago to grant that they *ought* to help out, even to feel guilty if they don't. But there's often a long way between word and deed. It's also true that many more husbands do, in fact, pick up some of the chores that formerly were done by their wives alone. Some men get dinner started if they come home earlier than their wives; others help with the cleanup, with bathing the children, or with putting them to bed. But it's almost always cast in terms of him helping her, not of an equitable sharing of tasks and responsibilities of family life. Which means that he's free to be too tired or too burdened when it suits him.

Even in families where wife and husband work different shifts, many of the women I interviewed complain about husbands who do only the minimum required and only after being reminded of what's necessary. "He never sees what has to be done, so if I don't tell him, it's not done," complained one thirty-four-year-old woman whose husband works the swing shift while she's on days. "Like, he tells everybody he gets dinner started every day, but that's only if I have everything prepared and in the pot. Then he lights the fire on the stove or turns on the oven. So who's doing the cooking, I ask you?"

Why, when so much else has changed, when women now share with men the burden of supporting the family, can men still successfully resist full partnership in its care and feeding? The reasons are complex, and I have written about them in some detail elsewhere.[19] The bottom line is that women continue to be more vulnerable than men, whether in the economic or the social sphere. Socially, a divorced man has a far greater chance of remarrying than a woman. A divorced woman between the ages of twenty-five and forty-four is only 65 percent as likely to remarry as a man in the same age group. And the chances drop precipitously for a woman over forty-five. Economically, when a marriage ends in divorce, women and children are often left in desperate straits, leading to what analysts today call "the feminization of poverty"—a phrase that was unknown twenty years ago.[20]

The discriminatory practices in the labor market remain a potent instrument for maintaining the power imbalance between women and men. In 1989 median income for women was $17,606 compared to $26,656 for men, which means that women earned only 70 cents for every dollar made by men.[21] That's better than the 59-cent discrepancy of twenty years earlier, to be sure. It gives women not only a greater sense of independence but also slightly more leverage in their negotiations with their husbands. But it's not nearly enough to allow women to meet their men on equal economic terms.

The usual explanation for the discrepancy in male-female earnings is that most women work at low-skill, low-paying jobs. But this doesn't take into account the fact that women's work pays considerably less than men's, *regardless of the level of skill required*. A fork-lift operator with an eighth-grade education earns substantially more than a secretary with a college degree. *It's gender, not skill, that makes the difference.* In fact, women earn less than men simply because they're paid less, often even when they do the same work and are equally experienced.[22] Finally, the glass ceiling that limits women's job mobility isn't given only to the executive suite. It's felt powerfully at every level of the occupational hierarchy, whether it's a promotion to a supervisory position on the factory floor or an acceptance to a medical residency in surgery.

These social and economic inequities outside the marriage make themselves felt inside it. When a wife confronts her husband's resistance to sharing the responsibilities of the home, she's likely to count the cost and decide it's safer to back off, to try to preserve the peace in the interest of safeguarding the marriage.[23] It's true that more women initiate divorce now than ever before—a fact that undoubtedly is related to their increased economic independence. Nevertheless, given the social and economic deficits they know they'll take with them, most women swallow their resentment and still their tongues. Thus, a husband no longer has to keep his wife "barefoot and pregnant to keep her," as the old saying goes. He can send her out into the world of work secure in the knowledge that her earnings will not threaten his dominance. And most of the time he can avoid taking responsibility for the tasks of the household without fear of serious reprisal from his wife.

With so many women working outside the home as well as in it, families have less time for leisure pursuits and social activities than ever before. In 1972 weekends saw occasional family outings, Friday-evening bowling, a Saturday trip to the shopping mall, a Sunday with extended family, once in a while an evening out without the children. In summer, when the children weren't in school, a weeknight might find the family paying a short visit to a friend, a relative, or a neighbor. In 1992 almost everyone I interviewed complains that it's hard to find time even for these occasional outings.[24] Instead, most off-work hours today are spent trying to catch up with the dozens of family and household tasks that were left undone during the regular work week. When they aren't doing chores, parents guiltily try to make up to their children for the fact that they're gone for so many daytime hours.

As I wrote those last sentences, a nagging voice inside my head complained: *That's not unique to the working class; middle-class families suffer the same issues today.* And that, of course, is one of the most important changes in recent years. Middle-class women, too, now hold full-time jobs in ever-increasing numbers, which means that life inside their families has changed just as it has in the working class. For most of these families the "companionate marriage" isn't very companionable anymore, as more and more off-work hours are given over to family and household responsibilities. The pressures of time, the impoverishment of social life, the anxieties about child care, the fear that their children will live in a world of increasing scarcity, the threat of divorce—all these are part of family life today, regardless of class.

Why focus on class then? Because there are important differences that are distinctly class-related. In the twenty years between 1972 and 1992, the median hourly pay for blue-collar and service workers fell from $8.52 to $7.46. Although weekly income among lower- and mid-level white-collar workers followed the same downward course, tumbling from $516 to $501 during this period, a sizeable difference remains.[25] At the top figure, a working-class person earned $340, *if* he or she worked a full forty-hour week—a wage substantially below even the lowest weekly earnings of the white-collar worker. And, of course, the differences are even more striking as we move up the class ladder.

I don't mean to deny that even families at the high end of middle-class incomes can feel strapped by the cost of housing, feeding, clothing, and educating a family today. They may have trouble paying for their children's private school, may have to go into debt to buy a new car or take a vacation. But will anyone argue that these problems are as wrenching as those of the working-class family earning $35,000 that struggles to come up with the money for the rent, the mortgage payment, a doctor bill, or a winter coat for a growing child? The subjective experience of deprivation in both instances is real. But there's also an objective reality that cannot be dismissed.

For an increasing number of two-job working-class families there's another complication. Unable to afford the cost of day care for small children, they take jobs on different shifts, one working days, the other swing or graveyard. That way one parent is home with the children at all times. But the cost to the marriage can be very high. Ask these husbands and wives when they have time to talk, and you're likely to get a look of annoyance at a question that, on its face, seems stupid to them. "Talk? How can we talk when we hardly see each other?"

Mostly, conversation is limited to the logistics that take place at shift-changing time when children and chores are handed off from one to the other. With children dancing around underfoot, the incoming parent gets a quick summary of the day's or night's events, a list of reminders about things to be done, perhaps about what's cooking in the pot on the stove. If the arriving spouse gets home early enough, there may be an hour when both are there. But with the pressures of the work day fresh for one and awaiting the other, and with children clamoring for parental attention, this isn't a propitious moment for any serious conversation. In any case, most of the time even this brief hour isn't available. Then the ritual changing of the guard takes only a few minutes—a quick peck on the cheek in greeting, a few words, and it's over.

For these families especially, social life falls by the wayside. Some of the luckier couples work different shifts on the same days, so they're home together on weekends. But with so little time for normal family life, there's little room for anyone or anything outside. Friendships founder, and adult social activities are put on hold as parents try to do in two days a week what usually takes seven—that is, to establish a sense of family life for themselves and their children. For those whose days off don't match, the problems of sustaining both the couple relationship and family life are magnified enormously.

Finding time and energy for sex is also a problem—this one for two-job families of any class, although more difficult for those in the working class because they have so few resources with which to buy some time and privacy for themselves. Ask about their sex lives and you'll be met with an angry, "What's that?" or a wistful, "I wish." When it happens, it is, as one woman put it, "on the run"—a situation that's particularly unsatisfactory for most women. For them the pleasure of sex is related to the whole of the interaction—to a sense of intimacy and connection, to at least a few relaxed, loving moments. When they can't have these, they're likely to avoid sex altogether—a situation the men find equally unsatisfactory. I don't mean that the men are content with the kind of quick sexual exchanges to which these couples find themselves consigned. But for them it's generally better than no sex at all, while for the women it's often the other way around.

In 1972 it was relatively easy to find working-class families in which mother, father, and children all lived in the same household. Certainly divorce was a reality then; one-fourth of the women and one-fifth of the men I interviewed for *Worlds of Pain* were living in a second marriage. But there's a considerable difference between 1972 and 1992. Then roughly one-third of all marriages ended in divorce; now the figure stands at about one-half.[26]

In preparation for writing this new introduction, I contacted some of the families whose lives are chronicled in this book. It was no surprise to find that their divorce rate matches the national statistics. Of the thirty-two families I was able to locate, eighteen (56 percent) had been divorced. All but one of the men had remarried, all to divorcées with children.[27] Three had a second set of children in the new marriage, so that their families now included his, hers, and our children. The rest remained content with only his and hers.

The women, as expected, hadn't fared nearly so well. Seven of the eighteen had been single for five years or more. As mothers raising children alone, often with little or no support from their former husbands, their lives were even more economically unstable than they had been when they were married. Of the eleven who had remarried, all had married men who had children from a previous marriage, and three also had children in the new marriage.

Thus has the divorce revolution transformed family life. The relatively stable cast of family characters of the past is harder and harder to find. Instead, we have single-parent families, blended families, reconstituted families, and "divorce-extended" families,[28] each with its own particular blend of parents, stepparents, siblings, half-sibs, step-sibs, and a variety of fictive aunts, uncles, and grandparents. It was a common experience in my recent research to have children and young adults spend considerable time sorting out for me their relationships with various blood-, step-, and half-relatives. One twenty-year-old, for example, spoke at length about his grandparents, telling me how important they have been in his life. "They're great, not like most grandparents. I can really talk to them, I mean about anything," he explained.

"Whose parents are they?" I asked. "Your mother's or your father's?"

Laughing, he replied, "It's funny, people always ask me that, but they're not my mom's or my dad's. I don't see my real grandparents much; they don't live around here. These grandparents are…" He paused, looked up at the ceiling as he sorted out the relationships, then continued, "Let's see how I can explain it. It's not so complicated; it just sounds that way. They're my ex-stepmother's mother and her stepfather."

THE SHATTERED DREAM

As we move into the 1990s, the shifts in the economy that have been taking place over the last several decades are making themselves felt in ever more painful ways. The well-paying manufacturing and construction jobs that used to support the high end of the working class continue to disappear.[29] In the thirteen months between June 1990 and July 1991, 804,000 jobs in manufacturing, 495,000 in construction, and 365,000 in retailing were lost.[30] Every major corporation in the nation has been trimming its work force sharply in a process we have come to know as "downsizing." From October to December 1991, 2,600 jobs were cut each day.[31] Consequently, in the twelve months ending September 30, 1991, personal bankruptcy filings soared 24 percent nationwide, with the Northeast spiraling up to between 40 and 50 percent.[32]

And the layoffs continue. Some are a response to the most protracted recession since World War II. But labor experts predict that as many as half these jobs are gone for good, the price of structural changes in the economy that will not be reversed even when good times return. A spokesperson for Eastman Kodak explained, for example: "The recession was a lot worse than we thought, and it triggered this round of cutbacks. But if it were just the recession, we would be hiring these people back again. And we aren't going to do that."[33] When Xerox announced that it would cut 20 percent of its work force, its chairman commented that the economic slump was only speeding up cost-cutting plans that were already in place.[34] Even the service sector, which saw fairly high levels of growth during the 1980s, has suffered a shake-out that is expected to continue well into the 1990s.

No surprise, then, that in 1992 the mood of the nation is somber and fearful. Magazines like *Newsweek* feature cover stories titled "The Glooming of America: A Nation Down in the Dumps,"[35] and newspapers across the country headline article after article chronicling the nightmare of unemployment and its effect on family life. Even those people lucky enough to have jobs are apprehensive, waiting uneasily for the other shoe to drop. Only life in the executive suite remains relatively unchanged. While joblessness rises and profits fall, the lower-paid chief executives of some of our largest companies typically earn $3.2 million; those in the higher brackets count their annual earnings in the tens of millions.[36]

For millions of working-class families, then, life is even harder in 1992 than it was in 1972. Back then it was credible for young parents to believe that their children would reap the reward of whatever sacrifices they might have to make. They could forgo small comforts, put off pleasures, work longer hours without complaint, all in the expectation that they were ensuring a better, easier life for their children. This, after all, has been the unique and quintessential American promise: Each generation would surpass the one before it.

Then, too, it was possible for young couples to dream of owning a home of their own, to believe if they worked hard and lived frugally the dream would become a reality. And it did for many of the families I interviewed for this book. Their houses were generally small, unpretentious, modestly furnished, the pride of ownership visible in the many loving little touches that said, *This is mine, the achievement of a lifetime.* But in the years between 1972 and 1992, inflation sent the median price of a starter home up 21 percent at the same time that real income for young working-class families *declined* by 30 percent[37]—a situation that turned the dream of owning a home into a mirage.

It's true that, as housing prices have increased, buying a home has become a problem for young families in any class. But parents in the middle- and upper-income brackets are far more likely than those below to be able to offer all or part of a down payment to their children. For the working-class young, outside help rarely is available. Therefore, even a modest first home is usually beyond their reach.[38]

Those few who do manage to become homeowners are forced into the low end of the housing market, which means that their houses have even less space and fewer comforts than the unassuming homes in which they grew up. Or the only housing they can afford is in distant fringe cities, leaving them with long commutes that add not only to the daily stress but also to the time pressure that husbands and wives both complain about so bitterly. As one thirty-year-old warehouse worker living in a small city outside Chicago put it: "The driving back and forth is a killer; traffic's murder. I get off work at five and don't get home until six, six-thirty. By then I'm dead beat. But can I just take a load off and take it easy? Hell, no. First there's the kids, then the wife's always got something for me to do. Christ, there's no time left to live; it's work and shit, that's all, work and shit. But what can I do? No way could we afford a house closer to the city—no way."

The parental generation watches the struggle of their adult children in pain and puzzlement. *They make three times as much as we did at that age, and we managed to buy a house. What happened?* they ask themselves. When they look at their own lives in the present and compare them with the past, their bewilderment grows. In 1972 median family income hovered around $12,000; by 1992 it had nearly tripled to just over $34,000. To people old enough to have been wage earners twenty years earlier, the idea that they could earn over $30,000 and still feel poor is almost impossible to grasp. As one forty-nine-year-old machinist I interviewed exclaimed: "Dammit, I don't get it. Between me and the wife we make $38,000 a year, and we're always behind. I remember when I thought that was a fortune. If anybody'd ever told me I wouldn't be rich on that kind of money, I'd have told him he was nuts. Back when I was making twelve or thirteen grand a year, I used to think if I could just get up to twenty I'd have it made. Now thirty-eight doesn't make it. How do you figure it?"

Psychologically, it's hard indeed to "figure it," to fit the fantasies of his twenties into the reality of his forties, to integrate the fact that dollars no longer mean the same thing. What he knows is that his income has tripled. He remembers his dreams of years ago and wonders: *How is it possible? $38,000!* When he says the number it still seems like "a fortune." He knows that everything costs more, that taxes are higher, that they take a bigger cut out of his paycheck now than they did before.[39] He may even have read in the newspaper that, after taking inflation into account, his $38,000 isn't worth much more than his $12,000 was two decades ago, or that the average pay for men in his line of work fell by about 4 percent in 1991.[40] But this cognitive knowledge lies alongside a deeply embedded sensibility born in the past, making it difficult to incorporate fully the new reality. So when he comes up against the economic squeeze he feels in the present, he's caught, not quite able to understand why he's hurting financially when the numbers tell him he *ought* to feel rich.

This discontinuity between past and present realities is, I believe, one reason why white working-class anger has escalated so sharply in recent years. Since they were earning what seemed like so much money, they *felt* rich even when they weren't. When, in addition, a wife went to work and her income was added to her husband's, the amount seemed even more impressive. In fact, for a long time, the entry of so many women into the work force created a false aura of affluence, since the addition of their earnings to the family coffers helped to mask the fact that men's real wages either remained stagnant or fell. The result has been a peculiar disjunction between the belief that they ought to be affluent juxtaposed against the end-of-the-month shortfall, leaving people perplexed and uncertain about just how to feel and whom to blame.

RACE AND THE RISE OF ETHNICITY

These economic realities form the backdrop against which racial and ethnic tensions have escalated over the last two decades. In 1972 it was reasonable to plan a study about white working-class families without reference to race. In 1992 it makes no sense to leave it out of this brief essay. I don't mean to suggest that there wasn't plenty of racial anger around two decades ago. But it wasn't high on the list of issues the people I interviewed wanted to talk about then.[41] In my recent research it was a recurrent theme, most of the time arising spontaneously as people aired their grievances and gave vent to their wrath.[42]

One important reason for the difference is that in 1972 we were living in the immediate aftermath of the civil rights revolution that had convulsed the nation since the mid-1950s. Significant gains had been won. And despite the tenacity with which this headway had been resisted by some, most white Americans were feeling good about themselves. Legal segregation was effectively ended; the Civil Rights Act of 1964 and the Voting Rights Act of 1965 laid the basis for a new equality for black Americans. In 1969 even such a racial conservative as President Richard Nixon signed a series of executive orders designed to set aside a fixed proportion of federal contracts for minority-owned businesses and to increase black access to union jobs.

No one expected the nation's racial problems and tensions to dissolve easily or quickly. The rancorous controversies over school busing that were making headlines around the country were reminders that racial strife would not soon become a thing of the past.[43] But there was also a sense that we were moving in the right direction, that there was a national commitment to redressing at least some of the worst aspects of black-white inequality.

Between 1972 and 1992, however, the national economy buckled under the weight of three recessions. At the same time, government policies requiring preferential treatment were enabling African-Americans and other minorities to make small but visible inroads into what had been, until then, largely white terrain. The sense of scarcity, always a part of American life but intensified sharply by the history of these three recessions, made minority gains seem particularly threatening to white working-class families. The fluctuations in the economy left them feeling as if they were on a roller coaster—a climb followed by a fall, hope followed by despair. As the economic vise tightened, despair turned to anger. But partly because we have so little concept of class resentment and conflict in America, this anger was not directed so much at those above as at those below. And when whites at or near the bottom of the ladder look down in this nation, they generally see blacks and other minorities.

True, during all of the 1980s and well into the 1990s, white ire was fostered by national administrations that fanned racial discord as a way of fending off white discontent, of diverting it from the voting booth to the streets, the school, and the factory floor. But our history of racial animosity coupled with our lack of class consciousness made it easier to accomplish that aim than it might otherwise have been.[44]

That same history buttressed by the economic pain whites have been suffering is at least partly responsible for the rise of ethnicity as well. There have, of course, always been white ethnic enclaves throughout the land. Cities like New York and Chicago have long been known for the variety of ethnic neighborhoods that importantly influence their culture. But ethnicity was essentially a private matter, a part of the family heritage to be passed on to the children and celebrated on ritual occasions. In the public arena, the emphasis generally was on assimilation, the process of Americaniza- tion being viewed not only as inexorable but also desirable.[45] So much so that recent researchers in the field insist that, although some subjective sense of ethnic identity remains, it has little objective reality. And it certainly hasn't been strong enough to contain the soaring rates of ethnic intermarriage, which now involves roughly three in four American-born whites.[46]

What, then, can we make of the fervor with which, since the 1970s, Americans of European descent have proclaimed attachment to their various ethnic pasts with increasing force? The debate among students of ethnicity is too complex to deal with adequately in this essay. That must await my forthcoming book, which will explore this issue in some detail. Here it is enough to say that some students of ethnicity argue that the various ethnic groups continue to exhibit subcultural variations that derive from the culture their ancestors brought to these shores, and that these differ- ences in behavior and attitude are a deep and meaningful part of ethnic group life. Others insist that as the structural realities of ethnic group life have changed—that is, people no longer live in the same neighborhood, work at the same occupations, socialize almost exclusively with members of their group—language facility has fal- tered, manners and mores have changed, and ethnic identity has become symbolic rather than real.[47]

It seems to me that the either/or quality of the debate is misguided. There's not much doubt that ethnic identity has receded as a deeply significant part of life for most second-, third-, and fourth-generation Americans of European ancestry. But I think it's a mistake to dismiss ethnic identification—even if only symbolic—as unreal and meaningless. Symbols, after all, become symbolic precisely because they have meaning. In this case, as I see it, the symbol has meaning at two levels: One is the psychological; the other is the sociopolitical.

At the psychological level, in a nation as large and diverse as ours, defining oneself in the context of an ethnic group is comforting. It provides a sense of belong- ing to some recognizable and manageable collectivity—a group that has particular meaning because it's connected to the family, and because it's there, when we were small children, that we first learned about our relationship to the group.

Moreover, being American is different from being French or Dutch or any number of other nationalities because, except for Native Americans, there's no such thing as an American without a hyphen somewhere in the past. To identify with the front end of that hyphen is to maintain a connection, however tenuous, with our roots. It sets us apart from others, allows us a sense of uniqueness, while, paradoxi- cally, it also gives us a sense of belonging—of being one with others like self—that helps to overcome the isolation of modern life.

But this doesn't explain our infatuation with ethnicity that seemed to spring from nowhere two decades ago and that remains with us today. To understand that we must move from the personal to the social level. When we do, it seems clear to me that this ethnic fever is significantly related to two major sociopolitical events—one beginning in the late 1950s, the other a product of the mid-1960s. The first was the Civil Rights Movement with its demand for racial equality. It was easy for northern whites to support the early demands of that movement when blacks were asking for the desegregation of buses and drinking fountains in the South. But supporting the black drive to end discrimination in jobs, housing, and education in the urban North was quite another matter—especially among those white ethnics whose hold on the ladder of mobility was tenuous at best and with whom blacks would be most likely to compete, whether in the job market, the neighborhood, or the classroom. As the courts and the legislatures around the country began to honor some black claims for redress of past injustices, white hackles began to rise.

The second watershed event came in 1965, when the laws restricting immigration were liberalized—a change that resulted in a rush of immigration from Asia, Latin America, and the Caribbean, and colored the urban landscape in ways unknown before. Suddenly, whites became a rapidly declining proportion of the total population. In 1972, for example, the California cities that were the site of the original research for *Worlds of Pain* were almost exclusively white; by 1992 their minority populations ranged from 54 to 69 percent. The 1990 census figures showed nearly one in four Americans with African, Asian, Hispanic, or American Indian ancestry, up from one in five in 1980.[48] The same census found that whites of European descent made up just over two-thirds of the population in New York State, while in California, where the shift was most dramatic, they were only 57 percent. In cities like New York and San Francisco, whites were a minority—accounting for only 43 and 47 percent of residents, respectively.[49]

As racial minorities became more visible and more vocal, whites began to feel more anxious and more vulnerable. Blacks, Hispanics, Native Americans, Asians, all were making claims on the nation. To white workers it seemed as if everyone else was getting a piece of the action while they got nothing. Perhaps equally galling was the fact that the others were all part of a group; they had a name; they were defined as "something." But the whites were, well ... just "white"—nothing special, belonging to no one, with no particular claim that anyone would honor. Suddenly, it was they who knew the discomfort of feeling left out and unrecognized. Feeling economically deprived on the one hand and without a publicly acknowledged social identity on the other, it was natural and logical to reach back to their ethnic past. Then they, too, were "something"; they also belonged to a group; they had a name, a history, a culture, and a voice.

At the same time that the complexion of their social world was changing so dramatically, the contracting economy was putting continuing pressure on the economy of the family. As those strains increased, policies such as affirmative action in employment and education began to appear increasingly threatening to white workers.[50] Given the American ideology, if not reality, about justice, fairness, and equality, whites could hardly agitate openly for the continuing oppression of our minority populations. But in reclaiming their ethnic roots, they could recount with pride the tribulations and the transcendence of their ancestors and insist that blacks and others take their place in the line from which they had only recently came.

From there it was only a short step to the conviction that those who don't progress up that line are hampered by nothing more than their own inadequacies or, worse yet, by their unwillingness to take advantage of the opportunities offered them. Ironically, blacks unwittingly aided in reinforcing this white scenario when, in the heat of the emphasis on ethnicity, they began to define themselves in ethnic terms. Partly this was related to the movement to elevate black consciousness, pride, and self-esteem—to reclaim a heritage that, however distant, once had been their own. And partly it was a political strategy—one that affirmed their American experience and identity and gave hope that they would be seen simply as another group of hyphenated Americans.

Unfortunately, we have lots of experience to remind us that changing a word will not alter the reality—in this case, the reality that race is an enduring factor in the American consciousness, and no amount of change in the language will erase that fact. I don't mean to suggest that language is not a significant element in the development of consciousness. In fact, elsewhere I have argued strongly for this very connection.[51] Here I want simply to stress that we have seen several such name changes in recent decades, none of them effective in changing white America's view of blacks.

In this instance—that is, the shift from black to African-American—the focus on ethnicity made it easier for whites to sustain the denial of their racial consciousness and the fear and hostility it engendered. If African-Americans were just another ethnic group, no different from Italian-Americans or Irish-Americans or German-Americans, then it was their problem if they couldn't make it in America. After all, the reasoning went, nobody made it easy for us either. We worked hard, and we made it. Now let them do the same.

I can almost hear some African-Americans responding angrily to what I've written here with one version or another of: *We don't care what it did for whites; this is for us, not for you.* I respect the reply and sympathize with the need that underlies it. And I would respond: *Yes, it's your business, not ours. You have the right to pick your name and expect us to honor it.* But I would also insist that the political costs I have outlined here are worth counting.

The increased visibility of other racial groups focused whites more self-consciously than ever on their own racial identification. Until recently, they didn't think of themselves as "white" in the same way that Chinese know they're "Chinese" and blacks know they're "black." Being white was simply a fact of life, one that didn't require any public statement since it was the definitive social value against which all others were measured. There were whites and nonwhites, the latter a diverse collection of peoples who were defined socially by the fact that they were not white. *This* was their public identity.

In recent decades, however, these nonwhites separated themselves out from the mass and insisted on being seen, heard, measured, and valued on their own terms. African-Americans, Asians, Hispanics, and Native Americans joined with others like themselves, each affirming a distinctive cultural heritage, while at the same time raising their voices in protest against the injustices visited upon them. True, these groups sometimes have been at war among themselves as they pressed their own particular claims. But whatever their differences, they also have stood together as peoples of color in opposition to the power and privilege of whites.

As racial polarization escalated, white ethnics, once so separate and distinct, began to find some common ground in being white. As discrete groups, their power was limited. United, they could be a formidable countervailing force, one that could stand fast against the threat posed by minority demands. Thus was born a new entity in the history of American ethnic groups—the "European-Americans."[52] Members of this group remain hyphenated Americans, but rather than being divided by their various ancestries, they are united by virtue of their shared European origin.

Never mind that the historical experience of the Irish in the potato fields, the Italians in the villages of southern Italy, and the Jews in the *shtetls* of eastern Europe were so different. Or that there had, until recently, been few common bonds between them in the New World. All this is muted in favor of the similarity of the immigrant experience as it is embodied in the "we came, we suffered, we conquered" myth, which by now has gained legendary proportions.

And all of it without a single reference to race. Instead, the quintessential American experience is defined in terms of immigration, its burdens, and the ability to overcome them through sacrifice and hard work. These are the real Americans, the only ones worthy of the name. It just happens that they're all white.

As I write, European-American clubs are beginning to spring up around the nation. Their members insist that these organizations have nothing to do with race, that their purpose is to affirm the common bond of people of European extraction.[53] It's undoubtedly true that one reason for the emergence of such alliances is that many whites now find themselves in social situations where they feel they are the outsiders.[54] But it's disingenuous to maintain that race is not the relevant issue, as these words of a sixteen-year-old San Francisco high-school student I interviewed show so clearly: "There's all these things for all the different ethnicities, you know, like clubs for black kids and Hispanic kids, but there's nothing for me and my friends to join. They won't let us have a white club because that's supposed to be racist. So we figured, I don't know, maybe we have to call it something else, you know, some ethnic thing." Ethnicity, then, becomes a cover for "white," not necessarily because these high-school students are racist but because racial identity is now such a prominent feature of the discourse in their social world.

There's little doubt that in gathering together under a single umbrella and defining themselves as European-Americans, white ethnics are seeking to build an organization through which they can make their needs and wishes heard. In talking about the conditions for membership in his club, for example, the head of the European-American Study Group in San Jose, California, declared that members are expected to share the belief that whites of European background must recognize themselves as an ethnic group and organize around their interests. "We've left our chair at the multicultural table empty," he explained, "and the multicultural table is where the debate is, where the deals are being made."[55]

It's this perception—this fear that white privilege is under siege—that has moved whites to gather their wagons in a circle. But such responses cannot be dismissed by name-calling or by exhortations to greater charity or nobility. They are the price we pay for a society that rests on the notion of scarcity and a class structure that pits those at or close to the bottom against each other in a struggle for survival.

THE END OF INNOCENCE

In the opening sentences of *Worlds of Pain* I wrote that America was choking on its differences. If we were choking then, we're being asphyxiated now. Unemployment, underemployment, and an escalating cost of living have drained the resources of the stable working class and have made their prospects for the future look bleak. As the economy continues to falter and local, state, and federal governments keep cutting services, there are more and more acrimonious debates about who will share in the shrinking pie. Racial and ethnic groups, each in their own corners, square off as they ready themselves for what seems to each of them the fight of their lives. Meanwhile, the quality of life for all Americans is spiraling downward—a plunge that's felt most deeply by those at the lower end of the class spectrum, regardless of color.[56]

In this atmosphere, the steadily increasing numbers of homeless on our streets have become an ever-present and frightening reminder of just how precarious life in this society can be. Twenty years ago we wept when we read about the homeless people on the streets of India. *What kind of society doesn't provide this most basic of life's needs?* we asked ourselves. Today they're in our face, on our streets, an accepted category of American social life—"the homeless." We recoil as we walk by, trying not to see, unable to meet their eyes, ashamed of our own good fortune, anger and sympathy tugging us in opposite directions. Neither feels good. The anger is a challenge to our belief that we're kind, humane, caring. But the sympathy is even more threatening. To allow ourselves to feel compassion is to open the floodgates of our own vulnerability, of our denied understanding of how delicately our own lives and fortunes are balanced.

The shrunken economy has taken its toll on life inside the family as well. While women's presence in the labor force has given them a measure of independence unknown before, most also are stuck with doing two days' work in one—one on the job, the other when they get home at night. Unlike their counterparts in the earlier era, today's women are openly resentful about the burdens they carry, which makes for another dimension of conflict between wives and husbands.

As more and more mothers of young children work full-time outside the home, the question of who will raise the children comes center stage. Decent, affordable child care is scandalously scarce, with no government intervention in this crucial need in sight. In poor and working-class families, therefore, child care often is patched together in ways that leave parents anxious and children in jeopardy.

In families with two working parents, time has become their most precious commodity—time to attend to the necessary tasks of family life; time to nurture relationships between wife and husband, between parents and children; time for oneself, time for others; time for solitude, time for a social life. Today more than ever before, family life has become impoverished for want of time, adding another threat to the already fragile bonds that hold families together.

As I reflect on the beginnings of *Worlds of Pain* and compare it to what I have written here, it seems to me now that I was writing then about a more innocent age—a time, difficult though it was for the working-class families of our nation, when we could believe anything was possible. Whether about the economy, race relations, or life inside the family, most Americans believed that the future promised progress, that the solution to the social problems and inequities of the age were within our grasp, that sacrifice today would pay off tomorrow. This is perhaps the biggest change in the last twenty years: The innocence is gone; we're no longer so sure. But is this necessarily a cause for mourning?

It's true that life in the working-class family is, in many ways, more precarious now than it was then, especially at the economic level. The changes we have seen have left families stressed and fragile, sometimes seeming as if they are balanced delicately on the edge of a precipice. But there's also another side. The same changes have created families that, in some ways at least, are more responsive to the needs of their members, more democratic than any we have known before. These are the twin realities of family life today. Yes, there are new sources of conflict as increasing numbers of women engage in the struggle to reorder the traditional gender roles in the family. But who is to say that this is worse than the resignation and depression of the past?

Just so, the strife among the racial and ethnic groups that make up our society has mushroomed well beyond anything we knew in 1972. But at the same time, many more members of these warring groups than ever before live peaceably together in our schools, our factories, our shops, our corporations, and our neighborhoods.

Perhaps, then, the loss of innocence is not a social tragedy. Perhaps only when innocence is gone and our eyes unveiled are we able to look squarely at our problems and undertake a realistic search for solutions. Yes, it means heightened public and private discord, often more than most of us live with comfortably. But without such conflict, there will be no change. And this, ultimately, will be the real cause for mourning. For without substantial change in both our public and our private worlds, it is not just the future of the family that is imperiled, but the very life of the nation itself.

NOTES

My thanks to Troy Duster, Diane Ehrensaft, Jim Hawley, Michael Kimmel, Michael Rogin, Hank Rubin, Marci Rubin, Judith Stacey, and Stephen Steinberg, for their critical readings of early versions of this chapter.

1. Rubin (1976:204).

2. See Phillips (1990) for an excellent account of how the Reagan policies favored the rich and penalized the poor. In February 1992 a Census Bureau report documented what has been common knowledge for some time now—that is, that income inequality has grown enormously over the last two decades. The proportion of Americans with middle incomes fell from 71.2 percent in 1969 to 63.3 percent in 1989 (*New York Times,* February 22, 1992).

3. U.S. Bureau of the Census (1991:454, Table 730).

4. Economists offer a variety of complex explanations for the income stagnation that has plagued workers in these last two decades. Here, let me mention a few of the most obvious. The decline of union power is high on the list of reasons for the wage stagnation of American workers—a decline that is at least in part attributable to the successful war on unions waged by the Reagan administration. In addition, many companies have moved production to countries where wages are substantially lower than they are here, leaving fewer well-paying jobs for American workers. Finally, as recession followed recession, as the government participated in strike-breaking while offering no protection to the workers, and as unemployment rose, many workers worried more about keeping a job than about getting a raise.

5. All figures cited are in constant 1989 dollars (*New York Times,* December 16, 1990).

6. U.S. Bureau of the Census (1991:425, Table 697).

7. *New York Times,* January 19, 1992.

8. Reported in the *New York Times,* January 11, 1992.

9. *New York Times,* January 11, 1992.

10. In 1989 the median income of families in which the wife was not in the labor force was $28,747 (U.S. Bureau of the Census [1991:455, Table 732]).

11. U.S. Bureau of the Census (1991:454, Table 730).

12. *New York Times,* January 8, 1992.

13. U.S. Department of Labor (December 1991:49, Table A-39).

14. U.S. Department of Labor (December 1991:49, Table A-39). Whether at the blue-collar or the white-collar level, these statistics vastly understate unemployment, since they do not include what the Labor Department calls "discouraged workers"—men and women who have been unemployed for so long that they have given up hope of finding a job and therefore are no longer counted in the unemployment statistics. Nor do these figures count those who are underemployed—people who lost high-paying jobs in manufacturing or construction and, if lucky, eventually resettled in service jobs at half their former earnings, or, if less fortunate, have been able to find only part-time work. In November 1991, for example, 2.25 percent (2,156,000) of the total labor force was *involuntary* part-time workers—women and men who usually work full time but were forced into part-time jobs by the lack of full-time work (U.S. Department of Labor [December 1991:23, Table A-9]).

15. Blankenhorn (1989).

16. U.S. Bureau of the Census (1991:391, Table 643).

17. U.S. Bureau of the Census (1991:391, Table 643).

18. For a recent study about these conflicts, see Hochschild (1989).

19. Rubin (1983).

20. See Weitzman (1985) for a compelling analysis of the unanticipated consequences of no-fault divorce on women and children. There she shows that while men enjoy a 42 percent rise in their standard of living immediately after divorce, their ex-wives and children suffer a 73 percent drop.

21. U.S. Department of Labor, Women's Bureau (September 1990).

22. See Robertson (1992) for a fascinating account of the enormous wage differences between female and male reporters and editors at the *New York Times.* In its editorial columns, the newspaper took the "correct" position, applauding the affirmative action policies that were meant to redress such inequalities. But until it was sued, it never got around to translating that public position into the private paychecks of the women on the staff. And

even now, years after the *Times* settled that suit and agreed to mend its ways, there are continuing complaints about the disparities between the salaries of women and men.

23. See Hochschild (1989) for some interesting vignettes about how such conflicts get played out in two-job families.

24. See Schor (1992) for an excellent analysis of what she calls "the overworked American" and the consequences for family and social life; also see Sirianni and Walsh (1991) for their discussion of the "time famine."

25. All figures cited are in constant 1989 dollars (*New York Times,* December 16, 1990).

26. U.S. Bureau of the Census (1991:62, Table 82).

27. The one man who hadn't remarried had separated from his wife only ten months earlier, and he was already involved with a woman in what he took to be a serious relationship.

28. The phrase "divorce-extended" is taken from Stacey (1990), who offers a finely textured description and analysis of what she calls "postmodern families" who live in divorce-extended kin networks.

29. The issues this shift in the labor force raises are too complicated to merit more than passing mention in this short essay. I want to note, however, that the problem is not simply job losses, but the fact that there are no government policies to ameliorate the costs of the shift from the manufacturing to the service sector, which is a prominent feature of the economy of all Western nations at this time. American workers suffer in particularly brutal ways because, unlike other Western nations, we do not have a full employment policy and effective labor market policies to implement it.

30. U.S. Department of Labor, Bureau of Labor Statistics, *Data Resources* (1991).

31. Cited in the *New York Times,* December 16, 1991.

32. *San Francisco Chronicle,* December 29, 1991.

33. Quoted in the *New York Times,* December 16, 1991.

34. See the front-page article in the *New York Times,* December 16, 1991, entitled "Executives Expect Many '91 Layoffs to Be Permanent."

35. *Newsweek,* January 13, 1992.

36. The top executives of big American companies are paid extraordinarily high sums when compared to their counterparts in other countries. For example, when salary and stock options are included, the co–chief executives of Time Warner earned $99.6 million; the head of Reebok International took home $33.3 million; U.S. Surgical paid its top man $15 million; ITT's CEO earned $11.5 million; and the chairman of Walt Disney pocketed $11.2. Compare this with chief executives of big firms in Great Britain, Germany, and Japan, where earnings were $1.1 million, $800,000, and $250,000, respectively (*New York Times,* January 20, 1992).

37. Children's Defense Fund. Only families headed by a college graduate saw a small (3 percent) rise in income.

38. The proportion of young families who owned their own home dropped from 51.4 percent in 1973 to 44.3 percent in 1990 (*New York Times,* October 20, 1991).

39. Although federal income taxes have not risen substantially and, in some cases, may even be less, other taxes—such as state income taxes, payroll taxes, property taxes, sales taxes, and various local taxes and use fees—have taken an increasingly larger share of the weekly paycheck of most workers. The important point here is that during the 1960s real wages were increasing by 1 or 2 percent a year, while taxes were taking about one-third of the extra income. So long as people were improving their living standards, the tax burden wasn't an

issue. But by the 1970s real wages began to stagnate or decline, while many taxes increased, which meant that they were taking a greater portion of people's already stagnant income. At the same time as wages stagnated and taxes increased, services in most local communities were declining. Together, these factors created the tax revolts that in recent years have made headlines in communities across the country.

40. U.S. Department of Labor (December 1991:90–91, Table C-2). This figure assumes an inflation factor of 4 percent in 1991.

41. The *New York Times* (February 6, 1992) published a graph tracing the results of Gallup polls from 1946–1991 in which Americans were asked about "the most important problems facing the country." Race relations was high on the list from the early to mid-1960s. It waned toward the end of the 1960s, and by the early 1970s, when I was doing the research for this book, it wasn't even mentioned. Indeed, in the early part of the decade, the only domestic issue of serious concern was the cost of living. By the mid-1970s, when the recession had set in, concerns about the cost of living escalated sharply and unemployment joined it as a major problem. Race was not mentioned as a significant issue.

42. There are, of course, many other issues that play their part in making the urban stew so tough to swallow today: an environment filled with pollution, rot, and decay; heavy taxes while services crumble; public schools that fail children of all races and ethnic groups; the obscene spectacle of one of the wealthiest nations in the world whose streets are filled with the homeless; and crime as a pervasive and unnerving reality. All are good reasons for the kind of anger that colors the national discourse now and that's expressed so virulently by both blacks and the white working and lower middle class. But discussion and analysis of how these fit into the picture must await the larger work now in process.

43. See Rubin (1972) for an in-depth study of a community in conflict over busing.

44. See Landry (1991) for a good summary of our racial history.

45. The thrust toward assimilation was not given to whites only. African Americans, Chinese Americans, Japanese Americans, and other peoples of color were similarly motivated, but prejudice and discrimination kept them out.

46. Interracial marriage also has increased in recent decades. For example, intermarriage among the Japanese in Seattle, which was less than 10 percent before 1950, climbed from 17 percent in the early 1960s to 30 percent later in the decade. By 1975 the rate of exogamy in this Japanese community stood at over 50 percent. Nationwide, in 1980, 29 percent of Hispanics and 28 percent of Asians married outside their group, mainly to white spouses. Only black-white intermarriage rates remained at a relatively low 2 percent. Cited in Sanjek (1991).

47. See Alba (1990); Daniels (1990); Gans (1979); Leiberson and Waters (1990); Portes and Rumbaut (1990); Steinberg (1989); Waters (1990).

48. U.S. Bureau of the Census (1991:—Table 22 and Table 27).

49. The differences in the racial composition of these two cities explains, at least in part, why black-white tensions are so much higher in New York City than they are in San Francisco. In New York, 43 percent of the population is now white, 25 percent black, 24 percent Hispanic, and 7 percent Asian. In San Francisco, whites are 47 percent, blacks 11 percent, Hispanics 14 percent, and Asians 29 percent. Thus, blacks in New York make up the kind of critical mass that generally sparks racial prejudices, fears, and tensions. True, San Francisco's Asian population—three in ten of the city's residents—also forms that kind of critical and noticeable mass. But whatever the American prejudice against Asians, and however much they have been acted out in the past, Asians do not stir the same kind of fear and hatred in white hearts as blacks do.

50. My current study of white working-class families suggests that reactions to affirmative action vary somewhat by gender. So, for example, those working-class women who now work in occupations that formerly were exclusively male are significantly more inclined to see some value in these programs. And even women in traditional female occupations often have a more complex and differentiated view than the men.

51. Rubin (1983).

52. See Alba (1990) for an excellent account of what he calls "the transformation of ethnicity."

53. The January 15, 1992, *San Francisco Chronicle* features two articles about such clubs, one in a high school in Anaheim, the other in San Jose.

54. This was the cry of many of the white students at the University of California, Berkeley, who participated in a study of racial attitudes on the campus. See "The Diversity Project: Final Report," a publication of the Institute for the Study of Social Change, University of California, Berkeley (November 1990).

55. *San Francisco Examiner,* February 2, 1992.

56. When adjusted for inflation, the average after-tax incomes of the 100 million Americans who make up the bottom two-fifths of the income spectrum have fallen since 1977. The average of the middle fifth of households has edged up 2 to 4 percent. But the average after-tax income of upper-middle-income households has climbed more than 10 percent. And among the wealthiest 5 percent of taxpayers—those with incomes of $91,750—after-tax income rose more than 60 percent during this period (Greenstein, 1991).

REFERENCES

Alba, Richard D. 1990. *Ethnic Identity.* New Haven, CT: Yale University Press.

Blankenhorn, David. 1989. "Ozzie and Harriet: Have Reports of Their Death Been Greatly Exaggerated?" *Family Affairs* 2 (Summer–Fall):10.

Children's Defense Fund Report. 1992. Center for Labor Market Studies. Boston: Northeastern University.

Daniels, Roger. 1990. *Coming to America: A History of Immigration and Ethnicity in American Life.* New York: HarperCollins.

Gans, Herbert J. 1979. "Symbolic Ethnicity: The Future of Ethnic Groups and Culture in America." *Ethnic and Racial Studies* 2 (January):1–18.

Greenstein, Robert. 1991. "The Kindest Cut." *American Prospect* (Fall):49–57.

Hochschild, Arlie Russell. 1989. *The Second Shift: Working Parents and the Revolution at Home.* New York: Viking.

Landry, Bart. 1991. "The Enduring Dilemma of Race in America." In *America at Century's End,* ed. Alan Wolfe. Berkeley: University of California Press.

Leiberson, Stanley, and Mary C. Waters. 1990. *From Many Strands.* New York: Russell Sage.

Phillips, Kevin. 1990. *The Politics of Rich and Poor.* New York: Random House.

Portes, Alejandro, and Ruben G. Rumbaut. 1990. Immigrant America. Berkeley: University of California Press.

Robertson, Nan. 1992. *The Girls in the Balcony.* New York: Random House.

Rubin, Lillian. 1972. *Busing and Backlash: White Against White in an Urban School District.* Berkeley: University of California Press.

————. 1976. *Worlds of Pain: Life in the Working-Class Family.* New York: Basic Books.

————. 1983. *Intimate Strangers: Men and Women Together.* New York: Harper & Row.

Sanjek, Roger. 1991. "Intermarriage and the Future of the Races in the United States." Paper presented at the American Anthropological Association meeting, August, Chicago, Illinois.

Schor, Juliet B. 1992. *The Overworked American: The Unexpected Decline of Leisure.* New York: Basic Books.

Sirianni, Carmen, and Andrea Walsh. 1991. "Through the Prism of Time: Temporal Structures in Postindustrial America." In *America at Century's End,* ed. Alan Wolfe. Berkeley: University of California Press.

Stacey, Judith. 1990. *Brave New Families.* New York: Basic Books.

Steinberg, Stephen. 1989. *The Ethnic Myth.* Boston: Beacon.

U.S. Bureau of the Census. 1991. *Statistical Abstract of the United States.* Washington, DC: Government Printing Office.

U.S. Department of Labor, Bureau of Labor Statistics. 1991. *Data Resources.* Washington, DC: Government Printing Office.

————. 1991. *Employment and Earnings* 38, no. 12 (December). Washington, DC: U.S. Government Printing Office.

U.S. Department of Labor, Women's Bureau. 1990. *Facts on Working Women* 90, no. 2 (September). Washington, DC: Government Printing Office.

Waters, Mary C. 1990. *Ethnic Options.* Berkeley: University of California Press.

Weitzman, Lenore J. 1985. *The Divorce Revolution.* New York: Free Press.

"Is This a White Country, or What?"

"They're letting all these coloreds come in and soon there won't be any place left for white people," broods Tim Walsh, a thirty-three-year-old white construction worker. "It makes you wonder: Is this a white country, or what?"

It's a question that nags at white America, one perhaps that's articulated most often and most clearly by the men and women of the working class. For it's they who feel most vulnerable, who have suffered the economic contractions of recent decades most keenly, who see the new immigrants most clearly as direct competitors for their jobs.

It's not whites alone who stew about immigrants. Native-born blacks, too, fear the newcomers nearly as much as whites—and for the same economic reasons. But for whites the issue is compounded by race, by the fact that the newcomers are primarily people of color. For them, therefore, their economic anxieties have combined with the changing face of America to create a profound uneasiness about immigration—a theme that was sounded by nearly 90 percent of the whites I met, even by those who are themselves first-generation, albeit well-assimilated, immigrants.

Sometimes they spoke about this in response to my questions; equally often the subject of immigration arose spontaneously as people gave voice to their concerns. But because the new immigrants are dominantly people of color, the discourse was almost always cast in terms of race as well as immigration, with the talk slipping from immigration to race and back again as if these are not two separate phenomena. "If we keep letting all them foreigners in, pretty soon there'll be more of them than us and then what will this country be like?" Tim's wife, Mary Anne, frets. "I mean, this is *our* country, but the way things are going, white people will be the minority in our own country. Now does that make any sense?"

Such fears are not new. Americans have always worried about the strangers who came to our shores, fearing that they would corrupt our society, dilute our culture, debase our values. So I remind Mary Anne, "When your ancestors came here, people also thought we were allowing too many foreigners into the country. Yet those earlier immigrants were successfully integrated into the American society. What's different now?"

"Oh, it's different, all right," she replies without hesitation. "When my people came, the immigrants were all white. That makes a big difference."

"Why do you think that's so?"

"I don't know; it just is, that's all. Look at the black people; they've been here a long time, and they still don't live like us—stealing and drugs and having all those babies."

"But you were talking about immigrants. Now you're talking about blacks, and they're not immigrants."

"Yeah, I know," she replies with a shrug. "But they're different, and there's enough problems with them, so we don't need any more. With all these other people coming here now, we just have more trouble. They don't talk English; and they think different from us, things like that."

Listening to Mary Anne's words I was reminded again how little we Americans look to history for its lessons, how impoverished is our historical memory. For, in fact, being white didn't make "a big difference" for many of those earlier immigrants. The dark-skinned Italians and the eastern European Jews who came in the late nineteenth and early twentieth centuries didn't look very white to the fair-skinned Americans who were here then. Indeed, the same people we now call white—Italians, Jews, Irish—were seen as another race at that time. Not black or Asian, it's true, but an alien other, a race apart, although one that didn't have a clearly defined name. Moreover, the racist fears and fantasies of native-born Americans were far less contained then than they are now, largely because there were few social constraints on their expression.

When, during the nineteenth century, for example, some Italians were taken for blacks and lynched in the South, the incidents passed virtually unnoticed. And if Mary Anne and Tim Walsh, both of Irish ancestry, had come to this country during the great Irish immigration of that period, they would have found themselves defined as an inferior race and described with the same language that was used to characterize blacks: "low-browed and savage, grovelling and bestial, lazy and wild, simian and sensual."[1] Not only during that period but for a long time afterward as well, the U.S. Census Bureau counted the Irish as a distinct and separate group, much as it does today with the category it labels "Hispanic."

But there are two important differences between then and now, differences that can be summed up in a few words: the economy and race. Then, a growing industrial economy meant that there were plenty of jobs for both immigrant and native workers, something that can't be said for the contracting economy in which we live today. True, the arrival of the immigrants, who were more readily exploitable than native workers, put Americans at a disadvantage and created discord between the two groups. Nevertheless, work was available for both.

Then, too, the immigrants—no matter how they were labeled, no matter how reviled they may have been—were ultimately assimilable, if for no other reason than that they were white. As they began to lose their alien ways, it became possible for native Americans to see in the white ethnics of yesteryear a reflection of themselves. Once this shift in perception occurred, it was possible for the nation to incorporate them, to take them in, chew them up, digest them, and spit them out as Americans—with subcultural variations not always to the liking of those who hoped to control the manners and mores of the day, to be sure, but still recognizably white Americans.

Today's immigrants, however, are the racial other in a deep and profound way. It's true that race is not a fixed category, that it's no less an *idea* today than it was yesterday. And it's also possible, as I have already suggested, that we may be witness to social transformation from race to ethnicity among some of the most assimilated—read: middle-class—Asians and Latinos. But even if so, there's a long way to go before that metamorphosis is realized. Meanwhile, the immigrants of this era not only bring their own language and culture, they are also people of color—men, women, and children whose skin tones are different and whose characteristic features set them apart and justify the racial categories we lock them into.[2] And integrating masses of people of color into a society where race consciousness lies at the very heart of our central nervous system raises a whole new set of anxieties and tensions.

It's not surprising, therefore, that racial dissension has increased so sharply in recent years. What is surprising, however, is the passion for ethnicity and the preoccupation with ethnic identification among whites that seem suddenly to have burst upon the public scene. Responding to this renewed emphasis on our ancestral past, students of ethnicity have been engaged in a lively debate about its meaning—a debate cast in terms of assimilation versus pluralism.[3]

The assimilationists rest their argument in structural realities, insisting that it's impossible to maintain ethnic group unity in the face of continuing social, residential, and occupational mobility. If people no longer live together, work together, marry each other, these theorists contend, ethnic solidarity ceases to exist anyplace but in the imagination.

The pluralists challenge the structural hypothesis, claiming instead that evidence for the importance of ethnicity lies in the persisting behavioral and attitudinal differences among ethnic groups. Italians, Irish, Germans, Jews, and so on, they maintain, all exhibit subcultural variations that derive from the culture their ancestors brought with them to these shores.

But even a casual comparison of the culture in the mother country and its expression here shows some very large differences. Sometimes these subcultural variations are so mixed with Americanisms that they seem only distantly related to the original culture, especially to an observer from the native land. And sometimes the immigrant generation clings tenaciously to the culture it left, enacting cultural forms and abiding by norms that are frozen in time, while the home country culture grows and changes. In this case, it doesn't take long before the group's culture in the new land looks more like a parody of the native culture than an emulation or a variation of it. Nor is this adaptation likely to survive the immigrant generation.

As further evidence for their premise, pluralists point to survey data that show that the vast majority of Americans identify themselves as ethnics. It's certainly true that when asked a question about ethnic background, most people respond with their ancestors' country of origin.[4] But whether this answer reflects a statement about their personal identity as well as their ancestry is an open question. Even if it does say something about identity, it tells us nothing about its *meaning* to the person who makes the claim, gives us no clue to whether ethnicity is central or peripheral to the definition of self. Sociologist Mary Waters argues that people can have a strong sense of ethnic identity without attaching any specific meaning either to their ethnic heritage or to the identity they claim—a formulation about ethnicity and identity that is itself without meaning.[5]

What does being German, Irish, French, Russian, Polish mean to someone who is an American? "It's undoubtedly different for recent immigrants than for those who have been here for generations. But even for a relative newcomer, the inexorable process of becoming an American changes the meaning of ethnic identification and its hold on the internal life of the individual. Nowhere have I seen this shift more eloquently described than in a recent op-ed piece published in the *New York Times*. The author, a Vietnamese refugee writing on the day when Vietnamese either celebrate or mourn the fall of Saigon, depending on which side of the conflict they were on, writes:

> Although I sometimes mourn the loss of home and land, it's the American landscape and what it offers that solidify my hyphenated identity. . . . Assimilation, education, the English language, the American "I"—these have carried me and many others further from that beloved tropical country than the C-130 ever could. . . . When did this happen? Who knows? One night, America quietly seeps in and takes hold of one's mind and body, and the Vietnamese soul of sorrows slowly fades away. In the morning, the Vietnamese American speaks a new language of materialism: his vocabulary includes terms like career choices, down payment, escrow, overtime.[6]

A new language emerges, but it lives, at least for another generation, alongside the old one; Vietnamese, yes, but also American, with a newly developed sense of self and possibility—an identity that continues to grow stronger with each succeeding generation. It's a process we have seen repeated throughout the history of American immigration. The American world reaches into the immigrant communities and shapes and changes the people who live in them.[7] By the second generation, ethnic identity already is attenuated; by the third, it usually has receded as a deeply meaningful part of life.

Residential segregation, occupational concentration, and a common language and culture—these historically have been the basis for ethnic solidarity and identification. As strangers in a new land, immigrants banded together, bound by their native tongue and shared culture. The sense of affinity they felt in these urban communities was natural; they were a touch of home, of the old country, of ways they understood. Once within their boundaries, they could feel whole again, sheltered from the ridicule and revulsion with which they were greeted by those who came before them. For whatever the myth about America's welcoming arms, nativist sentiment has nearly always been high and the anti-immigrant segment of the population large and noisy.

Ethnic solidarity and identity in America, then, were the consequence of the shared history each group brought with it, combined with the social and psychological experience of establishing themselves in the new land. But powerful as these were, the connections among the members of the group were heightened and sustained by the occupational concentration that followed—the Irish in the police departments of cities like Boston and San Francisco, for example, the Jews in New York City's garment industry, the east central Europeans in the mills and mines of western Pennsylvania.[8]

As each ethnic group moved into the labor force, its members often became concentrated in a particular occupation, largely because they were helped to find jobs there by those who went before them. For employers, this ethnic homogeneity made sense. They didn't have to cope with a babel of different languages, and they could count on the older workers to train the newcomers and keep them in line. For workers, there were advantages as well. It meant that they not only had compatible workmates, but that they weren't alone as they faced the jeers and contempt of their American-born counterparts. And perhaps most important, as more and more ethnic peers filled the available jobs, they began to develop some small measure of control in the workplace.

The same pattern of occupational concentration that was characteristic of yesterday's immigrant groups exists among the new immigrants today, and for the same reasons. The Cubans in Florida and the Dominicans in New York,[9] the various Asian groups in San Francisco, the Koreans in Los Angeles and New York—all continue to live in ethnic neighborhoods; all use the networks established there to find their way into the American labor force.[10]

For the white working-class ethnics whose immigrant past is little more than part of family lore, the occupational, residential, and linguistic chain has been broken. This is not to say that white ethnicity has ceased to be an observable phenomenon in American life. Cities like New York, Chicago, and San Francisco still have white ethnic districts that influence their culture, especially around food preferences and eating habits. But as in San Francisco's North Beach or New York's Little Italy, the people who once created vibrant neighborhoods, where a distinct subculture and language remained vividly alive, long ago moved out and left behind only the remnants of the commercial life of the old community. As such transformations took place, ethnicity became largely a private matter, a distant part of the family heritage that had little to do with the ongoing life of the family or community.

What, then, are we to make of the claims to ethnic identity that have become so prominent in recent years? Herbert Gans has called this identification "symbolic ethnicity"—that is, ethnicity that's invoked or not as the individual chooses.[11] Symbolic ethnicity, according to Gans, has little impact on a person's daily life and, because it is not connected to ethnic structures or activities—except for something like the wearing of the green on St. Patrick's Day—it makes no real contribution to ethnic solidarity or community.

The description is accurate. But it's a mistake to dismiss ethnic identification, even if only symbolic, as relatively meaningless. Symbols, after all, become symbolic precisely because they have meaning. In this case, the symbol has meaning at two levels: one is the personal and psychological, the other is the social and political.

At the personal level, in a nation as large and diverse as ours—a nation that defines itself by its immigrant past, where the metaphor for our national identity has been the melting pot—defining oneself in the context of an ethnic group is comforting. It provides a sense of belonging to some recognizable and manageable collectivity— an affiliation that has meaning because it's connected to the family where, when we were small children, we first learned about our relationship to the group. As Vilma Janowski, a twenty-four-year-old first-generation Polish American who came here as a child, put it: "Knowing there's other people like you is really nice. It's like having a big family, even if you don't ever really see them. It's just nice to know they're there. Besides, if I said I was American, what would it mean? Nobody's just American."

Which is true. Being an American is different from being French or Dutch or any number of other nationalities because, except for Native Americans, there's no such thing as an American without a hyphen somewhere in the past. To identify with the front end of that hyphen is to maintain a connection—however tenuous, illusory, or sentimentalized—with our roots. It sets us apart from others, allows us the fantasy of uniqueness—a quest given particular urgency by a psychological culture that increasingly emphasizes the development of the self and personal history. Paradoxically, however, it also gives us a sense of belonging—of being one with others like ourselves—that helps to overcome some of the isolation of modern life.

But these psychological meanings have developed renewed force in recent years because of two significant sociopolitical events. The first was the civil rights movement with its call for racial equality. The second was the change in the immigration laws, which, for the first time in nearly half a century, allowed masses of immigrants to enter the country.

It was easy for northern whites to support the early demands of the civil rights movement when blacks were asking for the desegregation of buses and drinking fountains in the South. But supporting the black drive to end discrimination in jobs, housing, and education in the urban North was quite another matter—especially among those white ethnics whose hold on the ladder of mobility was tenuous at best and with whom blacks would be most likely to compete, whether in the job market, the neighborhood, or the classroom. As the courts and legislatures around the country began to honor some black claims for redress of past injustices, white hackles began to rise.

It wasn't black demands alone that fed the apprehensions of whites, however. In the background of the black civil rights drive, there stood a growing chorus of voices, as other racial groups—Asian-Americans, Latinos, and Native Americans—joined the public fray to seek remedy for their own grievances. At the same time that these homegrown groups were making their voices heard and, not incidentally, affirming their distinctive cultural heritages and calling for public acknowledgment of them, the second great wave of immigration in this century washed across our shores.

After having closed the gates to mass immigration with the National Origins Act of 1924, Congress opened them again when it passed the Immigration Act of 1965.[12] This act, which was a series of amendments to the McCarran-Walter Act of 1952, essentially jettisoned the national origins provisions of earlier law and substituted overall hemisphere caps. The bill, according to immigration historian Roger Daniels, "changed the whole course of American immigration history" and left the door open for a vast increase in the numbers of immigrants.[13]

More striking than the increase in numbers has been the character of the new immigrants. Instead of the large numbers of western Europeans whom the sponsors had expected to take advantage of the new policy, it has been the people of Asia, Latin America, and the Caribbean who rushed to the boats. "It is doubtful if any drafter or supporter of the 1965 act envisaged this result," writes Daniels.[14] In fact, when members of Lyndon Johnson's administration, under whose tenure the bill became law, testified before Congress, they assured the legislators and the nation that few Asians would come in under the new law.[15]

This is a fascinating example of the unintended consequences of a political act. The change in the law was sponsored by northern Democrats who sought to appeal to their white ethnic constituencies by opening the gates to their countrymen once again—that is, to the people of eastern and southern Europe whom the 1924 law had kept out for nearly half a century. But those same white ethnics punished the Democratic Party by defecting to the Republicans during the Reagan-Bush years, a defection that was at least partly related to their anger about the new immigrants and the changing racial balance of urban America.

During the decade of the 1980s, 2.5 million immigrants from Asian countries were admitted to the United States, an increase of more than 450 percent over the years between 1961 and 1970, when the number was slightly less than half a million. In 1990 alone, nearly as many Asian immigrants—one-third of a million—entered the country as came during the entire decade of the 1960s. Other groups show similarly noteworthy increases. Close to three-quarters of a million documented Mexicans crossed the border in the single year of 1990, compared to less than half a million during all of the 1960s. Central American immigration, too, climbed from just under one hundred thousand between 1961 and 1970 to more than triple that number during the 1980s. And immigrants from the Caribbean, who numbered a little more than half a million during the 1960s, increased to over three-quarters of a million in the years between 1981 and 1989.[16]

Despite these large increases and the perception that we are awash with new immigrants, it's worth noting that they are a much smaller proportion of the total population today, 6.2 percent, than they were in 1920, when they were a hefty 13.2 percent of all U.S. residents.[17] But the fact that most immigrants today are people of color gives them greater visibility than ever before.

Suddenly, the nation's urban landscape has been colored in ways unknown before. In 1970, the California cities that were the site of the original research for *Worlds of Pain* were almost exclusively white. Twenty years later, the 1990 census reports that their minority populations range from 54 to 69 percent. In the nation at large, the same census shows nearly one in four Americans with African, Asian, Latino, or Native American ancestry, up from one in five in 1980.[18] So dramatic is this shift that whites of European descent now make up just over two-thirds of the population in New York State, while in California they number only 57 percent. In cities like New York, San Francisco, and Los Angeles whites are a minority— accounting for 38, 47, and 37 percent of residents, respectively. Twenty years ago the white population in all these cities was over 75 percent.[19]

The increased visibility of other racial groups has focused whites more self-consciously than ever on their own racial identification. Until the new immigration shifted the complexion of the land so perceptibly, whites didn't think of themselves as white in the same way that Chinese know they're Chinese and African-Americans know they're black. Being white was simply a fact of life, one that didn't require any public statement, since it was the definitive social value against which all others were measured. "It's like everything's changed and I don't know what happened," complains Marianne Bardolino. "All of a sudden you have to be thinking all the time about these race things. I don't remember growing up thinking about being white like I think about it now. I'm not saying I didn't know there was coloreds and whites; it's just that I didn't go along thinking, *Gee, I'm a white person.* I never thought about it at all. But now with all the different colored people around, you have to think about it because they're thinking about it all the time."

"You say you feel pushed now to think about being white, but I'm not sure I understand why. What's changed?" I ask.

"I told you," she replies quickly, a small smile covering her impatience with my question. "It's because they think about what they are, and they want things their way, so now I have to think about what I am and what's good for me and my kids." She pauses briefly to let her thoughts catch up with her tongue, then continues. "I mean, if somebody's always yelling at you about being black or Asian or something, then it makes you think about being white. Like, they want the kids in school to learn about their culture, so then I think about being white and being Italian and say: What about my culture? If they're going to teach about theirs, what about mine?"

To which America's racial minorities respond with bewilderment. "I don't understand what white people want," says Gwen Tomalson. "They say if black kids are going to learn about black culture in school, then white people want their kids to learn about white culture. I don't get it. What do they think kids have been learning about all these years? It's all about white people and how they live and what they accomplished. When I was in school you wouldn't have thought black people existed for all our books ever said about us."

As for the charge that they're "thinking about race all the time," as Marianne Bardolino complains, people of color insist that they're forced into it by a white world that never lets them forget. "If you're Chinese, you can't forget it, even if you want to, because there's always something that reminds you," Carol Kwan's husband, Andrew, remarks tartly. "I mean, if Chinese kids get good grades and get into the university, everybody's worried and you read about it in the papers."

While there's little doubt that racial anxieties are at the center of white concerns, our historic nativism also plays a part in escalating white alarm. The new immigrants bring with them a language and an ethnic culture that's vividly expressed wherever they congregate. And it's this also, the constant reminder of an alien presence from which whites are excluded, that's so troublesome to them.

The nativist impulse isn't, of course, given to the white working class alone. But for those in the upper reaches of the class and status hierarchy—those whose children go to private schools, whose closest contact with public transportation is the taxi cab—the immigrant population supplies a source of cheap labor, whether as nannies for their children, maids in their households, or workers in their businesses. They may grouse and complain that "nobody speaks English anymore," just as working-class people do. But for the people who use immigrant labor, legal or illegal, there's a payoff for the inconvenience—a payoff that doesn't exist for the families in this study but that sometimes costs them dearly.[20] For while it may be true that American workers aren't eager for many of the jobs immigrants are willing to take, it's also true that the presence of a large immigrant population—especially those who come from developing countries where living standards are far below our own—helps to make these jobs undesirable by keeping wages depressed well below what most American workers are willing to accept.[21]

Indeed, the economic basis of our immigration policies too often gets lost in the lore that we are a land that says to the world, "Give me your tired, your poor, your huddled masses, yearning to breathe free."[22] I don't mean to suggest that our humane impulses are a fiction, only that the reality is far more complex than Emma Lazarus's poem suggests. The massive immigration of the nineteenth and early twentieth centuries didn't just happen spontaneously. America may have been known as the land of opportunity to the Europeans who dreamed of coming here—a country where, as my parents once believed, the streets were lined with gold. But they believed these things because that's how America was sold by the agents who spread out across the face of Europe to recruit workers—men and women who were needed to keep the machines of our developing industrial society running and who, at the same time, gave the new industries a steady supply of hungry workers willing to work for wages well below those of native-born Americans.

The enormous number of immigrants who arrived during that period accomplished both those ends. In doing so, they set the stage for a long history of antipathy to foreign workers. For today, also, one function of the new immigrants is to keep our industries competitive in a global economy. Which simply is another way of saying that they serve to depress the wages of native American workers.

It's not surprising, therefore, that working-class women and men speak so angrily about the recent influx of immigrants. They not only see their jobs and their way of life threatened, they feel bruised and assaulted by an environment that seems suddenly to have turned color and in which they feel like strangers in their own land. So they chafe and complain: "They come here to take advantage of us, but they don't really want to learn our ways," Beverly Sowell, a thirty-three-year-old white electronics assembler, grumbles irritably. "They live different than us; it's like another world how they live. And they're so clannish. They keep to themselves, and they don't even *try* to learn English. You go on the bus these days and you might as well be in a foreign country; everybody's talking some other language, you know, Chinese or Spanish or something. Lots of them have been here a long time, too, but they don't care; they just want to take what they can get."

But their complaints reveal an interesting paradox, an illuminating glimpse into the contradictions that beset native-born Americans in their relations with those who seek refuge here. On the one hand, they scorn the immigrants; on the other, they protest because they "keep to themselves." It's the same contradiction that dominates black-white relations. Whites refuse to integrate blacks but are outraged when they stop knocking at the door, when they move to sustain the separation on their own terms—in black theme houses on campuses, for example, or in the newly developing black middle-class suburbs.

I wondered, as I listened to Beverly Sowell and others like her, why the same people who find the lifeways and languages of our foreign-born population offensive also care whether they "keep to themselves."

"Because like I said, they just shouldn't, that's all," Beverly says stubbornly. "If they're going to come here, they should be willing to learn our ways—you know what I mean, be real Americans. That's what my grandparents did, and that's what they should do."

"But your grandparents probably lived in an immigrant neighborhood when they first came here, too," I remind her.

"It was different," she insists. "I don't know why; it was. They wanted to be Americans; these here people now, I don't think they do. They just want to take advantage of this country."

She stops, thinks for a moment, then continues, "Right now it's awful in this country. Their kids come into the schools, and it's a big mess. There's not enough money for our kids to get a decent education, and we have to spend money to teach their kids English. It makes me mad. I went to public school, but I have to send my kids to Catholic school because now on top of the black kids, there's all these foreign kids who don't speak English. What kind of an education can kids get in a school like that? Something's wrong when plain old American kids can't go to their own schools.

"Everything's changed, and it doesn't make sense. Maybe you get it, but I don't. We can't take care of our own people and we keep bringing more and more foreigners in. Look at all the homeless. Why do we need more people here when our own people haven't got a place to sleep?"

"Why do we need more people here?"—a question Americans have asked for two centuries now. Historically, efforts to curb immigration have come during economic downturns, which suggests that when times are good, when American workers feel confident about their future, they're likely to be more generous in sharing their good fortune with foreigners. But when the economy falters, as it did in the 1990s, and workers worry about having to compete for jobs with people whose standard of living is well below their own, resistance to immigration rises. "Don't get me wrong; I've got nothing against these people," Tim Walsh demurs. "But they don't talk English, and they're used to a lot less, so they can work for less money than guys like me can. I see it all the time; they get hired and some white guy gets left out."

It's this confluence of forces—the racial and cultural diversity of our new immigrant population; the claims on the resources of the nation now being made by those minorities who, for generations, have called America their home; the failure of some of our basic institutions to serve the needs of our people; the contracting economy, which threatens the mobility aspirations of working-class families—all these have come together to leave white workers feeling as if everyone else is getting a piece of the action while they get nothing. "I feel like white people are left out in the cold," protests Diane Johnson, a twenty-eight-year-old white single mother who believes she lost a job as a bus driver to a black woman. "First it's the blacks; now it's all those other colored people, and it's like everything always goes their way. It seems like a white person doesn't have a chance anymore. It's like the squeaky wheel gets the grease, and they've been squeaking and we haven't," she concludes angrily.

Until recently, whites didn't need to think about having to "squeak"—at least not specifically as whites. They have, of course, organized and squeaked at various times in the past—sometimes as ethnic groups, sometimes as workers. But not as whites. As whites they have been the dominant group, the favored ones, the ones who could count on getting the job when people of color could not. Now suddenly there are others—not just individual others but identifiable groups, people who share a history, a language, a culture, even a color—who lay claim to some of the rights and privileges that formerly had been labeled "for whites only." And whites react as if they've been betrayed, as if a sacred promise has been broken. They're white, aren't they? They're *real* Americans, aren't they? This is their country, isn't it?

The answers to these questions used to be relatively unambiguous. But not anymore. Being white no longer automatically ensures dominance in the politics of a multiracial society. Ethnic group politics, however, has a long and fruitful history. As whites sought a social and political base on which to stand, therefore, it was natural and logical to reach back to their ethnic past. Then they, too, could be "something"; they also would belong to a group; they would have a name, a history, a culture, and a voice. "Why is it only the blacks or Mexicans or Jews that are 'something'?" asks Tim Walsh. "I'm Irish, isn't that something, too? Why doesn't that count?"

In reclaiming their ethnic roots, whites can recount with pride the tribulations and transcendence of their ancestors and insist that others take their place in the line from which they have only recently come. "My people had a rough time, too. But nobody gave us anything, so why do we owe them something? Let them pull their share like the rest of us had to do," says Al Riccardi, a twenty-nine-year-old white taxi driver.

From there it's only a short step to the conviction that those who don't progress up that line are hampered by nothing more than their own inadequacies or, worse yet, by their unwillingness to take advantage of the opportunities offered them. "Those people, they're hollering all the time about discrimination," Al continues, without defining who "those people" are. "Maybe once a long time ago that was true, but not now. The problem is that a lot of those people are lazy. There's plenty of opportunities, but you've got to be willing to work hard."

He stops a moment, as if listening to his own words, then continues, "Yeah, yeah, I know there's a recession on and lots of people don't have jobs. But it's different with some of those people. They don't really want to work, because if they did, there wouldn't be so many of them selling drugs and getting in all kinds of trouble."

"You keep talking about 'those people' without saying who you mean," I remark.

"Aw c'mon, you know who I'm talking about," he says, his body shifting uneasily in his chair. "It's mostly the black people, but the Spanish ones, too."

In reality, however, it's a no-win situation for America's people of color, whether immigrant or native-born. For the industriousness of the Asians comes in for nearly as much criticism as the alleged laziness of other groups. When blacks don't make it, it's because whites like Al Riccardi insist their culture doesn't teach respect for family; because they're hedonistic, lazy, stupid, and/or criminally inclined. But when Asians demonstrate their ability to overcome the obstacles of an alien language and culture, when the Asian family seems to be the repository of our most highly regarded traditional values, white hostility doesn't disappear. It just changes its form. Then the accomplishments of Asians, the speed with which they move up the economic ladder, aren't credited to their superior culture, diligence, or intelligence—even when these are granted—but to the fact that they're "single-minded," "untrustworthy," "clannish drones," "narrow people" who raise children who are insufficiently "well rounded."[23]

True, the remarkable successes of members of the Asian immigrant community have engendered grudging, if ambivalent, respect. "If our people were as hard working and disciplined as the Asians, we'd be a lot better off," says Doug Craigen, a thirty-two-year-old white truck driver.

But the words are barely out of his mouth before the other side surfaces and he reaches for the stereotypes that are so widely accepted. "I'm not a racist, but sometimes they give me the creeps. You've got to watch out for them because they'll do anything for a buck, anything. I guess the thing that bothers me most is you can't get away from them," he explains, as if their very presence is somehow menacing. "They're all over the place, like pushy little yellow drones. You go to the bank, they're working there. You go to a store, they're behind the counter. It's like they're gobbling up all the jobs in town."

The job market isn't the only place where Asians are competing successfully with whites. From grade school to college, Asian students are taking a large share of the top honors, leaving white parents in a state of anxious concern.[24] "I don't know if our kids can compete with those Chinese kids," worries Linda Hammer, a thirty-year-old white beautician who hopes to see her children in college one day. "My kids aren't bad students, but those Asian kids, that's all they live for. I don't think it's good to push kids so hard, do you? I mean, I hear some of those people beat their kids if they don't get A's. They turn them into little nerds who don't do anything but study. How can American kids compete with that?"

Whites aren't alone in greeting Asian successes so ambivalently. Like Doug Craigen, Lurine Washington, a black thirty-year-old nurse's aide, speaks admiringly of the accomplishments of her Asian neighbors. "I could get killed for saying this, but I don't care. The Asians are a lot more disciplined than blacks as a whole: That's not a racist statement; it's a fact because of their culture. Saying that doesn't mean I don't like my people, but I'm not blind either. All I know is if our kids worked as hard in school as theirs do, they could make something of themselves, too. And those families, all of them working together like that. You've got to respect that, don't you?"

Moments later, however, Lurine complains, "If we don't watch out, they'll take over everything. I mean, they already own half the country, even Rockefeller Center. You know what I mean. They're like ants; there's so many of them, and they're so sneaky and everything. And they think they're better than other people; that's what really makes me mad."

Not surprisingly, as competition increases, the various minority groups often are at war among themselves as they press their own particular claims, fight over turf, and compete for an ever-shrinking piece of the pie. In several African-American communities, where Korean shopkeepers have taken the place once held by Jews, the confrontations have been both wrenching and tragic. A Korean grocer in Los Angeles shoots and kills a fifteen-year-old black girl for allegedly trying to steal some trivial item from the store.[25] From New York City to Berkeley, California, African-Americans boycott Korean shop owners who, they charge, invade their neighborhoods, take their money, and treat them disrespectfully.[26] But painful as these incidents are for those involved, they are only symptoms of a deeper malaise in both communities—the contempt and distrust in which the Koreans hold their African-American neighbors, and the rage of blacks as they watch these new immigrants surpass them.

Latino-black conflict also makes headlines when, in the aftermath of the riots in South Central Los Angeles, the two groups fight over who will get the lion's share of the jobs to rebuild the neighborhood. Blacks, insisting that they're being discriminated against, shut down building projects that don't include them in satisfactory numbers. And indeed, many of the jobs that formerly went to African-Americans are now being taken by Latino workers. In an article entitled "Black vs. Brown," Jack Miles, an editorial writer for the *Los Angeles Times,* reports that "janitorial firms serving downtown Los Angeles have almost entirely replaced their unionized black work force with nonunionized immigrants."[27]

On their side of the escalating divide, the Latino community complains bitterly that they always take second place to black demands. "Nobody pays attention to us like they do to the blacks," protests Julio Martinez, a thirty-year-old Latino warehouseman. "There's a saying in Spanish: You scratch where it itches. There's plenty of problems all around us here," he explains, his sweeping gesture encompassing the Latino neighborhood where he lives, "but they don't pay attention because we don't make so much trouble. But people are getting mad. That's what happened in L.A.; they got mad because nobody paid attention."

But the disagreements among America's racial minorities are of little interest or concern to most white working-class families. Instead of conflicting groups, they see one large mass of people of color, all of them making claims that endanger their own precarious place in the world. It's this perception that has led some white ethnics to believe that reclaiming their ethnicity alone is not enough, that so long as they remain in their separate and distinct groups, their power will be limited. United, however, they can become a formidable countervailing force, one that can stand fast against the threat posed by minority demands. But to come together solely as whites would diminish their impact and leave them open to the charge that their real purpose is simply to retain the privileges of whiteness. A dilemma that has been resolved, at least for some, by the birth of a new entity in the history of American ethnic groups—the "European-Americans."[28]

Presently, this is little more than an idea in the minds of those who would mobilize white ethnics to organize under a common umbrella. But it's a powerful idea, one that's beginning to develop an organizational base, as is evident from the emergence of European-American clubs in various cities around the country. No one knows just how many of these clubs exist or what proportion of their membership is made up of working-class ethnics. But in the three clubs I visited during the course of this research, their members were drawn almost exclusively from the white working class.

Although these European-American clubs probably aren't widespread yet, the outlines of things to come are visible. "It's time for European-Americans to defend themselves against all these minority people who are ruining the country," says Ben Wiltsey, a twenty-seven-year-old white construction worker who joined a European-American club a few months before we met. "We're getting people from all over the county joining up with us to call a halt. This multicultural business is garbage. White people need their own space to practice their culture."

While most of the people I talked with wouldn't put it so crudely, virtually all would give assent to the idea embodied in the words Ben spoke. They don't usually speak so self-consciously about themselves as European-Americans, either. But the notion of European-Americans as an ethnic group has permeated their consciousness, even if in a relatively inchoate way.[29] Consequently, they see themselves as people whose European immigrant heritage gives them some common ground, a socially acceptable place to stand in opposition to "them." "They all get together to fight for what they want, so why shouldn't we?" asks Tony Bardolino, with mounting irritation. "You can't just have a white organization anymore because they call you a racist, so maybe you need something else, like all the people who were once immigrants get together."

However it's framed and articulated, the idea has profound social and political significance. At the political level, an organization of European-Americans can provide the vehicle through which white ethnics can make their needs and wishes heard most effectively.[30] As one large confederation instead of a diverse collection of groups, each with its own agenda, European-Americans would have greater standing in the policy debates that have swept the nation in recent years. "We've left our chair at the multicultural table empty, and the multicultural table is where the debate is, where the deals are being made," explains the head of the European-American Study Group in one California city.

As European-Americans, whites remain hyphenated Americans, but rather than being divided by their various ancestries, they're united by virtue of their shared

European origin. Never mind that the historical experience of the Irish in the potato fields, the Italians in the villages of southern Italy, and the Jews in the shtetls of eastern Europe were so different. Or that there had been, until recently, few common bonds between them in the New World. All this gets muted in favor of the similarity of the immigrant experience as it is embodied in the "we came, we suffered, we conquered" myth, which by now has gained legendary proportions. And all of it without a single reference to race. Instead, the quintessential American experience is defined in terms of immigration, its burdens, and the ability to overcome such burdens through sacrifice and hard work. These are the real Americans, the only ones worthy of the name. It just happens that they're all white.

"It has nothing to do with race," maintains Delia Kronin, a thirty-eight-year-old working-class woman of Hungarian ancestry who, with her German American husband, recently joined a group calling themselves the "European-Americans." Other members of the group repeat Delia's words and contend that their purpose in joining together is simply to affirm the common bond of people of European extraction. "Why should we be the ones who feel like we have no place?" asks Ron Morgan, a forty-one-year-old police officer. "We come here and meet with other people like us. What's wrong with that? Nobody complains when black people or Asians or Hispanics go to their own clubs, so why can't we?"

It's undoubtedly true that one reason for the emergence of such alliances is that many whites now find themselves in social and political situations where they feel they are the outsiders. But it's disingenuous to maintain that race is not a relevant issue. Communities like Canarsie in Brooklyn, where Italians and Jews have banded together to keep blacks out, offer evidence of the growing tendency for whites of European ancestry to join together in common cause around racial issues.

Historically, these two ethnic groups have had little in common. And despite the fact that they share a neighborhood, Jonathan Rieder's account of life in Canarsie makes it clear that this has not changed.[31] The lifestyles and values of that community's Jews and Italians are conspicuously different, and neither has much respect for the other. Italian conservatism, both political and cultural, clashes with the Jewish liberal and cosmopolitan worldview. The willingness of some Italian activists to risk violence frightens the more pacific Jews. But these differences pale when they're confronted with what they perceive to be an invasion of blacks. Then they come together, bound by their whiteness, to protect their turf.

It's generally not expressed in these terms, of course. Instead, the talk is of differences in culture, class, values, and lifestyles. Yet professional middle-class black families—people with more education and higher class status than most Canarsie residents—are no more welcome there than those who are poor and working-class. Sometimes whites explain this contradiction by saying they worry that the neighborhood will tip once the walls are breached. "Some black people, I wouldn't mind, you know, those who are decent people, the educated kind," says Jake Rosenbaum, a forty-year-old white taxi driver who, by his own account, barely made it through high school. "The problem is once one of them, even the nice ones, comes on the block, the whole neighborhood's gone, just like that," he explains, snapping his fingers on the word *that* for emphasis.

Others speak fearfully about who will come into the neighborhood once an acceptable black family moves in. "I don't know. I've got nothing against the nice ones; they're people just like us," says Janet Marcantonio, a white thirty-eight-year-old office worker. "But they've got these big families and who knows who they'll bring with them. I mean everybody's got people who come to visit, or maybe even stay for a while, things like that. But with them, even if they're okay themselves, you worry that they'll bring an element into the neighborhood that you don't want. And once they move in, you can't control who comes to their house, can you?

"I don't like what some people around here do and how they talk, but I had to move once before because they came in and it ruined the neighborhood. So now I think we've all got to be together on this, even if you don't like some of the people and how they talk and act."

Whatever they say, then, it's clear that it's minority demand for equal treatment, whether in housing, jobs, or education, that has brought whites together. Indeed, until racial minorities came to be seen as a serious threat, white ethnics didn't join with others to celebrate their European heritage. We need only look at the high school and college campuses of the nation to see the shift. There, where the relatively closed nature of these institutions allows a view not ordinarily available in the world outside, we see white students struggling to deal with the minority presence and to find legitimacy for the kind of public expression of their identity that, in the current climate, is readily acceptable for other racial groups but not for whites as whites.

So, for example, many of the white students who participated in a recent study of racial attitudes on the University of California's Berkeley campus worry that they will soon find themselves disadvantaged in the competition for jobs with minorities. Alongside this fear, and not unrelated to it, is their feeling of being left out, without an easily recognizable social identity.[32] The others are all part of a group; they have some basis for coming together, both socially and politically. But the whites are, well ... just white—with no particular claim that anyone would honor. Indeed, to ask to be heard as a white person is to open oneself to the charge of racism.

I don't mean to suggest that racism, although often in coded form, isn't a central issue in the discourse of discontent in America today. Nevertheless, it's also true that in recent years there has been no escaping the indictment, regardless of the intent.

Now, as other racial groups on campus have found common cause and a shared social space—whether informally in the eating halls or other public spaces that have come to be their designated meeting places, or more formally in racially separated dormitories and theme houses—white students also want a place and an identity of their own. But since they can't comfortably ask for recognition as whites, they embrace their ethnic past and demand public acknowledgment of their newly acquired group status.

At the University of California at Berkeley, for example, white students and their faculty supporters insisted that the recently adopted multicultural curriculum include a unit of study on European-Americans. At Queens College in New York City, where white ethnic groups retain a more distinct presence, Italian-American students launched a successful suit to win recognition as a disadvantaged minority and gain the entitlements accompanying that status, including special units of Italian-American studies.

White high school students, too, talk of feeling isolated and, being less sophisticated and wary than their older sisters and brothers, complain quite openly that there's no acceptable and legitimate way for them to acknowledge a white identity. "There's all these things for all the different ethnicities, you know, like clubs for black kids and Hispanic kids, but there's nothing for me and my friends to join," Lisa Marshall, a sixteen-year-old white high school student explains with exasperation. "They won't let us have a white club because that's supposed to be racist. So we figured we'd just have to call it something else, you know, some ethnic thing, like Euro-Americans. Why not? They have African-American clubs."

Ethnicity, then, often becomes a cover for "white," not necessarily because these students are racist but because racial identity is now such a prominent feature of the discourse in our social world. In a society where racial consciousness is so high, how else can whites define themselves in ways that connect them to a community and, at the same time, allow them to deny their racial antagonisms?

Ethnicity and race—separate phenomena that are now inextricably entwined. Incorporating newcomers has never been easy, as our history of controversy and violence over immigration tells us.[33] But for the first time, the new immigrants are also people of color, which means that they tap both the nativist and racist impulses that are so deeply a part of American life. As in the past, however, the fear of foreigners, the revulsion against their strange customs and seemingly unruly ways, is only part of the reason for the anti-immigrant attitudes that are increasingly being expressed today. For whatever xenophobic suspicions may arise in modern America, economic issues play a critical role in stirring them up.

NOTES

1. Roediger, David, *The Wages of Whiteness* (New York: Verso, 1991), 133.
2. I'm aware that many Americans who have none of the characteristic features associated with their African heritage are still defined as black. This is one reason why I characterize race as an idea, not a fact. Nevertheless, the main point I am making here still holds—that is, the visible racial character of a people makes a difference in whether white Americans see them as assimilable or not.
3. See, for example, Richard D. Alba, *Ethnic Identity* (New Haven, Conn.: Yale University Press, 1990); Herbert Gans, "Symbolic Ethnicity: The Future of Ethnic Groups and Cultures in America" (*Ethnic and Racial Studies* 2 [January 1979]: 1–18); Stanley Leiberson and Mary C. Waters, *From Many Strands* (New York: Russell Sage, 1990); Alejandro Portes and Ruben G. Rumbaut, *Immigrant America* (Berkeley: University of California Press, 1990); Werner Sollors, ed., *The Invention of Ethnicity* (New York: Oxford University Press, 1989); Stephen Steinberg, *The Ethnic Myth* (Boston: Beacon, 1989); Waters, Mary C. *Ethnic Options* (Berkeley: University of California Press, 1990).
4. As I have already indicated, Jews and African Americans are notable exceptions.
5. Mary C. Waters, *Ethnic Options* (Berkeley: University of California Press, 1990).
6. *New York Times*, April 30, 1993.

7. For an excellent historical portrayal of the formation of ethnic communities among the east central European immigrants in Pennsylvania, the development of ethnic identity, and the process of Americanization, see Ewa Morawska, *For Bread with Butter* (New York: Cambridge University Press, 1985).

8. Ibid.

9. Alejandro Portes, and Rubén G. Rumbaut, *Immigrant America* (Berkeley: University of California Press, 1990).

10. One need only walk the streets of New York to see the concentration of Koreans in the corner markets and the nail care salons that dot the city's landscape. In San Francisco the Cambodians now own most of the donut shops in the city. It all started when, after working in such a shop, an enterprising young Cambodian combined the family resources and opened his own store and bakery. He now has twenty shops and has been instrumental in helping his countrymen open more, all of them buying their donuts from his bakery.

11. Herbert Gans, "Symbolic Ethnicity: The Future of Ethnic Groups and Cultures in America," *Ethnic and Racial Studies* 2 (January 1979): 1–18).

12. Despite nativist protests, immigration had proceeded unchecked by government regulation until the end of the nineteenth century. The first serious attempt to restrict immigration came in 1882 when, responding to the clamor about the growing immigration of Chinese laborers to California and other western states, Congress passed the Chinese Exclusion Act. But European immigration remained unimpeded. In the years between 1880 and 1924, 24 million newcomers arrived on these shores, most of them eastern and southern Europeans, all bringing their own language and culture, and all the target of pervasive bigotry and exploitation by native-born Americans. By the early part of the twentieth century, anti-immigration sentiments grew strong enough to gain congressional attention once again. The result was the National Origins Act of 1924, which established the quota system that sharply limited immigration, especially from the countries of southern and eastern Europe.

13. Roger Daniels, *Coming to America: A History of Immigration and Ethnicity in American Life* (New York: HarperCollins, 1990), 338–344.

14. Daniels, *Coming to America*, p. 341, writes further, "In his Liberty Island speech Lyndon Johnson stressed the fact that he was redressing the wrong done [by the McCarran-Walter Act] to those 'from southern or eastern Europe,' and although he did mention 'developing continents,' there was no other reference to Asian or Third World immigration."

15. For a further review of the Immigration Act of 1965, see chapter 13 (pp. 328–349) of *Coming to America*.

16. *Statistical Abstract*, U.S. Bureau of the Census (1992), Table 8, p. 11.

17. *Statistical Abstract*, U.S. Bureau of the Census (1992), Table 45, p. 42.

18. *Statistical Abstract*, U.S. Bureau of the Census (1992), Table 18, p. 18, and Table 26, p. 24.

19. U.S. Bureau of the Census, *Population Reports*, 1970 and 1990. Cited in Mike Davis, "The Body Count," *Crossroads* (June 1993). The difference in the racial composition of New York and San Francisco explains, at least in part, why black-white tensions are so much higher in New York City than they are in San Francisco. In New York, 38 percent of the population is now white, 30 percent black, 25 percent Hispanic, and 7 percent Asian. In San Francisco, whites make up 47 percent of the residents, blacks 11 percent, Hispanics 14 percent, and Asians 29 percent. Thus, blacks in New York reflect the kind of critical mass that generally sparks racial prejudices, fears, and conflicts. True, San Francisco's Asian population—three in ten of the city's residents—also form that kind of critical and noticeable mass. But whatever the American prejudice against Asians, and however much it has been acted out in the past, Asians do not stir the same kind of fear and hatred in white hearts as do blacks.

20. Zoë Baird, the first woman ever to be nominated to be attorney general of the United States, was forced to withdraw when it became known that she and her husband had hired an illegal immigrant as a nanny for their three-year-old child. The public indignation that followed the revelation came largely from people who were furious that, in a time of high unemployment, American workers were bypassed in favor of cheaper foreign labor.

21. This is now beginning to happen in more skilled jobs as well. In California's Silicon Valley, for example, software programmers and others are being displaced by Indian workers, people who are trained in India and recruited to work here because they are willing to do so for lower wages than similarly skilled Americans (*San Francisco Examiner,* February 14, 1993).

22. From Emma Lazarus's "The New Colossus," inscribed at the base of the Statue of Liberty in New York's harbor, the gateway through which most of the immigrants from Europe passed as they came in search of a new life.

23. These were, and often still are, the commonly held stereotypes about Jews. Indeed, the Asian immigrants are often referred to as "the new Jews."

24. In the fall 1992 freshman class at the University of California at Berkeley, Asians accounted for 37 percent of the students, the largest single group admitted; at the university's Los Angeles campus, they were nearly 40 percent of incoming freshmen; and at Irvine, Asian students made up just under half of the first-year class. Final admission figures for the 1993–94 academic year are not available at this writing, but it's already clear that the proportion of Asians will increase substantially.

25. Soon Ja Du, the Korean grocer who killed fifteen-year-old Latasha Harlins, was found guilty of voluntary manslaughter, for which she was sentenced to 400 hours of community service, a $500 fine, reimbursement of funeral costs to the Harlins family, and five years' probation.

26. The incident in Berkeley didn't happen in the black ghetto, as most of the others did. There, the Korean grocery store is near the University of California campus, and the woman involved in the incident is an African-American university student who was maced by the grocer after an argument over a penny.

27. Jack Miles, "Blacks vs. Browns," *Atlantic Monthly* (October 1992), pp. 41–68.

28. For an interesting analysis of what he calls "the transformation of ethnicity," see Alba, *Ethnic Identity.*

29. On college campuses the idea of whites as an ethnic group is not so unformed. A recent publication of the University of California at Berkeley detailing the racial breakdown in undergraduate admissions conflates race and ethnicity and refers to whites who were admitted to advanced standing as "the single largest ethnic group" (Office of Student Research, University of California, Berkeley, December 16, 1992).

30. While such an organization is still in an embryonic state, if the 1992 presidential election can be taken as a measure, the idea itself seems to have had some effect. Race, a central issue in earlier campaigns, dropped from view, as the candidates of both parties focused their political energy on winning the votes of the white working-class ethnics who are coming to be known as European-Americans.

31. For a detailed account of this struggle, see Jonathan Rieder, *Canarsie* (Cambridge: Harvard University Press, 1985).

32. "The Diversity Project: Final Report," a publication of the Institute for the Study of Social Change, University of California, Berkeley (November 1991).

33. In the past, many of those who agitated for a halt to immigration were immigrants or native-born children of immigrants. The same often is true today. As anti-immigrant sentiment grows, at least some of those joining the fray are relatively recent arrivals. One man in this study, for example—a fifty-two-year-old immigrant from Hungary—is one of the leaders of an anti-immigration group in the city where he lives.

The Approach-
Avoidance Dance:
Men, Women, and Intimacy

For one human being to love another, that is perhaps the most difficult of all our tasks, the ultimate, the last test and proof, the work for which all other work is but preparation.

Rainer Maria Rilke

Intimacy. We hunger for it, but we also fear it. We come close to a loved one, then we back off. A teacher I had once described this as the "go away a little closer" message. I call it the approach-avoidance dance.

The conventional wisdom says that women want intimacy, men resist it. And I have plenty of material that would *seem* to support that view. Whether in my research interviews, in my clinical hours, or in the ordinary course of my life, I hear the same story told repeatedly. "He doesn't talk to me," says a woman. "I don't know what she wants me to talk about," says a man. "I want to know what he's feeling," she tells me. "I'm not feeling anything," he insists. "Who can feel nothing?" she cries. "I can," he shouts. As the heat rises, so does the wall between them. Defensive and angry, they retreat—stalemated by their inability to understand each other.

Women complain to each other all the time about not being able to talk to their men about the things that matter most to them—about what they themselves are thinking and feeling, about what goes on in the hearts and minds of the men they're relating to. And men, less able to expose themselves and their conflicts—those within themselves or those with the women in their lives—either turn silent or take cover by holding women up to derision. It's one of the norms of male camaraderie to poke fun at women, to complain laughingly about the mystery of their minds, wonderingly about their ways. Even Freud did it when, in exasperation, he asked mockingly, "What do women want? Dear God, what do they want?"

But it's not a joke—not for the women, not for the men who like to pretend it is.

> The whole goddamn business of what you're calling intimacy bugs the hell out of me. I never know what you women mean when you talk about it. Karen complains that I don't talk to her, but it's not talk she wants, it's some other damn thing, only I don't know what the hell it is. Feelings, she keeps asking for. So what am I supposed to do if I don't have any to give her or to talk about just because she decides it's time to talk about feelings? Tell me, will you; maybe we can get some peace around here.

The expression of such conflicts would seem to validate the common understandings that suggest that women want and need intimacy more than men do—that the issue belongs to women alone; that, if left to themselves, men would not suffer it. But things are not always what they seem. And I wonder: "If men would renounce intimacy, what is their stake in relationships with women?"

Some would say that men need women to tend to their daily needs—to prepare their meals, clean their houses, wash their clothes, rear their children—so that they can be free to attend to life's larger problems. And, given the traditional structure of roles in the family, it has certainly worked that way most of the time. But, if that were all men seek, why is it that, even when they're not relating to women, so much of their lives is spent in search of a relationship with another, so much agony experienced when it's not available?

These are difficult issues to talk about—even to think about—because the subject of intimacy isn't just complicated, it's slippery as well. Ask yourself: What is intimacy? What words come to mind, what thoughts?

It's an idea that excites our imagination, a word that seems larger than life to most of us. It lures us, beckoning us with a power we're unable to resist. And, just because it's so seductive, it frightens us as well—seeming sometimes to be some mysterious force from outside ourselves that, if we let it, could sweep us away.

But what is it we fear?

Asked what intimacy is, most of us—men and women—struggle to say something sensible, something that we can connect with the real experience of our lives. "Intimacy is knowing there's someone who cares about the children as much as you do." "Intimacy is a history of shared experience." "It's sitting there having a cup of coffee together and watching the eleven-o'clock news." "It's knowing you care about the same things." "It's knowing she'll always understand." "It's him sitting in the hospital for hours at a time when I was sick." "It's knowing he cares when I'm hurting." "It's standing by me when I was out of work." "It's seeing each other at our worst." "It's sitting across the breakfast table." "It's talking when you're in the bathroom." "It's knowing we'll begin and end each day together."

These seem the obvious things—the things we expect when we commit our lives to one another in a marriage, when we decide to have children together. And they're not to be dismissed as inconsequential. They make up the daily experience of our lives together, setting the tone for a relationship in important and powerful ways. It's sharing such commonplace, everyday events that determines the temper and the texture of life, that keeps us living together even when other aspects of the relationship seem less than perfect. Knowing someone is there, is constant, and can be counted on in just the ways these thoughts express provides the background of emotional security and stability we look for when we enter a marriage. Certainly a marriage and the people in it will be tested and judged quite differently in an unusual situation or in a crisis. But how often does life present us with circumstances and events that are so out of the range of ordinary experience?

These ways in which a relationship feels intimate on a daily basis are only one part of what we mean by intimacy, however—the part that's most obvious, the part that doesn't awaken our fears. At a lecture where I spoke of these issues recently, one man commented also, "Intimacy is putting aside the masks we wear in the rest of our lives." A murmur of assent ran through the audience of a hundred or so. Intuitively we say "yes." Yet this is the very issue that also complicates our intimate relationships.

On the one hand, it's reassuring to be able to put away the public persona—to believe we can be loved for who we *really* are, that we can show our shadow side without fear, that our vulnerabilities will not be counted against us. "The most important thing is to feel I'm accepted just the way I am," people will say.

But there's another side. For, when we show ourselves thus without the masks, we also become anxious and fearful. "Is it possible that someone could love the *real* me?" we're likely to ask. Not the most promising question for the further development of intimacy, since it suggests that, whatever else another might do or feel, it's we who have trouble loving ourselves. Unfortunately, such misgivings are not usually experienced consciously. We're aware only that our discomfort has risen, that we feel a need to get away. For the person who has seen the "real me" is also the one who reflects back to us an image that's usually not wholly to our liking. We get angry at that, first at ourselves for not living up to our own expectations, then at the other, who becomes for us the mirror of our self-doubts—a displacement of hostility that serves intimacy poorly.

There's yet another level—one that's further below the surface of consciousness, therefore, one that's much more difficult for us to grasp, let alone to talk about. I'm referring to the differences in the ways in which women and men deal with their inner emotional lives—differences that create barriers between us that can be high indeed. It's here that we see how those early childhood experiences of separation and individuation—the psychological tasks that were required of us in order to separate from mother, to distinguish ourselves as autonomous persons, to internalize a firm sense of gender identity—take their toll on our intimate relationships.

Stop a woman in mid-sentence with the question, "What are you feeling right now?" and you might have to wait a bit while she reruns the mental tape to capture the moment just passed. But, more than likely, she'll be able to do it successfully. More than likely, she'll think for a while and come up with an answer.

The same is not true of a man. For him, a similar question usually will bring a sense of wonderment that one would even ask it, followed quickly by an uncomprehending and puzzled response. "What do you mean?" he'll ask. "I was just talking," he'll say.

I've seen it most clearly in the clinical setting where the task is to get to the feeling level—or, as one of my male patients said when he came into therapy, to "hook up the head and the gut." Repeatedly when therapy begins, I find myself having to teach a man how to monitor his internal states—how to attend to his thoughts and feelings, how to bring them into consciousness. In the early stages of our work, it's a common experience to say to a man, "How does that feel?" and to see a blank look come over his face. Over and over, I find myself listening as a man speaks with calm reason about a situation which I know must be fraught with pain. "How do you feel about that?" I'll ask. "I've just been telling you," he's likely to reply. "No," I'll say, "you've told me what happened, not how you *feel* about it." Frustrated, he might well respond, "You sound just like my wife."

It would be easy to write off such dialogues as the problems of men in therapy, of those who happen to be having some particular emotional difficulties. But it's not so, as any woman who has lived with a man will attest. Time and again women complain: "I can't get him to verbalize his feelings." "He talks, but it's always intellectualizing." "He's so closed off from what he's feeling, I don't know how he lives that way." "If there's one thing that will eventually ruin this marriage, it's the fact that he can't talk about what's going on inside him." "I have to work like hell to get anything out of him that resembles a feeling that's something besides anger. That I get plenty of—me and the kids, we all get his anger. Anything else is damn hard to come by with him." One woman talked eloquently about her husband's anguish over his inability to get problems in his work life resolved. When I asked how she knew about his pain, she answered:

> I pull for it, I pull hard, and sometimes I can get something from him. But it'll be late at night in the dark—you know, when we're in bed and I can't look at him while he's talking and he doesn't have to look at me. Otherwise, he's just defensive and puts on what I call his bear act, where he makes his warning, go-away faces, and he can't be reached or penetrated at all.

To a woman, the world men live in seems a lonely one—a world in which their fear of exposing their sadness and pain, their anxiety about allowing their vulnerability to show, even to a woman they love, is so deeply rooted inside them that, most often, they can only allow it to happen "late at night in the dark."

Yet, if we listen to what men say, we will hear their insistence that they *do* speak of what's inside them, *do* share their thoughts and feelings with the women they love. "I tell her, but she's never satisfied," they complain. "No matter how much I say, it's never enough," they grumble.

From both sides, the complaints have merit. The problem lies not in what men don't say, however, but in what's not there—in what, quite simply, happens so far out of consciousness that it's not within their reach. For men have integrated all too well the lessons of their childhood—the experiences that taught them to repress and deny their inner thoughts, wishes, needs, and fears; indeed, not even to notice them. It's real, therefore, that the kind of inner thoughts and feelings that are readily accessible to a woman generally are unavailable to a man. When he says, "I don't know what I'm feeling," he isn't necessarily being intransigent and withholding. More than likely, he speaks the truth.

Partly that's a result of the ways in which boys are trained to camouflage their feelings under cover of an exterior of calm, strength, and rationality. Fears are not manly. Fantasies are not rational. Emotions, above all, are not for the strong, the sane, the adult. Women suffer them, not men—women, who are more like children with what seems like their never-ending preoccupation with their emotional life. But the training takes so well because of their early childhood experience when, as very young boys, they had to shift their identification from mother to father and sever themselves from their earliest emotional connection. Put the two together and it does seem like suffering to men to have to experience that emotional side of themselves, to have to give it voice.

This is the single most dispiriting dilemma of relations between women and men. He complains, "She's so emotional, there's no point in talking to her." She protests, "It's him you can't talk to, he's always so darned rational." He says, "Even when I tell her nothing's the matter, she won't quit." She says, "How can I believe him when I can see with my own eyes that something's wrong?" He says, "Okay, so something's wrong! What good will it do to tell her?" She cries, "What are we married for? What do you need me for, just to wash your socks?"

These differences in the psychology of women and men are born of a complex interaction between society and the individual. At the broadest social level is the rending of thought and feeling that is such a fundamental part of Western thought. Thought, defined as the ultimate good, has been assigned to men; feeling, considered at best a problem, has fallen to women.

So firmly fixed have these ideas been that, until recently, few thought to question them. For they were built into the structure of psychological thought as if they spoke to an eternal, natural, and scientific truth. Thus, even such a great and innovative thinker as Carl Jung wrote, "The woman is increasingly aware that love alone can give her her full stature, just as the man begins to discern that spirit alone can endow his life with its highest meaning. Fundamentally, therefore, both seek a psychic relation one to the other, because love needs the spirit, and the spirit love, for their fulfillment."*

For a woman, "love"; for a man, "spirit"—each expected to complete the other by bringing to the relationship the missing half. In German, the word that is translated here as spirit is *Geist*. But *The New Cassell's German Dictionary* shows that another primary meaning of *Geist* is "mind, intellect, intelligence, wit, imagination, sense of reason." And, given the context of these words, it seems reasonable that *Geist* for Jung referred to a man's highest essence—his mind. There's no ambiguity about a woman's calling, however. It's love.

---

*Carl Gustav Jung, *Contributions to Analytical Psychology* (New York: Harcourt, Brace & Co., 1928), p. 185.

Intuitively, women try to heal the split that these definitions of male and female have foisted upon us.

> I can't stand that he's so damned unemotional and expects me to be the same. He lives in his head all the time, and he acts like anything that's emotional isn't worth dealing with.

Cognitively, even women often share the belief that the rational side, which seems to come so naturally to men, is the more mature, the more desirable.

> I know I'm too emotional, and it causes problems between us. He can't stand it when I get emotional like that. It turns him right off.

Her husband agrees that she's "too emotional" and complains:

> Sometimes she's like a child who's out to test her parents. I have to be careful when she's like that not to let her rile me up because otherwise all hell would break loose. You just can't reason with her when she gets like that.

It's the rational-man-hysterical-woman script, played out again and again by two people whose emotional repertoire is so limited that they have few real options. As the interaction between them continues, she reaches for the strongest tools she has, the mode she's most comfortable and familiar with: She becomes progressively more emotional and expressive. He falls back on his best weapons: He becomes more rational, more determinedly reasonable. She cries for him to attend to her feelings, whatever they may be. He tells her coolly, with a kind of clenched-teeth reasonableness, that it's silly for her to feel that way, that she's just being emotional. And of course she is. But that dismissive word "just" is the last straw. She gets so upset that she does, in fact, seem hysterical. He gets so bewildered by the whole interaction that his only recourse is to build the wall of reason even higher. All of which makes things measurably worse for both of them.

> The more I try to be cool and calm her the worse it gets. I swear, I can't figure her out. I'll keep trying to tell her not to get so excited, but there's nothing I can do. Anything I say just makes it worse. So then I try to keep quiet, but ... wow, the explosion is like crazy, just nuts.

And by then it *is* a wild exchange that any outsider would agree was "just nuts." But it's not just her response that's off, it's his as well—their conflict resting in the fact that we equate the emotional with the nonrational.

This notion, shared by both women and men, is a product of the fact that they were born and reared in this culture. But there's also a difference between them in their capacity to apprehend the *logic* of emotions—a difference born in their early childhood experiences in the family, when boys had to repress so much of their emotional side and girls could permit theirs to flower.

For men, generally the idea of the "logic of emotions" seems a contradiction in terms. For women, it's not. The complexity of their inner life—their relatively easy shifts between the intuitive and the cognitive, the emotional and the rational—provides some internal evidence with which to stand in opposition to the ideology the culture propounds so assiduously. So they both believe and disbelieve it all at once. They believe because it's so difficult to credit their own experience in the face of such a cultural assault. And they disbelieve because it's also so difficult to completely discredit that same experience. Thus, a woman will say:

> When he gets into that oh-so-reasonable place, there are times when I feel like I'm going crazy. Well, I don't know if I'm really nuts, but I'm plenty hysterical. When I can get a hold of myself, I can tell myself it's not me, it's him, that he's driving me crazy because he refuses to listen to what I'm saying and behaves as if I'm talking in Turkish or something.

All this, however, tells us only about the differences between men and women in how accessible their inner thoughts are to them. There remains the question: When they're available, how willing are they to speak those thoughts to one another?

"The word," wrote Thomas Mann in *The Magic Mountain,* "even the most contradictory word, preserves contact—it is silence which isolates." Words that go right to a woman's heart. For her, intimacy without words is small comfort most of the time. It's not that she needs always to talk, but it's important to her to know what's going on inside him if she's to feel close. And it's equally important for her to believe he cares about what's going on inside her. Thus a vivacious thirty-one-year-old woman, married six years, said:

> It's always the same. I'm the one who tries to get things going. I'm always doing my bla-bla-bla number, you know, keeping things moving and alive around here. But he's the original Mr. Shutmouth most of the time, so I'd just as leave be with a friend and I go call somebody up and talk to her for a while. At least she cares about what I have to say, and she always has something to say back. Then—I swear, I don't know why it bothers him because he wasn't talking to me or noticing me or anything—but anyway, then he gets mad at me, or jealous or something, for talking on the telephone.

That, too, is a familiar tale, the cycle the same in family after family. Women have long conversations on the phone with friends; men are angered by it; women complain uncomprehendingly:

> I can never understand why he gets upset; it's not as if I'm taking anything from him when I get on the phone. Most of the time we haven't said a word to each other in hours.

For a man, it's reassuring just to be in a woman's presence again—to know that, like the mother of infancy, she's there and available when and as she's needed. Then, in that distant past, he didn't need words to feel soothed and comforted; mother's presence was enough. To re-create that experience in adulthood is to heal some of the pain of childhood. Words, therefore, are less important than proximity itself.

Obviously, I don't mean to suggest that men wholly devalue words and their importance to a relationship. But it's equally plain that they will often see difficulties about talking where women will not. For example, some men worry that talking about a problem will escalate it by giving the feelings that underlie it more concrete form. When a woman wants to discuss some issue in their relationship, therefore, her husband may demur out of fear. One thirty-eight-year-old electrician gave voice to those concerns with as clear a statement as I have ever heard:

> She wants to talk about something that worries her—maybe something between us—but it makes me nervous so I don't want to hear about it. As soon as she starts talking about her worries, she exaggerates the problem, and all of a sudden, we've got a big nut on our hands. Who needs it? So lots of times when she starts, I'll back off, figuring her talking is only going to make it worse. [With a crooked smile] But that doesn't work so well either because then she gets mad because I don't want to hear and then *that's* the problem. It's no win!

But this is only a specific example of the more general theme—the fact that connecting words with feeling and emotion is difficult and frightening for most men. It's difficult because the repression came so early in life—at the stage before the linguistic ability to express complex feelings had fully developed—thereby creating an internal split between the two. And it's frightening because the verbal expression of emotion seems to them to threaten to provoke conflict or to expose vulnerability.

Words, therefore, are not at the center of the definition of intimacy for most men; nonverbal activities will do for them at least as well, often better. Thus, the husband who is accused of being "Mr. Shutmouth" complains:

> She objects because I do a lot of reading, and she keeps hassling me that I don't talk to her enough. She tells me all the time we can't be really close if we're not talking to each other. It's hard for me to understand what she means. Doesn't she know that it feels close to me just to be in the same room with her? I tell her, but all I get back is more of her talk. Jesus, I get so tired of hearing words all the time. I don't understand how women can nag a subject to death.

His wife counters:

> Carl's always surprised that my friends and I have so much to talk about. But that's exactly what I would want from him. I'd like him to *want* to talk about all his thoughts and feelings with me. I mean, I'd love to be able to dissect and obsess over all the emotional issues in his life with him like I do with my friends.
>
> He says I need to live every experience at least twice—once in the living and then in talking about it. And I think he's right. [With mounting irritation] But what's

wrong with that? Why can't I get him to share the reliving of it, or examination or whatever you want to call it, like I can do with any of my women friends?

On the other side are the men who insist they talk plenty, who say they're quite willing to share their thoughts with the woman they love but that, all too often, she has trouble listening. Thus this complaint from a twenty-nine-year-old salesman in a five-year marriage:

> Our problem is not my talking but getting her to listen, I mean, to pay attention. It's like she drifts off when I'm trying to tell her how I feel about something, then I get mad as hell. First she complains I don't talk, then when I do, she disappears somewhere in her head.

His wife has another story:

> He says he's telling me how he feels, but he doesn't want anything from me—just that I'm expected to be there listening to every word. It's like dealing with my three-year-old. He wants to talk to me, too.

Puzzled, I said, "I'm not sure I understand what you mean. Could you explain it to me?" She sat quietly, thinking for a while, then:

> Well, when Jason—that's my son—comes running to talk to me, he doesn't want anything from me, he just wants me to be there to listen to him. That's what mommies are for. He'll come to cry if he hurts himself or to show me something he's excited about, but it's not what you could call two people communicating with each other. There's this little kid who wants his mommy's attention—you know, to fix the hurt or ... Oh hell, I don't know what—just to be there, I guess. Well, it's kind of the same thing with Paul. First of all, he's not talking *to* me, he's saying words *at* me. I mean, he doesn't want a *conversation,* he just wants to talk—like a kid who comes running to mom, has his say, and then goes away again without ever paying any attention to the person underneath the mommy. Do you know what I mean?

Her experience at such times is that these are not intimate moments, but covert expressions of his dependency. And it makes her both angry and lonely. It's all right to be "mommy" to the child; from the father she wants something else. Sometimes she tells him:

> I try to tell him that I don't want it to be all on his timetable. When he's ready to say something, we can talk. But why doesn't he care about me and my timetable; why doesn't he ask about how I'm feeling or what I'm thinking? Oh, sure, if I get real mad or hysterical or something, he'll notice. But otherwise ... you have to hit him over the head. I sometimes feel like I've got two kids, not one. And I tell him, too, but he doesn't really get it. [More gently] I think he tries, but he doesn't get it.

It is, indeed, hard for him to understand the message she keeps trying to convey, hard to know just what she wants and how to give it to her.

> She says lots of times when I want to talk to her that it's the same as Jason wanting her attention. But I don't know what she's talking about, and she's never been able to explain it to me.

What she's asking from him is a sharing of his inner life and thoughts not out of fear, not out of a need to be cared for, but out of the wish to expose that part of himself. But that alone wouldn't satisfy either, because along with his own openness she wants him to *want* hers. She doesn't want to have to ask him to listen to her innermost thoughts, she wants him to *want* to know them. That's one important definition of intimacy among adults—the wish to know another's inner life along with the ability to share one's own.

But we all know couples today who are struggling against such stereotypic ways of being and of living together. Perhaps we ourselves are among them. And sometimes, happily, we win the battle to free ourselves from our past. Then, at some unexpected moment when the guard is relaxed, we find ourselves caught again, as the story of this interaction between husband and wife tells so eloquently.

He's a musician; she manages a gift shop. At thirty-six and thirty-three respectively, they have been married for eight years and are the parents of two children aged four and six. His words come quickly, the tension evident not just in his voice but in the set of his head, in the furrowed brow that fits well with the anxious smile that comes and goes, in the taut way he leans forward in the chair.

> It hasn't been easy to work on this intimacy stuff because it sometimes feels like we're so far apart. But I think we're both getting better at it. I really try to tell her what's going on in my mind more. [Sighing] But it can still be damned hard; even when I know what I'm thinking, it's hard as hell to say it sometimes. I've tried to tell her that I'm not just being stubborn or hostile; I actually feel scared at times like that.

"What are you scared of?" I asked. He stared out the window for a bit, then, with some agitation, said:

> Damned if I know. It's like a kid in a way—scared I'll say or do the wrong thing and wind up in trouble, so better to just hole up and keep quiet.

The wife, a tall, auburn-haired woman, spoke more calmly, weighing her words carefully as if trying to be sure she would portray the issues fairly.

> I don't think anything is more difficult for us than this business of trying to be open. [Stops for a moment wanting to clarify her position, then] Look, I want you to understand that I'm not one of these people who thinks openness or honesty in a

relationship means spilling your guts or telling your partner every angry thought that comes into your head. There's plenty I don't talk about—like when I wonder do I really love him sometimes, or do I want to be married. Those things don't have to be said; they're damaging. But ... how can I say it, it's the real stuff that goes on in him I want to know about. I mean, I want him to be able to say something hurts him or scares him, not just to barricade himself off behind the paper or something.

But I've had to learn that I can't have it all my way. I have to let him come to it without my constant pushing all the time. And when it comes to a certain kind of sharing of your innards and examining it, maybe I have to know that I'll never get from him what I get from Sally—she's my closest friend. I also think I've come to understand better now that there are things I get from Stephen that I don't get from anyone else. [Laughing] Who else would put up with my moods and all the crap I put out in this relationship? So now, when I get upset and begin to feel sorry for myself because Sally knows me better than Stephen in some ways, I remind myself pretty quick that he knows me better than she does in other ways, and that maybe he has to put up with the worst part of me.

I guess the important thing we both feel is that we're growing and changing. [Again, an ironic laugh] It's just not like in the storybooks or the fantasies but, well ... what is?

The husband:

We keep trying, but I've got to tell you, sometimes nothing works. I don't know what happens, but something gets going in me and there's no stopping it.

"Tell me about that," I prompted, as his hesitation became apparent.

Well, it can go something like this. Molly can come into the room, take one look, and know something's wrong. So she'll ask: "What's the matter?" And then the craziest damn thing happens. Instead of saying, "I'm feeling really terrible, and I need to talk to you," what do I do? I stick my head deeper into the paper I'm reading and grunt something unintelligible. She'll say again, "Hey, what's the matter? Is anything wrong?" I'll just mutter, "Nothing." Then she'll say, "It doesn't sound like nothing; you sound angry at me. Are you?" I'll say, "I'm not angry at you." But the truth is, the vibes say I'm sitting there smoldering. But I don't give an inch. It's like she's going to take something priceless from me, that's how hard I hold on to it. [Hunching his shoulders and leaning still further forward] But I don't even know what the "it" is. I just know it's like when my mother would keep harping on me: "Where you going? What you doing? Who you seeing?" It's really nuts. There's some part of me that doesn't *want* her to leave me alone, like I want her to push me so maybe I won't feel so bad. But when she does I freeze up, like I have to protect myself from her.

It's inevitable, however, that the withdrawal will soon exact its price, that the other side of his ambivalent strivings will emerge. The child within clamors to be attended, to be cared for, to be reassured. He reaches out to his wife, who, by now, has retreated into her own hostile silence because his withdrawal feels so rejecting to her. He responds with disappointment, fear, then anger—each following the other in quick succession.

> When she finally goes away—no, she doesn't just go, I drive her away. Anyway, she leaves, and for a minute I feel better—like, "Aha, I made her suffer too." But it doesn't last long because I begin to feel like a jerk for how I've been acting. And I trash myself for feeling bad and for not having the strength to cope the way I should. I guess I get a little scared, too, that maybe she'll leave permanently. So I make a move. But by then she's having none of it.

Eventually husband and wife wind up in a fight. In such situations, it makes no difference what the adults actually say to each other as they fight it out, for it's the children who are playing out an old conflict that has nothing to do with the substance the grown-ups have given it.

> From there on, it's downhill all the way. She's mad, then I have a good reason to be mad instead of whatever the hell I was feeling that started the whole mess. And away we go.

It should be understood: Commitment itself is not a problem for a man; he's good at that. He can spend a lifetime living in the same family, working at the same job—even one he hates. And he's not without an inner emotional life. But when a relationship requires the sustained verbal expression of that inner life and the full range of feelings that accompany it, then it becomes burdensome for him. He can act out anger and frustration inside the family, it's true. But ask him to express his sadness, his fear, his dependency—all those feelings that would expose his vulnerability to himself or to another—and he's likely to close down as if under some compulsion to protect himself.

All requests for such intimacy are difficult for a man, but they become especially complex and troublesome in relations with women. It's another of those paradoxes. For, to the degree that it's possible for him to be emotionally open with anyone, it is with a woman—a tribute to the power of the childhood experience with mother. Yet it's that same early experience and his need to repress it that raise his ambivalence and generate his resistance.

He moves close, wanting to share some part of himself with her, trying to do so, perhaps even yearning to experience again the bliss of the infant's connection with a woman. She responds, woman style—wanting to touch him just a little more deeply, to know what he's thinking, feeling, fearing, wanting. And the fear closes in—the fear of finding himself again in the grip of a powerful woman, of allowing her admittance only to be betrayed and abandoned once again, of being overwhelmed by denied desires.

So he withdraws.

It's not in consciousness that all this goes on. He knows, of course, that he's distinctly uncomfortable when pressed by a woman for more intimacy in the relationship, but he doesn't know why. And, very often, his behavior doesn't please him any more than it pleases her. But he can't seem to help it.

That's his side of the ambivalence that leads to the approach-avoidance dance we see so often in relations between men and women.* What about her side?

On the surface, she seems to have little problem in dealing with closeness in a relationship. She's the one who keeps calling for more intimacy, who complains that he doesn't share himself fully enough, doesn't tell her what he's thinking and feeling. And while there's a partial truth in this imagery, the reality is more complex. Thus, when, as is sometimes the case, a woman meets a man who seems capable of the kind of intimacy she says she longs for, dreams about, we see that it's not just a matter of a woman who keeps asking for more in a relationship and a man who keeps protesting. Instead, we hear the other side of the story, as these words from a thirty-year-old patient show. Her blond curly head bent low, she sat in my office and wept bitterly:

> I can't figure out what's happening to me. I'm so anxious and churning inside I can't stand it. I try to read a book, and I find myself thinking of him. But it's not loving thoughts; it's critical, picky thoughts—anything negative, just to get me out of the relationship. Then, once I've convinced myself, I wonder: Why did I love him yesterday? And, if I did, how can it feel so miserable today? I get so confused I want to run and hide just to get away. But now I understand better what I'm scared of; I know it's my problem. I can't tolerate the intimacy, but I can't just break off the relationship like I used to and justify my escape by talking about his faults and inadequacies. But, at times, I actually feel myself being torn apart by this conflict going on inside me. [Tears streaming down her cheeks] How could it be such a burden to be loved?

It would be easy, and perhaps more comfortable, to write her off as some pathological case, a study in extremes that most of us have no reason to be concerned about. In fact, she's a woman in one of our most honored professions, a competent, highly functional person whose professional and personal life would seem to most of us the very model of accomplishment—good friends, a wide range of social and cultural activities, an active and committed work life. Altogether an intelligent, appealing, personable woman. The difference between her and so many others like her is only that, in the course of her therapy, she has learned to identify the cause of the anxiety that usually remains unrecognized, therefore, nameless and formless.

---

*Given the recent struggle to loosen traditional definitions of masculinity and femininity, we might assume that there would be differences in the intimate relations of men who are twenty-five and those who are fifty. And, although the younger men are likely to be more openly concerned with these issues, all the research evidence—my own and others'—suggests that integrating that concern into their behavior has been met with difficulties which, while usually not understood, parallel the issues I have been writing of here.

Most women know when a relationship makes them uncomfortable; they just have no idea why. They blame it on something particular about the person—he's too smart or not smart enough; he's too short or too tall; he's too passive or too aggressive; he's too successful or not successful enough; he's too needy or seems too self-contained. Some good reasons, some bad. Some true, some not. More to the point is how quickly a woman will rush for her checklist, how easily she will find ways to dismiss this person whose nearness is making her uneasy.

But even those women who are more able to tolerate closeness, who have fewer problems in sustaining a long-term relationship, are not without ambivalence about just how much of themselves they want to share, and when and how they want to do it. Trying to explain to me the one thing she thought most important in the success of her thirty-four-year marriage, one woman said almost casually, "It's worked so well because we both keep very busy and we don't see that much of each other." A sentiment she was not alone in expressing.

Surprisingly, women often have some sense—even if still an inchoate one—that their husbands' reticence about closeness serves their own needs as well. Thus, a twenty-nine-year-old woman responded to my questions about intimacy with some irritation.

> I can't stand all this talk about intimacy that's all around these days. Peter and I are plenty close—anyhow close enough to suit both of us, I guess. He's the strong, suffer-in-silence type. And maybe that's okay, I'm not sure anymore. Maybe I don't have the psyche for much more intimacy; maybe I couldn't tolerate any more than we have. There's something about the wall he builds around himself that's almost reassuring for me sometimes; I mean, like it's safe or something like that.

Even the fact that a husband is often less sensitive to what his wife is feeling than she might wish has both its positive side and its negative. On the one hand, a thirty-seven-year-old woman, married thirteen years, complains:

> I'm always genuinely interested in what's going on with him, and it's a problem for me—a pain, you know—that he never seems as interested in what's going on with me. I'd like him to want to know about me like I want to know about him.

On the other hand, she recognizes that there's a certain sense of relief for her in his not knowing or wanting to know—a reassurance that she can stay in control, that what's spoken and what isn't will be hers to choose. So, just minutes after she has voiced her complaint, she says thoughtfully:

> Talking about it this way makes me realize that it's not so simple as I'm saying. Actually, I have to admit that it's a double-edged thing. It's hard to explain, but sometimes I feel a real safe feeling in the fact that he doesn't notice what's happening with me. That way what I'm feeling and thinking is only up for notice and discussion if I bring it up. There's a way it feels safer even though there's also a

kind of loneliness about it. It means it's all up to me to have it on the agenda. If I don't bring it up, forget it, Lloyd's certainly not going to. So, like I said, it works both ways; it's got its good points and bad ones. But one thing's sure, I can hide myself as much as I need to.

What is it she needs to feel safe from? Why is it she wants to hide? I asked the questions; she struggled for answers.

I don't know exactly how to say it. It's not very clear, just a feeling. I mean, I know there are things he just wouldn't understand and it would only create a crisis. He gets very upset if I'm upset or depressed or something; it's like he can't stand it. He has trouble just listening without doing something, so he'll do or say something dumb like telling me I shouldn't feel bad. So then it ends up that I'm reassuring him and feeling ripped off, and like I got lost in the whole thing. It's too easy for me to lose myself and my thoughts. So why bother? It's better to go talk to a friend and get it off my chest that way than to try to deal with him.

Then there are the women who present the semblance of intimacy without much substance. We all know them—women who seem to have an ineffable ability to attract people, who develop a kind of court around themselves. They walk in an atmosphere that radiates warmth and openness, that promises an intense and intimate closeness. But the husband of one such woman spoke bleakly about what it's like to be married to her:

Everybody gets a piece of the action but me. She looks like she's wonderful at closeness just so you don't get too close. She's got a million friends and they all think she's great. Everyone comes to her for advice or to cry on her shoulder, and she loves it all. It makes her feel like the queen bee—always in the center of a swarm. But the truth is, she uses it to bind people to her, gets them to need her; that's the only way she feels secure. If someone catches on and wants something in return— I mean if they want something besides her big, loving mama number—they get run out of the court. I don't know exactly how she manages it, but she does, and it always turns out to be some problem with them, never with her. Now that the kids are grown, they're catching on, too. She's like mercury, she's so elusive; no one can get hold of her.

Surprised at the bitterness of the outburst from this quiet, contained man, I commented, "Yet you've been married to her for twenty-three years. What keeps you here?" With a small, sad smile, he replied:

I guess the same thing that keeps others around—the seduction. There's always the hope that she'll deliver what she promises, and that if she ever does, it'll be worth the wait. Meanwhile ... well, I'm hooked, that's all; I keep going towards her, she keeps backing off. Oh, she'll be there if I want to cry my guts out—that's just what she wants from everybody. But try to get at her guts and you're in for trouble. All of a sudden that sweet, wonderful warmth can turn icy cold. [Pausing thoughtfully for a moment, he backtracked] No, that's not right. On the outside, she manages to keep up the facade, and then somehow she turns things around as if you're the one who hurt her by asking for something impossible. But underneath there's ice.

What can we make of women like this? They excel in the social skills; they're artful at nurturance—both qualities for which they have been well schooled from girlhood on. But perhaps nurturance is not to be confused with intimacy.

I thought about this for a long time—about how to disentangle nurturance and intimacy, about whether it would make sense to do so. The issue began to puzzle me earlier when I looked at men whose ability to nurture was not in doubt but whose capacity for intimacy was. Of course I had noticed this in women before. But, since women are both the designated nurturers and the most articulate champions of intimacy in this society, the issue never came fully to the fore as a problem requiring explanation until I set out to understand men who nurture and their relationship to intimacy.

They're not a common lot, it's true, but they exist. I know them; I even live with one. And, as I struggled to make sense out of some of the issues that arose about men and intimacy, I kept asking myself, "Where do men who nurture fit? How can I explain the Allens, the Hanks, the Marks—few though they may be?" Friends with whom I talked of these problems when understanding still eluded me raised the same questions: "What about men who nurture? What about your own husband?"

I gave these pages to my husband to read, saying, "What about it? Am I being unfair to men in talking about their blocks to intimacy as I have?" We talked; we argued; we agreed; we disagreed. Thousands of words later, he finally said,

> I think you're right; what you've written is true about me, too. I keep trying to be more open and let you in on what goes on inside me, but it's damn hard. I know I've gotten better at it after twenty years of living with you, but it doesn't come easily and naturally. And lots of times I can't do it.

"But how do I make sense out of that when you're the most nurturing man I know," I lamented. To which he replied, laughing, "I don't know, but then I don't have to; it's your book."

Then we had a fight one day—a fight over the most classical of issues between men and women. I had asked him to do something to which I thought he had given assent. Actually, he had, as is his wont, said nothing. When, weeks later, the task was still not done, I asked again, only this time with some heat. "Stop pushing me," he said edgily. "I will if you'll answer me," I retorted. Then more quietly, "If you don't want to do it, why can't you just say so?" No answer. I waited a while. Finally, unable to tolerate the heavy silence, I said, "What's going on for you? What are you thinking?" "Nothing," came the surly reply. "How can you be thinking nothing?" I began to shout. "Christ, you never leave anything alone," he stormed as he left the room. And I, trailing after him, practically screamed, "It's because you never tell me what's going on in that head of yours so it could be finished." By then, both of us were standing in the hallway, and suddenly I was convulsed with laughter while he stared at me nonplused at this unexpected turnabout. "What's so funny," he growled. "We're right off the pages of my book," I gasped when I finally gained some control.

He talked then, his words coming with difficulty. "You ask me to do things and always assume that I know how. You don't ask me if I can, you just assume—as if I'm *supposed* to know all about those things. Then if I'm not sure how, it's hard to tell you that. So I think that I'll try to figure it out, then get it done. Meanwhile, I get busy and forget, then you remind me and I feel guilty, so I get defensive, and ... well, what's to say?"

In amazement, I said to myself and to him, "And it took twenty years to tell me that? All these years when we'd have one of these exchanges, I thought you were being hostile. And you were just *scared?* Why couldn't you tell me?" "I don't know, it's just hard," he said with difficulty. Then, smiling impishly, "But after reading your book, I'll be damned if I'll let you be *that* right about men." And, more seriously, "Besides, I'm learning."

It became clear to me then—not so much from anything in the content of our argument, but in its process. Nurturance is not intimacy. It may be connected to intimacy, may even sometimes be a result of it, but the two are distinct and separate phenomena. Nurturance is caretaking. Intimacy is some kind of reciprocal expression of feeling and thought, not out of fear or dependent need, but out of a wish to know another's inner life and to be able to share one's own. Nurturance can be used as a defense against intimacy in a relationship—a cover to confuse both self and other, to screen the fact that it doesn't exist. It can be used manipulatively—as a way to stay in control, as a way to bind another and ensure against the pain of loneliness.

We've all seen women who use their nurturant arts thus—binding children, husbands, friends to them through their generous, sometimes selfless, giving. But we don't think of men doing it. Yet it happens. A male friend, one who has thought deeply about his own nurturant tendencies, confessed:

> The kind of nurturance I offer to women makes them very dependent on me. After all, how many guys are good at caretaking or at listening? And, as a result, a woman will reveal her soul to me and will tell me she's never had such an intimate relationship. But the truth is that they're so seduced by my nurturant style that they don't notice that I'm pretty careful about revealing my own vulnerabilities. It all seems very benign, but I'm quite aware that it's one of the ways a man can retain power over a woman; he doesn't have to dominate her in any oppressive way, he can dominate by giving her so much that he ties her to him for as long as he wants. She becomes emotionally dependent, then he's safe.

A few men even talked about their capacity for sexual nurturance and the binding effect it has on a woman. It's not an easy subject to talk about, especially when facing a woman. But one thirty-six-year-old man in his second marriage spoke with particular eloquence:

I don't want this to sound Machiavellian, but I developed all the arts of being a very good lover because they serve me well. I don't mean that I don't enjoy giving a woman pleasure—I do, very much. But I also know that it's one way to hook her, too. If you can open a woman up to a level of sexual passion she hasn't known before, she can become very dependent on you for that and you can have some assurance that she'll be around when you need her. [Somewhat uncomfortably] I hope you understand what I'm saying and that these words won't be used against me. I mean, I don't want to be portrayed as some sexist pig who uses women sexually; that's not the point I'm trying to make. I'm saying that I can only allow myself to be vulnerable when a woman is thoroughly hooked. I don't mean that I want to disempower her, but I'm scared that I can't hold her otherwise.

For both men and women, then, nurturance is a complex phenomenon that can have several meanings; for both, it can be a way of gaining love, of palliating fears of abandonment, of ensuring safety and security. None malevolent in themselves. But, however benign the motive, when a person nurtures out of fear and insecurity, it can also be a barrier to intimacy since it means that there's anxiety about revealing the "true" self for fear of losing the loved and desired one.

What all this says is that, despite the cant about women being available for intimacy and men being unavailable, they are both likely to experience problems and pressures in an intimate relationship. But, given the combination of the social roles for which they were trained and their early developmental experiences inside the family, what makes intimacy feel risky is different for each of them.

For a woman, the problem of finding and maintaining the boundary between self and a loved other is paramount. The continuity of identification with mother means that the tie is never quite severed—an invisible cord that fastens them to each other in a powerful bond that doesn't exist between mother and son.

A mother understands her son's differences from herself, indeed emphasizes them with pride and pleasure. That helps him in the task of separation. But there are no obvious differences to separate mother and daughter—no differences in their physiology, none in the requirements of the social role for which the girl child is destined. Thus, even when she conscientiously struggles against it, a mother looks at her daughter and sees there a miniature of herself—a reincarnation of her own past—just as a daughter sees her own future in her mother's present existence.

This fusion of identities and the struggle a girl engages in to break those bonds foretells the future of her adult emotional relationships. "The basic feminine sense of self is connected to [others in] the world," writes Nancy Chodorow, "the basic masculine sense of self is separate." Compared to a man, therefore, a woman remains more preoccupied with relational issues, gives herself more easily to emotional relationships, and reaches for attachment and emotional connection with an insistence and intensity that often startles her as well as the man in her life.

But this need for intimacy and connection is not without its paradoxical side. Because her boundaries can be so easily breached, she begins to fear that she's losing some part of herself—not just because someone is taking something from her but because, unless she's constantly vigilant, she's all too likely to give it away. For her, therefore, maintaining herself as a separate person in the context of an intimate relationship is the dominant issue, the one she'll wrestle with from girlhood on.

A thirty-nine-year-old professional woman, married four years, spoke about just such fears. For her, they were so keenly felt that she had avoided intimate relationships with men until she met her husband five years ago. There were men in her life earlier, of course—even some relatively long-term relationships. But she fled from them in fear each time she began to feel, in her words, "too intensely"—not necessarily because of what a man might ask of her but because she was so frightened of her own internal responses.

> It took a long time before I could get married because I was so scared of getting that close to someone. I still worry because it's so easy to lose myself. I'm always afraid because I know I could sell myself out too easily and for a cheap price.

"What do you mean when you say you could 'sell yourself out'?" I asked.

> I mean that I can forget who I am and what I really need just to feel loved and taken care of and approved of. When John and I are having problems, I can't think about anything else; I can't do my work as competently as I feel I should—things like that. Then I feel like I'm disappearing, like maybe I'm just a product of someone's imagination.

"What happens when you begin to feel like that?" I wanted to know.

> [Laughing tensely] Oh boy, it's a mess. I get angry at John. I know it's a way to defend against him—or maybe it's more accurate to say it's the way I defend against what I might do to myself when I feel that isolated, I mean, what I might give away just not to feel that way.
>
> You know, men are different. I know John loves me, but no matter what's going on, it doesn't interfere with his work. Even when the baby is sick, or if our relationship would be in trouble, none of it interferes with his going to work and doing his job in a very single-minded way. I go, too, because I have to. You know, you meet your responsibilities, no matter what. But my body's there; my mind and my heart are distracted. It's terribly upsetting to feel that way—not good at all for my self-esteem to crumble that way.

"And is there some patterned way you handle those feelings?" I asked.

> You bet there is! I withdraw. Ask my husband, he'll tell you. It's like I put a steel wall around me. It's the way I protect myself from myself and that terrible passivity

that can come over me where it feels like I've disappeared. I have to talk to myself and remind myself that there's a competent me, I mean the one who got through graduate school and all. [Sheepishly] With honors, too.

"Is that withdrawal a source of conflict between you and John?" I wondered.

Sometimes it is, of course. But I think what makes this marriage possible for me is that he seems to be able to let me do it without getting too upset. The fact is that he has his own troubles with closeness, so as long as the distant times and close ones are not so out of whack that we might not recognize each other, it's okay.

It's partly because of a woman's problems in maintaining the boundaries of self that friendships play such an important part in her life. Unlike most men, a woman understands the depth of her craving for emotional connection. But the rules that structure relations between men, women, and marriage and her own internal needs come together to make it difficult to retain the integrity of the self she has built with such effort. The norms of friendship, however, permit physical distance and psychological separation—indeed, at various times, require both for the maintenance of the relationship—thus providing the safety within which intimacy can occur without violation of self.

Parenthetically, it's the same with courtship—but not just for women. There, too, the structure of the relationship protects against the immediacy of the difficulties with intimacy. Whatever the level of intimacy and self-exposure, courting couples are not thrust into the kind of close, daily contact a marriage requires. There are acceptable ways of maintaining separation and distance, of protecting against vulnerability and intrusion. Before the marriage, too, expectations remain somewhat restrained; fears, feelings, needs generally are kept in check. What seems like a right after marriage is still considered a privilege in courtship. Whether in a legal marriage or not, when couples move from living separately to living together in a committed relationship, these issues of managing intimacy and expectation come to the surface—a shift that often comes so suddenly and unexpectedly after the marriage that it seems incomprehensible to the people involved.

How the conflicts are handled depends on the couple—on the ability of the individuals involved to tolerate both closeness and distance, to establish the boundaries of self while, at the same time, permitting a satisfactory level of emotional connection and attachment; in essence, on their capacity to move comfortably between separation and unity. But, however well or badly they are dealt with, these problems about which I have been writing will be there, requiring resolution. And they will be felt most keenly in any relationship that has the aura of permanence, that re-creates the old family.

For men, who come to define themselves in terms of the denial of the original connection, the issue of unity is the most pressing. The problem that plagues their emotional relationships is their difficulty in allowing another to penetrate the boundaries sufficiently to establish the communion, the unity, that's necessary for a deep and sustained intimacy with another.

For women, it's the other way around. Because they come to define themselves by affirming that original connection, the problem of separation is in the forefront. Their more permeable boundaries and greater relational concerns make women less certain that they can maintain the hard-won separation, even that they want to maintain it. The possibility of merger with another, therefore, remains both a threat and a promise—a persistent strain in their relationships as they move ambivalently from the fear of violation and invasion to the hunger for that old symbiotic union.

Yet we all know women who seem not to have difficulties in close relationships—women who seem gladly to give themselves over to another, who apparently take their definition of self from that relationship without the conflict I'm speaking of here. It's another of those paradoxes that make this subject of women and men and their relationships with each other so endlessly fascinating. For this stereotypic image is both true and not true.

The truth is the simple one, as feminist writers have been telling us for almost two decades now. There are benefits in the connection to a man and, even in this so-called liberated age, few rewards for the woman who seeks to maintain an independent self. From earliest childhood, she has been socialized to derive her status from another—to know that she would grow up to marry a man through whom she would live vicariously. Even today, if a woman is married, she's still generally "placed" in the world according to who her husband is. And, if she has children, their successes or failures are taken to be hers. No surprise, then, that she so often seems to give herself to relationships so easily.

But such relationships are not necessarily intimate ones. And, when we look below the surface, a reality emerges that's more complex than we have heretofore understood. Then we find that women have their own problems in dealing with intimacy and build their own defenses against it—that, like their men, women also experience internal conflict about closeness which creates anxiety and ambivalence, if not outright fear. In relating to men, however, women rarely have to face the conflict inside themselves squarely, precisely because men take care of the problem for them by their own unmistakable difficulties with closeness and connection—because men tend to be so self-contained and protected from intrusion, except in the matter of sex. This, more than any other, is the area in which the conflicts of both—their differences and similarities—can be seen most clearly.

PART III
STUDYING SEXUALITY, ADDRESSING AGE

Erotic Wars: What Happened to the Sexual Revolution?

Sex! Say the word and instantly our mind leaps into action. Like scenes from a film, images flash by, remembrances of real experiences, fantasies of those we wish we'd had. Memories of pleasure, excitement, and joy live side by side with moments of anxiety, disappointment, and shame. We recall roads not taken, opportunities missed, uncertain about whether to feel regret or relief. And along with it all, there's a yearning, a longing for something that seems to elude us, something we missed perhaps, some pleasure not experienced, some promise not fulfilled—something . . . something . . . something that has no name.

"What a subject!" friends exclaimed when they heard I was flying all over the country talking to people about the sexual revolution, asking about the intimate details of their sex lives, probing not just their sexual experiences but their feelings about them. "It's great," they said. "But what made you start working on it?"

The easy answer is that, during the waning years of the 1980s, my attention was caught by the contradiction between my own observations of the sexual behavior and attitudes of the people around me and the media pronouncements that the AIDS crisis had sounded the death knell for the sexual revolution. Every time I read another newspaper or magazine story about how we were in the midst of a return to the sexual conservatism of the past, I'd wonder what these writers and reporters knew that I didn't. What did they mean when they said the sexual revolution was over? Who were they talking to? Surely not the women and men I'd met in over two decades of doing research and writing about intimate relationships. Certainly not my straight single friends and colleagues all over the country, nor the patients who filled my clinical practice, nor the teenagers who were becoming sexually active at younger and younger ages.

It's true that the conservative electoral victory of 1980, which ushered in the Reagan years, gave impetus to the growth of a highly politicized, repressive response to the enormous social-sexual changes of the decades of the sixties and seventies. The liberation of female sexuality, which has been the most significant consequence of the sexual revolution, and the struggle for greater equality, which has been the charge of the gender revolution, have brought an increasingly vocal counterattack from conservative leaders, legislators, and courts across the land. Despite all the noise, however, it seemed to me that we knew little about what effect these campaigns to turn back the clock were having on the private lives and behavior of the people to whom they were addressed.

But those external events are only part of the answer to the question about what started me on the path to this study. The other reaches back into my own life. I was first married during World War II, a virgin, a girl who followed the rules of her day, who would never have thought to "go all the way." It wasn't I alone who drew the boundary. My husband-to-be was an active participant in protecting my honor, his sense of "sexual rights and wrongs" well matched with my own.

Then, on the day we were married all that changed. Just because a few words had been spoken, a benediction given, I was expected to drop the restraints that had circumscribed both my sexuality and my sexual activities until then. It wasn't fun. Not for me, not for him. My body said, "Let go"; my mind wouldn't let me. "What would he think if I did?" I asked myself. But it wasn't really a question. I knew the answer: "Nice girls don't!"

How do we learn these sexual rules? I don't remember anyone explicitly saying those words to me. Yet I knew, as surely as I knew the time of day or the day of the week. For the sexual norms of an age are passed on to the young in a thousand unseen and unspoken ways, as much in what is never said or named as in what is.

I swore to myself that no daughter of mine would ever suffer the struggle with sexual repression that had been mine, that I'd bring her up to feel differently about her body and her sexuality. Little did I know how much help a rapidly changing sexual culture would provide in that task. Nor what conflicts those changes would stir inside me as I watched my daughter enter a life so different from my own. For in the brief span of one generation—from the 1940s to the 1960s—we went from mothers who believed their virginity was their most prized possession to daughters for whom it was a burden.

Intellectually, I knew the young women of my daughter's generation were right to cast off the old sexual norms, to insist upon their right to express their sexuality openly, freely, and fully. Emotionally, however, it was another matter. My heart cried out, "This is my child, my flesh; she could get exploited, hurt, damaged." *Damaged!* A word from my past, when a girl who "slipped" was considered "damaged goods." For my daughter, an alien notion. I could imagine her saying to me, "Damaged? What are you talking about, Mom? How could I be damaged?"

I struggled silently with myself—watching, wondering, worrying, not just about my own daughter but about all the other mothers' daughters who were caught up in the sexual revolution. "What, if anything, should I be saying to my daughter?" I asked myself. For a long time I had no idea. By the late 1960s, when these questions were upon me, her life, the world she was living in, was so different from the one I had known. What use could my experience possibly be to her? Yet there was a certain virtue in the distance my age and my own life circumstance gave me. While not *in* the sexual revolution, I was *of* it, touched by the depth and breadth of the changes it spurred, exhilarated by the permission they afforded for the release from yet another level of sexual repression. At the same time, I could see the possibility for problems ahead. "Sexual freedom," I finally said to her one summer day as we walked across the lovely, hilly terrain of Berkeley's Tilden Park, "is about choice. It's the freedom to say no as well as yes."

Was it on that day more than twenty years ago that my work on sexuality began? Or the day before, when I was still haunted by what words I might have for my child? Or the one before that, when I listened to the brave words being spoken, watched the bold deeds being done by the young women of my daughter's generation and wondered: Were we as a society ready to accept the sexual freedom they were insisting upon? Were they?

Two decades later, it was time to answer some of the questions that troubled me then. I started the research, which eventually became a book entitled *Erotic Wars,* with a series of questions: What happened to the sexual revolution? How do the women and men who made it feel about their past? Their present? How have succeeding generations internalized and institutionalized the changes for which their older sisters and brothers fought? What changes in sexual attitudes and behavior have taken place over the years? How well do behavior, attitude, and feeling match in this difficult and delicate arena of human life?

But if we're to understand the sexual revolution, it cannot be studied in isolation from the other movements of its time—in particular, two others with which it has been intimately entwined: the gender revolution and the psychological revolution. Therefore, I asked also: How has the gender revolution with its demand for reordering traditional roles and relationships affected male-female sexual interactions and behavior? What effect has the increasing psychologization of everyday life—what I call the therapeutic revolution—had on sexual expectations, attitudes, and behavior? How have the sexual revolution and its companions, the gender and therapeutic revolutions, influenced our lives and relationships, in bed and out?

As with all my previous work, I was interested not just in what people *do* but how they *feel* about what they do. For to dwell on an act without understanding the feeling behind it is to miss a profoundly important dimension in human experience— the *meaning* people attribute to their behavior.

Since the only way to understand those deeper levels of meaning is to talk to people directly, my search for the answers to the questions that were puzzling me took me into the lives of 375 people—75 adolescents, ages thirteen to seventeen, and 300 adults, ages eighteen to forty-eight—each of whom submitted to a very long, in-depth interview about the intimate details of their sexual history and its meaning to them. In addition, I analyzed the data from a thirteen-page questionnaire that I distributed to 600 others, mostly college students from eight colleges and universities around the country. The breadth of the age range meant that I could not only study the generation that made the sexual revolution (those over thirty-five) but the ways each succeeding generation, right down to today's teenagers, internalized the new sexual norms.

The data, then, are a distillation of the sexual histories of almost a thousand people, heterosexuals all, who live in cities throughout the country, come from diverse class and ethnic backgrounds, are engaged in a wide variety of occupations, from factory workers to investment bankers and most jobs in between, and represent a wide range of beliefs from Christian fundamentalism to agnosticism to atheism.

The research was directed at heterosexuals only, not because I think the experience of homosexuals and lesbians is irrelevant to the state of sexuality in our nation today. Far from it. No one who has lived through these last decades can doubt the important ways the gay and lesbian movements have affected our sexual attitudes and behavior. Still, as I planned this work, it became clear that trying to sort out the complexities of the heterosexual experience was already a mammoth task—more than enough for a single book.

In the public arena, sex screams at us at every turn—from our television and movie screens, on our roadways, from the pages of our magazines, from the advertisements for goods, whether they seek to sell automobiles, soap, or undergarments. Bookstore shelves bulge with volumes about sex, all of them dedicated to telling us what to do and how to do it. TV talk shows feature solemn discussions of pornography, impotence, premarital sex, marital sex, extramarital sex, swinging, sadomasochism, and as many other varieties of sexual behavior their producers can think of, whether ordinary or bizarre. Even the comic strips offer graphic presentations of every aspect of adult sexuality.

But in our private lives, it's another matter. There, sex still is relegated to a shadow existence, and silence is the rule. There, the old taboos still hold: Sex is a private affair, something we don't talk about, not with friends, often not even with lovers or mates. What do we really know about the sexual relationships of even our nearest and dearest? What turns them on, what leaves them cold? It's this peculiar combination of public discourse and private silence, the paradox of a "society that speaks verbosely of its own silence," as Michel Foucault put it so crisply, that is one of the hallmarks of sex in our age.

Given this reality, I came to this study with some trepidation, fearful that people would be anxious about talking with me about something so private. I was surprised, therefore, at the alacrity with which so many women and men, strangers all, accepted my invitation to participate in this study. As I met and talked with them, however, several things became clear. First, in this era when so much has changed, when sex is both so public and so private, people feel a need to talk about it, not in some impersonal discussion of what "people" do, but about their own sexual behavior, attitudes, feelings, and fantasies. Our conversation allowed them to process their experiences in some systematic way, which, in turn, helped them to assign sense and meaning to those experiences.

Second, they wanted to share their sexual experience with someone they could define as an expert, to check it out, to ask, as so many did, if they were "normal." Who better to meet this need than a total stranger, one who's perfectly safe precisely because she's part of a fleeting encounter, never to be seen again.

And finally, the willingness of the people to speak so openly about the most intimate aspects of their sexual feelings and fantasies is in itself evidence of the depth and breadth of the sexual revolution. I don't mean to suggest that they didn't have moments of discomfort as they struggled to describe their sexual fantasies or just what they do when they masturbate. But they were a model of ease when compared with the way people responded two decades ago, when, in the context of a study of family life, I asked questions that were tame by today's standards.

Throughout our history the official sexual ideology has lived side by side with a deviant sexual reality. Most of the time such deviance from "respectable" norms is silent, people doing what they want quietly and privately. Because the behavior is shrouded in secrecy, it's invisible in the public domain and, therefore, no threat to the established codes of sexual conduct. But every now and then a group of sexual radicals appears who, unlike the quiet ones, refuse to make some surface adaptation to existing social values. Instead, they take aim at respectable society by publicly violating its norms and confronting it with its hypocrisies, contradictions, and failures.

The bohemians of Greenwich Village in the early part of the twentieth century were such a group. Their daring lifestyle, their insistence that women were sexual beings, that marriage and sex need not necessarily go together, dazzled the media and gave them the public notice they sought. By the 1920s, their message caught the attention of the middle-class college youth, and the sexual revolution of the "roaring twenties"—a revolution in manners and mores as spectacular and profound as any we have yet seen—was on in earnest.

The strict parental supervision that had until then marked the social life of the unmarried young was suddenly out. Roadhouses and dance halls with no chaperones in sight replaced the carefully supervised meetings of the past. Alcohol, made illegal by Prohibition, was consumed with abandon. Dance styles went from cool to hot as the Charleston and fox trot replaced the waltz. The syncopated rhythms of jazz bands heralded the birth of modern popular music. And while premarital sexual intercourse still was unacceptable, women's sexuality came out of the closet. Petting parties that included "everything but" became common events in campus social life.

Just as the bohemians had before them, the behavior of the campus crowd scandalized the keepers of the public morality. But these were not some disreputable creatures with foreign ideas; these were the children of the stable, law-abiding, decorous middle class, the very foundation of respectable society. Pulpits shook as preachers roared; campus administrators and professors agonized; and the media had a field day. Through it all, the students danced, drank, and found quiet corners in which to explore each other's bodies.

Before long the very behaviors that were creating such an uproar were adopted by the same adults who earlier had condemned them. "By 1923," wrote F. Scott Fitzgerald, "their elders, tired of watching the carnival with ill-concealed envy, had discovered that young liquor will take the place of young blood, and with a whoop the orgy began."

No longer would women suffer the tight corsets or the clothes made of sturdy fabrics that covered their bodies from neck to ankle. Not for them the long hair restrained in a prim bun. Corsets were abandoned; hair was bobbed and seductively waved; body contours were visible under the light, filmy fabrics that clothed them; silk stockings covered legs that were on display as skirts rose to uncover a knee. In our own era, when miniskirts, short shorts, and bathing suits cut to there don't raise an eyebrow, none of this may seem very revolutionary. But a look at photographs of women just a few years earlier—photos, for example, of women greeting the returning soldiers in 1918—reveals how startling the changes actually were.

While the 1920s affirmed women as sexual beings, it took the sexual revolution of the 1960s to smash the virginity mandate and leave the sexual norms that ruled until then lying in the dustbin of history. To understand the depth and breadth of those differences, it's useful to look at the generational differences in the people I spoke with. For those over thirty-five "everything but"—which meant touching, genital fondling, perhaps mutual masturbation—described their premarital sexual history. They recalled their awkward gropings that became more daring with time: the boy's hand moved from breast to vagina; the girl tentatively touched his penis and withdrew in surprise. Among teens today, oral sex—especially female on male—is commonplace.

I don't mean that every teenager does it, only that it's understood by all to be one of the sexual options and that it's practiced by many. So much so, in fact, that one 16-year-old explained, without a trace of embarrassment or self-consciousness, how she satisfied her curiosity about oral sex: "I had this friend—not a boyfriend, a boy *friend*—and I didn't know what to give him for his birthday, so I gave him a blow job. I wanted to know what it was like; it was just for kicks."

While generational responses to engaging in intercourse before marriage (what many still call "the big IT") differ sharply—guilt and anxiety dominating the experience of the older generation, a free-spirited ease among the younger ones—there's also a common thread of disappointment for both women and men. But their reasons for the dissatisfaction, then and now, differ by gender. Men talked about it being "over so fast" they hardly knew what was happening; women were disappointed because it didn't match their romantic fantasies. As one older woman put it, "It was so male-oriented; there was nothing soft and pleasurable. The so-called kid's experiences I had before were much more in the nature of mutual pleasuring. I used to think about those experiences and miss them and wonder why I ever got into doing the so-called real thing."

Despite their disappointment, however, men felt empowered by the experience, using such phrases as "crossing a divide" and "becoming a man" to describe what it meant to them. Not one woman of either generation saw the act as defining her womanhood. Indeed, for most, it was something to be gotten over in the hope something better would follow in the relationship. Even now, with all that has changed in the behavior and attitudes of the young, it's still often pressure from a boy she likes that's responsible for a girl's initiation into sexual intercourse. True, she makes the decision. But for too many girls it's a step taken out of the fear, not unfounded, that if she doesn't acquiesce, he'll find someone who will, and she'll lose the relationship.

As the sexual revolution has reached down the age scale from college to high school, two-thirds of the teenagers I met had sexual intercourse by the time they finished high school—a figure that matches every major national study. Equally telling, the age at which adolescents make their sexual debut continues to decline, so that while eighteen or nineteen might have been the norm among the thirty-year-olds, now it's probably down to sixteen and falling.

Even kids brought up in conservative Christian families show very high rates of sexual activity. A study in high schools of eight evangelical denominations found that 43 percent of the young people surveyed—all of whom attended church regularly—had sexual intercourse before their eighteenth birthday. Even more noteworthy, well over one-third of these students—whether they were sexually experienced or not—refused to brand sex outside marriage as morally unacceptable.

But these figures tell only one part of the story, for alongside such major shifts, some things remain very much the same. So, for example, the two words that most closely describe the sexual sensibility of today's youth are "tolerance" and "entitlement." Girls as well as boys believe unequivocally in their right to be sexual, to decide when, where, and how without interference. But when it comes to tolerance, the double standard is alive and well, and the word "slut" still is commonly used by boys to define a girl who violates the current peer norms.

True, today's norms are very different from yesterday's. Then, a girl who had premarital sexual intercourse qualified for the label. Today it's the girl who violates the norm of serial monogamy. In other words, it's okay for a girl to have sex, but only with one boy at a time. Notice, however, that while the norm supposedly applies to both boys and girls, there are no words in the language of teenage life that vilify and stigmatize a boy who breaks the rules. Which means that, despite enormous changes in acceptable sexual behavior for girls, the power to determine the limits of their behavior remains in the hands of men.

I've written elsewhere that consciousness change—the ability to drop or shift internal psychological restraints—doesn't follow easily on the heels of a changed social script. Consequently, many of today's young people are caught in conflict between the new norms of the external social world and the old consciousness of their internal one. Enter alcohol, the most commonly used drug among the high school set. Getting drunk is a way of providing an excuse to throw caution to the wind—a way of absenting the conscious self from behavior so that it can't be held responsible, whether engaging in sexual behaviors that aren't fully comfortable or being careless about birth control and the lurking panoply of diseases, including AIDS. "I don't remember," they say. "I didn't know what I was doing; I was drunk."

So much for high schoolers. What about the transition generation, the men and women who made the sexual revolution? It's among this group that we can follow the historical process as we move from the heady idealism of the '60s with its exhortation to "Make Love, Not War," to the more cynical "Girls say yes to guys who say no"—the recruiting slogan of the antiwar movement.

For men, the possibility of sex between equals, sex with a "good" woman who was neither guilt-ridden nor shamed by the expression of her sexuality, was an exhilarating first. But the women were caught in one of the several paradoxes that characterized the sexual revolution. For while it freed them to say yes, to explore their sexual needs and desires in ways never before possible, it also made it very hard to say no. As one woman explained, "The guys just took it for granted that you'd go to bed with them, and you felt like you had to explain it if you didn't want to. Then if you tried, you couldn't think of a good reason why not to, so you did it."

Looking back on those years, most people describe the fleeting sexual encounters that characterized the period as empty, although the men at least could find sexual satisfaction in them. Not so for the women who rarely claimed to have orgasms in a one-night stand. In fact, about half the women who were products of the '60s and '70s say they have some regrets and wish they could do it over again. These generally are the women who allowed themselves to be exploited for too long and, consequently, say they feel cheap when they think of their behavior then.

The other half look back positively. Even those who agree that there was what some called "a dark side" insist that "they were also wonderful, exciting times. Of course, I wouldn't mind being a twenty-year-old with the understanding of a forty-two-year-old. Who would?" one woman asked. "But I got to be the person I am now by living through that period as a twenty-year-old. It was all part of the job description."

What accounts for these differences in perspective? Partly, of course, our own psychology is responsible for how we view the past. Those of us who see a half-empty glass are more likely to live with regret than those who see a glass half full. Women who have a sense of entitlement, for whom the words "I deserve" don't evoke guilt or anxiety, will tend to experience the pleasure more keenly than the pain. But beyond such distinctly individual differences, the kind of social and political commitments that have governed their lives also affect their responses. Women who identified early with the women's movement and still call themselves feminists are more likely to look back with satisfaction. Whether single or coupled, they usually feel that the years of sexual exploration were crucial to the development of a healthy sexuality and of an autonomous, bounded self they can now rely on. As one of them said, "We were the transition generation. It's all part of the process of how we got to where we are now, so it was necessary."

That said, the bedroom also remains one of the primary places where men and women meet as intimate adversaries, where unspoken negotiations go on as they seek to get something they want—to gain an edge, to get control, to feel more powerful in relation to the other. Take fellatio, for example. "For me," a woman explained, "it's like having him tied up. When a guy's penis is in my mouth, he's absolutely, totally vulnerable. It's the one time I'm totally in control. It's the ultimate power." For men the script gets turned on its head. "When a woman puts my penis into her mouth," said a man, "it's the ultimate act of submission. I get a feeling of real power, and that adds to the whole sexual thrill."

Conversely, when I asked about cunnilingus, both men and women had some version of what I think of as a "yuck" response, both using words like "dark," "unclean," "smelly" to describe their aversion. Even women who had experienced it and said "it feels good" weren't always free of discomfort. But it was also clear that for men it meant a level of submission with which they were distinctly uncomfortable.

When it comes to sex, power, it seems, depends more on the symbolic meanings of the act—on how it's perceived—than on any hard and fast reality.

Meanwhile, the AIDS crisis in the homosexual community has begun to be felt in the heterosexual world. Not that it has dealt a deathblow to the sexual revolution as many in the media have suggested. But it seems to have given significant numbers of straight women and men the opportunity and the excuse to stop what they had already tired of doing, to step back and try to redefine the dance of sex in ways that are more emotionally satisfactory for them. As one man put it, "Nothing happened to the sexual revolution; it's still going on. It just looks different now." "Different," it seems, is that along with a more open sexuality, people now talk also about wanting relationships of love and intimacy.

This doesn't mean that they're having less sex, or that they're consistently practicing safe sex, or even that they're being very much more careful in their choice of partners. Indeed, although men and women are both likely to carry condoms in pocket or purse, at the moment of decision, they often remain lying there unused. And while they may no longer hop into bed on the first date, there's not a lot of hesitation about doing so on the second or third one when they know very little more about the person than they did on the first.

In bed or out, however, the power differences between men and women play a vital role as they seek the commitment and constancy they now say they want. And in this arena, it's not possible to talk about the sexual revolution without giving equal weight to the gender revolution. For the kind of ambivalence about intimate relationships that's so common now is rooted in women's demand for reordering gender roles and relationships. As the pressure for change has grown, both women and men are increasingly caught in conflict as the new age norms war with a deeply rooted old-age consciousness. It's not unusual, therefore, to hear men talk about wanting a woman who's independent, achieving, assertive—one who, as one man said, "can throw her share of logs on the fire." But as this same man acknowledged, he wants to be able to control the fire. And while women talk eloquently about wanting a sensitive, gentle, tender man, they're also looking for one who's head of a Fortune 500 company—a man who's a pussycat at home and a tiger in the world outside.

Despite the enormous changes that have come in this transition generation, the largest share of power still remains with men, even as it relates to something so seemingly personal as attractiveness and sexual desire. Thus, a forty-year-old man has many more choices than a woman of the same age, partly at least because the definitions of sexual desirability favor older men and punish older women. Consequently, men come to the negotiation for a relationship with much more power than women and, therefore, can nurture the conflicting voices inside them in ways that most women can't.

Until now, I've talked about single people, whether adolescent or adult. But no study like this would be complete without an analysis of sex in the coupled life. Here the data show unequivocally what most of us who are coupled know from personal experience: Sexual interest and activity are at their height during dating and courtship, take a drop when people begin to live together, then another fall after marriage, and show the most precipitous decline after the first child is born.

Since most people mourn the loss of the excitement that had been theirs in the past, I asked: What happened? Just about everyone talks about time and pressure. Undoubtedly there's some truth there, but it surely isn't the whole story. There were plenty of pressures before marriage, and some people, at least, had the added burden of having to travel across town to spend time together. Yet they found time for sex. So what happens?

Obviously, the answer is not the same for every couple, but some common themes stand out and are worth labeling. The most obvious one is that for a substantial number of couples, sex is the battleground on which other more serious conflicts were played out. More subtle is the one Freud long ago noted when he wrote that "an obstacle is required to heighten libido, and where natural resistances to satisfaction have not been sufficient, men have at all times erected conventional ones so as to be able to enjoy love." As if in confirmation of those thoughts, a woman in a 14-year marriage said ruefully, "There's no challenge anymore and no more mountains to climb, so some of the excitement is gone."

Anxiety, the natural companion of uncertainty, can be a great stimulator of sexual desire as well. So, for example, women and men often talk of masturbating more frequently in periods of high anxiety. And it also plays a part in writing the sexual script when divorce comes into the picture. It's not uncommon for wives and husbands to report having the best sex in years when they knew they would be divorcing—part of an internal psychological trick where anxiety about the impending rupture can be held in abeyance by transforming it into sexual need.

But anxiety is also a two-edged sword. So while it can at times be a stimulator of sexual desire, it can also be an inhibitor. Nothing in human life poses the possibility of fusion with another as powerfully as the act of sex. And for those people, more often women than men, who have trouble asserting and protecting their boundaries, the anxiety about losing oneself to the ecstasy of orgasm—what the French call *le petit mort,* the little death—can feel like an unendurable threat.

Does this suggest, then, that we need insecurity and anxiety to sustain sexual passion? Perhaps. In single life sex represents not just challenge but mystery—the unknown, the uncharted, the illicit. There's potential danger, a sense of vulnerability, an emotional intensity born of insecurity about the relationship—what it is, where it's going. All powerful aphrodisiacs that are largely absent from the marital bed.

I started this exploration with the question: What happened to the sexual revolution? But there's so simple and easy answer, for a social movement is like life—unruly, unpredictable, defying easy categories or neat endings. This one washed over us like a great wave, crashing over the rocks on the shore, sweeping aside the debris that had lain there for decades, erasing the footprints of the past that had been etched so deeply in the sand. When the wave receded, the sand seemed to lay sparkling in the sun, smoothed clean, ready for a new beginning. A compelling vision that disabled us, for the moment, from seeing that the rocks were still there, their contours eroded by the force of the water, new shapes emerging but not yet formed.

It seemed for a while as if this revolution might accomplish what others had not: a revolution in which everybody won. For women, it meant freedom from the sexual constraints under which they had lived for so long. For men, it meant sexual access to a wider range of women than had ever before been available. Win-win, right? But the history of revolutions—whether social or political—is a tale of triumph and failure, of winners and losers, of excess and backlash, of good intentions and unanticipated consequences. And this one was no different. For no revolution creates a wholly new universe. Rather, it reflects the history and culture that spawned it.

From our earliest beginnings, we have been a nation obsessed with sex, titillated by it at the same time that we fear it, elaborating rules to contain it at the same time that we violate them. So despite the extraordinary changes we have seen, the sexual revolution could not wholly escape its heritage. It wasn't long, therefore, before the revolution began to exhibit the same compulsive obsession with sex that characterized the society that produced it, only this time the avowed purpose was to embrace sex, not contain it. Nor surprisingly, the celebration of sex for its own sake turned out to have its own problems, and we found ourselves left with a peculiar malaise, a haunting hunger that, no matter how often and how much, sex alone cannot satisfy. We feel empty in the midst of plenty, we long for something to fill the void, but it continues to elude us.

That's the downside. But the upside is no less important. For while the great revolutionary wave of the '60s and '70s has receded, its ripples continue to make themselves felt, not just in our sexual behavior and the continuing expansion of the borders of the acceptable but in the whole mindset we bring to sexuality today. The changes wrought by the sexual revolution have, for good or ill, profoundly altered both the sociology and the psychology of sex in the United States, not just for the generation who made the revolution and those who came after, but for those who preceded it as well. A few weeks ago, I talked with a convent-educated woman in her mid-fifties who commented with the utmost casualness that her twenty-two-year-old daughter was living with her boyfriend. When I remarked on the ease with which she seemed to accept a situation so at odds with the training of her own past, she laughed and said, "If you think that's surprising, what would you think of my seventy-nine-year-old Catholic mother who invites them to dinner?"

NOTE

"Erotic Wars: What Happened to the Sexual Revolution?" previously unpublished. Keynote Address, Tenth Annual Congress of Sexology, Amsterdam, June 18, 1991.

Blue-Collar Marriage and the Sexual Revolution

Experimental? Oh, he's much more experimental than I am. Once in awhile, I'll say, "Okay, you get a treat; we'll do it with the lights on." And I put the pillow over my head. [Thirty-year-old woman, married twelve years]

Experimental? Not Ann. I keep trying to get her to loosen up; you know, to be more—What would you call it?—adventurous. I mean, there's lots of different things we could be doing. She just can't see it.

Sometimes I mind; but then sometimes I think, "After all, she was brought up in a good family, and she always was a nice, sweet girl." And that's the kind of girl I wanted, so I guess I ain't got no real right to complain. [Twenty-seven-year-old man, married seven years]

These comments, typical of a significant number of the fifty white working-class couples with whom I spoke, made me wonder: Is *this* the revolution in sexual behavior I had been reading about? And if so, were these the issues of the working class alone? To answer the second question, I also talked with twenty-five professional middle-class couples whose characteristics matched the working-class group in all but education and occupation.

Not one couple is without stories about adjustment problems in this difficult and delicate area of marital life—problems not just in the past, but in the present as well. Some of the problem areas—such as differences in frequency of sexual desire between men and women—are old ones. Some—such as the men's complaints about their wives' reluctance to engage in variant and esoteric sexual behaviors—are newer. All suggest that there is, in fact, a revolution in sexual behavior in the American society that runs wide and deep—a revolution in which sexual behaviors that formerly were the province of the college-educated upper classes now are practiced widely at all class and education levels.

The evidence is strong that more people are engaging in more varieties of sexual behavior than ever before—more premarital, postmarital, extramarital sex of all kinds. In 1948, for example, Kinsey found that only 15 percent of high-school-educated married men ever engaged in cunnilingus, compared to 45 percent of college-educated men. But the world changes quickly. Just twenty-five years later, a national survey shows that the proportion of high-school-educated men engaging in cunnilingus jumped to 56 percent.[1] And among the people I met, the figure stands at 70 percent.

But to dwell on these impressive statistics which tell us what people *do* without attention to how they *feel* about what they do is to miss a profoundly important dimension of human experience—that is, the *meaning* that people attribute to their behavior. Nowhere is the disjunction between behavior and attitude seen more sharply than in the area of sexual behavior. For when, in the course of a single lifetime, the forbidden becomes commonplace, when the border between the conceivable and the inconceivable suddenly disappears, people may do new things, but they don't necessarily *like* them.

For decades, novelists, filmmakers, and social scientists all have portrayed working-class men as little more than boorish, insensitive studs—men whose sexual performance was, at best, hasty and perfunctory; at worst, brutal—concerned only with meeting their own urgent needs. Consideration for a woman's needs, variety in sexual behaviors, experimentation—these, it is generally said, are to be found largely among men of the upper classes; working-class men allegedly know nothing of such amenities.[2]

If such men ever lived in large numbers, they surely do no longer. Morton Hunt's study, *Sexual Behavior in the 1970s,* which does not control for class but does give data that are controlled for education, provides evidence that men at all educational levels have become more concerned with and more sensitive to women's sexual needs—with the greatest increase reported among high-school-educated men. Comparing his sample with the 1948 Kinsey data on the subject of foreplay, for example, he notes that Kinsey reported that foreplay was "very brief or even perfunctory" among high-school-educated husbands, while college-educated husbands reported about ten minutes. Twenty-five years later, Hunt found that the median for non-college- and college-educated husbands was the same—fifteen minutes. Similar changes were found in the variety of sexual behaviors, the variety of positions used, and the duration of coitus—with especially sharp increases reported among high-school-educated men.

Not surprisingly, it is the men more often than the women who find these changing sexual norms easier to integrate—generally responding more positively to a cultural context that offers the potential for loosening sexual constraints. For historically, it is men, not women, whose sexuality has been thought to be unruly and ungovernable—destined to be restrained by a good (read: asexual) woman. Thus, it is the men who now more often speak of their wish for sex to be freer and with more mutual enjoyment:

> I think sex should be that you enjoy each other's bodies. Judy doesn't care for touching and feeling each other though.

… who push their wives to be sexually experimental, to try new things and different ways:

> She thinks there's just one right position and one right way—in the dark with her eyes closed tight. Anything that varies from that makes her upset.

… who sometimes are more concerned than their wives for her orgasm:

> It's just not enjoyable if she doesn't have a climax, too. She says she doesn't mind, but I do.

For the women, these attitudes of their men—their newly expressed wish for sexual innovation, their concern for their wives' gratification—are not an unmixed blessing. For in any situation, there is a gap between the ideal statements of a culture and the reality in which people live out their lives—a time lag between the emergence of new cultural forms and their internalization by the individuals who must act upon them. In sexual matters, that gap is felt most keenly by women. Socialized from infancy to experience their sexuality as a negative force to be inhibited and repressed, women can't just switch "on" as the changing culture or their husbands dictate. Nice girls don't! Men *use* bad girls but marry good girls! Submit, but don't enjoy—at least not obviously so! These are the injunctions that have dominated their lives—injunctions that are laid aside with difficulty, if at all.

The media tell us that the double standard of sexual morality is dead. But with good reason, women don't believe it. They know from experience that it is alive and well, that it exists side-by-side with the new ideology that heralds their sexual liberation. They know all about who are the "bad girls" in school, in the neighborhood; who are the "good girls." Everybody knows! Nor is this knowledge given only among the working class. The definition of "good girl" and "bad girl" may vary somewhat according to class, but the fundamental ideas those words encompass are not yet gone either from our culture or our consciousness at any class level.

We need only to look at our own responses to two questions to understand how vital the double standard remains. When we are asked, "What kind of woman is she?" we are likely to think about her sexual behavior; is she "easy" or not. But the question, "What kind of man is he?" evokes thoughts about what kind of work he does; is he strong, weak, kind, cruel? His sexual behavior is his private business, no concern of ours.

Whether these issues are especially real for working-class women, or whether women of that class are simply more open in talking about them than their middle-class counterparts, is difficult to say. Most of the middle-class women I spoke with came to their first sexual experiences at college where, during the early-to-middle 1960s, they suddenly entered a world where sexual freedom was the byword. These were the years when it was said, "Sex is no different than a handshake"; when it was insisted that if women would only "do what comes naturally," they'd have no problems with sexual enjoyment; when the young women who did have such problems experienced themselves as personally inadequate; when it was "uncool" for a girl to ask questions about these issues—even, God forbid, to say no. Thus for well over a decade, these college-educated women have lived in an atmosphere that was at once sexually permissive and coercive—permissive in that it encouraged them to unfetter and experience their sexuality; coercive, in that it gave them little room to experience also the constraints upon that sexuality that their culture and personal history until then had imposed upon them. That combination, then, would make them at once less guilty about their sexuality *and* less ready to speak of the inhibitions that remain.

All that notwithstanding, one thing is clear. Among the people I met, working-class and middle-class couples engage in essentially the same kinds of sexual behaviors in roughly the same proportions. But working-class wives express considerably more discomfort about what they do in the marriage bed than their middle-class sisters.

Take, for example, the conflict that engages many couples around the issue of oral-genital stimulation. Seventy percent of the working-class and 76 percent of the middle-class couples engage in such sexual activity. A word of caution is necessary here, however, because these gross figures can be misleading. For about one-third of each group, engaging in oral-genital stimulation means that they tried it once, or that it happens a few times a year at most. Another 30 percent of the middle-class couples and 40 percent of the working-class couples said they have oral sex only occasionally, meaning something over three times but less than ten times a year. Thus, only about one-fourth of the working-class couples and one-third of the middle-class couples who engage in oral sex use this sexual mode routinely as a standard part of their repertoire of sexual techniques. Still, fewer of the working-class women say they enjoy it unreservedly or without guilt. Listen to this couple, married twelve years. The husband:

> I've always been of the opinion that what two people do in the bedroom is fine; whatever they want to do is okay. But Jane, she doesn't agree. I personally like a lot of foreplay, caressing each other and whatever. For her, no. I think oral sex is the ultimate in making love; but she says it's revolting. [With a deep sign of yearning] I wish I could make her understand.

The wife ...

> I sure wish I could make him stop pushing me into that (ugh, I even hate to talk about it), into that oral stuff. I let him do it, but I hate it. He says I'm old-fashioned about sex and maybe I am. But I was brought up that there's just one way you're supposed to do it. I still believe that way, even though he keeps trying to convince me of his way. How can I change when I wasn't brought up that way? [With a pained sigh] I wish I could make him understand.

Notice her plaintive plea for understanding—"I wasn't brought up that way." In reality, when it comes to sex, she, like most of us, wasn't brought up any way. Girls generally learn only that it's "wrong" before marriage. But what that "it" is often is hazy and unclear until after the first sexual experience. As for the varieties of sexual behavior, these are rarely, if ever, mentioned to growing children, let alone discussed in terms of which are right or wrong, good or bad, permissible or impermissible.

Still, the cry for understanding from both men and women is real. Each wishes to make the other "understand," to transform the other into oneself for a brief moment so that the inner experience can be apprehended by the other. Yet, given the widely divergent socialization practices around male and female sexuality, the wish is but another impossible fantasy. The result: He asks; she gives. And neither is satisfied with the resolution. Despairing of finding a solution with which both are comfortable, one husband comments …

> Either I'm forcing my way on her or she's forcing her way on me. Either way, you can't win. If she gives in, it isn't because she's enjoying it, but because I pushed her. I suppose you could say I get what I want, but it doesn't feel that way.

It's true, on the question of oral sex, most of the time, she "gives in"—hesitantly, shyly, uncomfortably, even with revulsion. Sometimes women act from a sense of caring and consideration …

> We don't do it much because it really makes me uncomfortable, you know [making a face], a little sick. But sometimes, I say okay because I know it means a lot to him and I really want to do it for him.

Sometimes from a sense of duty …

> Even though I hate it, if he needs it, then I feel I ought to do it. After all, I'm his wife.

Sometimes out of fear of losing their men …

> He can find someone to give it to him, so I figure I better do it.

Sometimes out of resignation and a sense of powerlessness …

> I tell him I don't want to do it, but it doesn't do any good. If it's what he wants, that's what we do.

And sometimes it is offered as a bribe or payment for good behavior—not surprising in a culture that teaches a woman that her body is a negotiable instrument.

> He gets different treats at different times, depending on what he deserves. Sometimes I let him do that oral stuff you're talking about to me. Sometimes when he's *very* good, I do it to him.

While most of the working-class women greet both cunnilingus and fellatio with little enthusiasm or pleasure, cunnilingus is practiced with slightly greater frequency and with slightly less resistance than fellatio. Partly, that's because many women are talked into cunnilingus by their husbands' "If-I'm-willing-why-do-you-care?" argument ...

> I don't like him to do it, but I can't figure out what to say when he says that I shouldn't care if *he* doesn't.

... and partly, and perhaps more important, because cunnilingus is something that is done *to* a woman—an act not requiring her active engagement as fellatio does; and one, therefore, not quite so incongruent with her socialization to passivity. In all areas of life, she has been raised to wait upon the initiative of another, to monitor both behavior and response carefully so as not to appear too forward or aggressive. Nowhere are these lessons more thoroughly ingrained than in her sexual behavior; nowhere has she learned better to be a reflector rather than a generator of action. Thus, fellatio, perhaps more than any other sex act, is a difficult one for a woman.

Even those women who do not express distinctly negative feelings about oral sex are often in conflict about it—unsure whether it is really all right for them to engage in, let alone enjoy, such esoteric sexual behavior, worrying about whether these are things "nice girls" do. One twenty-eight-year-old mother of three, married ten years, explained ...

> I always feel like it's not quite right, no matter what Pete says. I guess it's not the way I was brought up, and it's hard to get over that. He keeps telling me it's okay if it's between us, that anything we do is okay. But I'm not sure about that. How do I know in the end he won't think I'm cheap.

> Sometimes I enjoy it, I guess. But most of the time I'm too worried thinking about whether I ought to be doing it, and worrying what he's *really* thinking to get much pleasure.

"How do I know he won't think I'm cheap?"—a question asked over and over again, an issue that dominates these women and their attitudes toward their own sexuality. Some husbands reassure them ...

> She says she worries I'll think she's a cheap tramp, and she doesn't really believe me when I keep telling her it's not true.

Such reassurances remain suspect, however, partly because it's so hard for women to move past the fears of their own sexuality with which they have been stamped; and partly because at least some men are not without their own ambivalence about it, as is evident in this comment from one young husband ...

> No, Alice isn't that kind of girl. Jesus, you shouldn't ask questions like that. [A long, difficult silence] She wasn't brought up to go for all that [pause] fancy stuff. You

know, all those different ways and [shifting uncomfortably in his chair, lighting a cigarette, and looking down at the floor] that oral stuff. But that's okay with me. There's plenty of women out there to do that kind of stuff with. You can meet them in any bar any time you want to. You don't have to marry those kind.

As long as that distinction remains, as long as men distinguish between the girl they marry and the girl they use, many women will remain unconvinced by their reassurances and wary about engaging in sexual behaviors that seem to threaten their "good girl" status.

The those assurances are doubly hard to hear and to believe when women also know that their husbands are proud of their naivete in sexual matters—a pride which many men take little trouble to hide.

It took a long time for me to convince her that it didn't have to be by the books. She was like an innocent babe. I taught her everything she knows.

Even men whose wives were married before will say with pleasure ...

It's funny how naive she was when we got married. She was married before, you know, but still she was kind of innocent. I taught her just about everything she knows.

For the women, the message seems clear: He wants to believe in her innocence, to believe in the special quality of their sexual relationship, to believe that these things she does only for him. She is to be pupil to his teacher. So she echoes his words—"He taught me everything I know." Repeatedly that phrase or a close equivalent is used as women discuss their sexual behavior and their feelings about it. And always it is said with a sure sense that it's what her husband wants and needs to believe, as these incongruent comments from a woman now in her second marriage show.

One thing I know he likes is that he taught me mostly all I know about sex, so that makes him feel good. It also means that I haven't any habits that have to be readjusted to his way or anything like that.

That seems a strange thing to say when you were married for some years before.

Startled, she looked at me, then down at her hands uncomfortably.

Yeah, I guess you'd think so. Well, you know, he likes to feel that way so why shouldn't he, and why shouldn't I let him?

Given that knowledge, even if it were possible to do so on command, most women would not dare risk unleashing their sexual inhibitions. From where a woman stands, the implicit injunction in her husband's pride in her innocence is that her sexuality be restrained. And restrain it she does—a feat for which she is all too well trained. The price for that training in restraint is high for both of them, however. He often complains because she doesn't take the initiative ...

> She never initiates anything. She'll make no advances at all, not even subtleties.

She often replies ...

> I just can't. I guess I'm inhibited, I don't know. All I know is it's very hard for me to start things up or to tell him something I want.

> On the other hand, not infrequently when women put aside that restraint and take the initiative, they may find themselves accused of not being feminine enough.

> It isn't that I mind her letting me know when she wants it, but she isn't very subtle about it. I mean, she could let me know in a nice, feminine way. Being feminine and, you know, kind of subtle, that's not her strong point.

Sensitive to the possibility of being thought of as "unfeminine" or "aggressive," most women shy away from any behavior that might bring those words down upon their heads. For it is painful for any woman of any class to hear herself described in these ways.

> I don't like to think he might think I was being aggressive, so I don't usually make any suggestions. Most of the time it's okay because he can usually tell when I'm in the mood. But if he can't, I just wait.

> These, then, are some of the dilemmas and conflicts people face around the newly required and desired sexual behaviors. Among working-class women, isolation and insulation compound their problems. It is one thing to read about all these strange and exotic sexual behaviors in books and magazines, another to know others like yourself who actually do these things.

> He keeps trying to get me to read those books, but what difference would it make? I don't know who those people are. There's a lot of people who do lots of things; it doesn't mean I have to do them.

If the books aren't convincing, and it's not culturally acceptable to discuss the intimate details of one's sex life with neighbors, friends, co-workers, or even family, most women are stuck with their childhood and adolescent fears, fantasies, and prohibitions. Small wonder that over and over again during my visit the atmosphere in the room changed from anxiety to relief when subjects such as oral sex were treated casually, with either the implicit or explicit understanding that it is both common and acceptable sexual practice.

Jim keeps telling me and telling me it's okay, that it's not dirty. But I always worry about it, not really knowing if that's true or not. I read a couple of books once, but it's different. I never talked to anyone but Jim about it before. [Smiling, as if a weight had been lifted from her shoulders] You're so cool about it; talking to you makes it seem not so bad.

In contrast, discussion of these issues with the middle-class women was considerably more relaxed. Regardless of their own feelings about engaging in oral sex, it was clear that most middle-class women recognize that it is a widely practiced and acceptable behavior. In fact, more often than not, they tended to feel guilty and uncomfortable about their own inhibitions, not because they weren't able to please their husbands but because they believed their constraint reflected some inadequacy in their personal sexual adjustment. It was also from middle-class women that I more often heard complaints when their husbands were unwilling to experiment with oral-genital sex. Of the working-class couples who never engage in oral sex, only one woman complained about her husband's unwillingness to do so. Of the middle-class couples in a similar situation, four women offered that complaint.

But it is also true that, generally, the husbands of these middle-class women send fewer ambiguous and ambivalent messages about their wives' sexuality, tend less to think in good girl–bad girl terms, more often expect and accept that their wives had other sexual experiences before they met. Further, these middle-class women are more often in contact with others like themselves in an environment where discussion of sexual issues is encouraged—a course in human sexuality, a women's group, for example.

Still, the recitation of these differences in experience ought not to be read to suggest that middle-class women are now sexually free and uninhibited. The most that can be said on that score is that more of them live in an atmosphere that more seriously encourages that goal, hence more—especially those under thirty—may be closer to its attainment. Meanwhile, at all class levels, most women probably feel comfortable enough with their own sexual responses to be willing participants in sexual intercourse. But when it comes to oral sex—especially among the working class—generally they submit just as their mothers before them submitted to more traditional sexual behaviors.

Sexual conflicts in marriage are not always constellated around such exotic issues, however; nor, as I have said, are any of them the exclusive problem of a particular class. Thus, although what follows rests on material taken from my discussions with working-class couples, much of it applies to the professional middle class as well. True, the middle-class couples more often are able to discuss some of their issues more openly with each other. But despite the current, almost mystical, belief in communication-as-problem-solving, talk doesn't always help. True, middle-class couples much more often seek professional help with these problems. But sexual conflicts in a marriage are among the most intractable—the recent development and proliferation of sex therapies notwithstanding. Those therapies can be useful in dealing with some specific sexual dysfunction—prematurely ejaculating men or nonorgasmic women. But the kinds of sexual conflicts to be discussed here are so deeply rooted in the sociocultural mandates of our world that they remain extraordinarily resistant regardless of how able the psychotherapeutic help we can buy. Thus, while there are subtle differences between the two classes in the language and tone with which the problems are dealt, in the amount of discussion about them, and in their ability and willingness to seek professional help, in this instance, those differences are not as important as the similarities that remain.

In fact, the earliest sexual problems rear their heads with the couple's first fight. Regardless of what has gone before, at bedtime, he's ready for sex; she remains cold and aloof. Listen to this couple in their mid-to-late-twenties, married nine years. The wife . . .

> I don't understand him. He's ready to go any time. It's always been a big problem with us right from the beginning. If we've hardly seen each other for two or three days and hardly talked to each other, I can't just jump into bed. If we have a fight, I can't just turn it off. He has a hard time understanding that. I feel like that's all he wants sometimes. I have to know I'm needed and wanted for more than just jumping into bed.

The husband . . .

> She complains that all I want from her is sex, and I try to make her understand that it's an expression of love. I'll want to make up with her by making love, but she's cold as the inside of the refrig. Sure I get mad when that happens. Why shouldn't I? Here I'm trying to make up and make love, and she's holding out for something—I don't know what.

The wife . . .

> He keeps saying he wants to make love, but it just doesn't feel like love to me. Sometimes I feel bad that I feel that way, but I just can't help it.

The husband . . .

> I don't understand. She says it doesn't feel like love. What does that mean, anyway? What does she think love is?

The wife . . .

> I want him to talk to me, to tell me what he's thinking about. If we have a fight, I want to talk about it so we could maybe understand it. I don't want to jump in bed and just pretend it didn't happen.

The husband . . .

Talk! Talk! What's there to talk about. I want to make love to her and she says she wants to talk. How's talking going to convince her I'm loving her.

In sex, as in other matters, the barriers to communication are high, and the language people use serves to further confuse and mystify. He says, "I want to make love." She says, "It doesn't feel like love." Neither quite knows what the other is talking about; both feel vaguely guilty and uncomfortable—aware only that somehow they're passing each other, not connecting. He believes he already has given her the most profound declaration of love of which a man is capable. He married her; he gives her a home; he works hard each day to support her and the children.

What does she want? Proof? She's got it, hasn't she? Would I be knocking myself out to get things for her—like to keep up this house—if I didn't love her. Why does a man do things like that if not because he loves his wife and kids? I swear, I can't figure what she wants.

This is one time when *she* knows what she wants.

I want him to let me know in other ways, too, not just sex. It's not enough that he supports us and takes care of us. I appreciate that, but I want him to share things with me. I need for him to tell me his feelings. He keeps saying no, but to me, there's a difference between making love and sex. Just once, I'd like him to love me without ending up in sex. But when I tell him that, he thinks I'm crazy.

For him, perhaps, it *does* seem crazy. Split off, as he is, from the rest of the expressive-emotional side of himself, sex may be the one place where he can allow himself the expression of deep feelings, the one place where he can experience the depth of that affective side. His wife, on the other hand, closely connected with her feeling side in all areas *but* the sexual, finds it difficult to be comfortable with her feelings in the very area in which he has the greatest—sometimes the only—ease. She keeps asking for something she can understand and is comfortable with—a demonstration of his feelings in nonsexual ways. He keeps giving her the one thing he can understand and is comfortable with—his feelings wrapped up in a blanket of sex. Thus do husbands and wives find themselves in an impossibly difficult bind— another bind not of their own making, but one that stems from the cultural context in which girls and boys grow to adulthood.

I am suggesting, then, that a man's ever-present sexual readiness is not simply an expression of urgent sexual need but also a complex compensatory response to a socialization process that *constricts the development of the emotional side of his personality in all but sexual expression.* Conversely, a woman's insistent plea for an emotional statement of a nonsexual nature is a response to a process that *encourages the development of the affective side of her personality in all but sexual expression.*[3]

Such differences between women and men about the *meaning* of sex make for differences between wives and husbands in frequency of desire as well—differences which lead to a wide discrepancy in their perceptions about the frequency of the sexual encounter.⁴ Except for a few cases where the women are inclined to be more sexually active than the men, he wants sex more often than she. To him, therefore, it seems as if they have sex less often than they actually do; to her, it seems more often. But the classical caricature of a wife fending off her husband's advances with a sick headache seems not to apply among working-class women. Once in a while, a woman says ...

> I tell him straight. I'm not in the mood, and he understands.

Mostly, however, women say ...

> I don't use excuses like headaches and things like that. If my husband wants me, I'm his wife, and I do what he wants. It's my responsiblity to give it to him when he needs it.

Whether she refuses outright or acquiesces out of a sense of duty or responsibility, the solution is less than satisfactory for both partners. In either case, he feels frustrated and deprived. He wants more than release from his own sexual tension; he wants her active involvement as well. Confronted with his ever-present readiness, she feels guilty ...

> I feel guilty and uncomfortable when he's always ready and I'm not, like I'm not taking care of him.

... coerced ...

> I feel like it hangs over my head all the time. He always wants it; twice a day wouldn't be too much for him. He says he doesn't want me just to give in to him, but if I didn't he'd be walking around horny all the time. If we waited for me to want it, it would never be enough for him.

... and also deprived.

> Before I ever get a chance to feel really sexy, he's there and waiting. I'd like to know what it feels like sometimes to really want it that bad. Oh, sometimes I do. But mostly I don't get the chance.

Thus, she rarely has the opportunity to experience the full force of her own sexual rhythm, and with it, the full impact of her sexuality. It is preempted by the urgency and frequency of his desires.

Finally, there is plenty of evidence that the battle between the sexes is still being waged in the marriage bed, and in very traditional ways. Several couples spoke of their early sexual adjustment problems in ways that suggest that the struggle was not over sex but over power and control. Often in the early years, when she wants sex, he's tired; when he wants sex, she's uninterested. For many couples, the pattern still repeats itself once in a while. For about one-fifth of them, the scenario continues to be played out with great regularity and sometimes with great drama, as this story of one early-thirties couple illustrates.

In six months of premarital and ten years of marital coitus, the woman had never had an orgasm.

> We had sex four or five times a week like clockwork all those years, and I just laid there like a lump. I couldn't figure out what all the noise was about.

Asked how he felt about her passivity during that period, her husband—a taciturn, brooding man, whose silence seemed to cover a wellspring of hostility—replied ...

> If she couldn't, she couldn't. I didn't like it, but I took what I needed. [After a moment's hesitation] She's always been hard to handle.

A year ago, attracted by ideas about women's sexuality that seemed to her to be "in the air," she began to read some of the women's literature on the subject. From there, she moved on to pornography and one night, as she tells it ...

> The earth shook. I couldn't believe anything could be so great. I kept wondering how I lived so long without knowing about it. I kept asking Fred why he'd never made me understand before. [Then, angrily] But you'll never believe what happened after that. My husband just lost interest in sex. Now, I can hardly ever get him to do it any more, no matter how much I try or beg him. He says he's too tired, or he doesn't feel well, or else he just falls asleep and I can't wake him up. I can hardly believe it's happening sometimes. Can you imagine such a thing? I even wonder whether maybe I shouldn't have made such a big fuss about it. Maybe it scared him off or something.

Her husband refused my attempts to explore the issue with him, insisting that all is well in their sex life, but adding ...

> She's always asking for something, or hollering about something. I don't have any control around this house any more. Nobody listens to me.

It would seem, then, that as long as he could "take what I needed," he could feel he was asserting some control over his wife and could remain sexually active and potent. When she unexpectedly became an assertive and active participant in the sex act, the only possibility for retaining control was to move from the active to the passive mode. Thus, he fell impotent. His wife, now acutely aware of her sexual deprivation, is left torn between anger, frustration, and the terrible fear that somehow she is responsible for it.

A dramatic story? Certainly, but one whose outlines are clear in 20 percent of these marriages where three women complained about their husbands' impotence and seven about sexual withholding—not surprisingly, a problem most of the men were unwilling to talk about. In the three cases where the husband did address the issue at all, either he denied its existence, "It's no problem; I'm just tired," or blamed his wife, "She doesn't appeal to me," or "She's too pushy." The last has been a subject of recent concern expressed publicly by psychologists and widely publicized in the mass media. The performance demands being laid on men are extraordinary, we are told, and women are cautioned that their emergent assertiveness—sexual and otherwise—threatens the sexual performance of their men. The time has come, these experts warn, to take the pressure off.

Nowhere, however, do we hear concern about the effects of the performance demand on women. Yet, never in history have heavier demands for sexual performance been laid on them. Until recently, women were expected to submit passively to sex; now they are told their passivity diminishes their husbands' enjoyment. Until recently, especially among the less educated working class, orgasm was an unexpected gift; now it is a requirement of adequate sexual performance.[5] These new definitions of adequacy leave many women feeling "under the gun"—fearful and anxious if they do not achieve orgasm, if it does not happen at the "right" moment—that is, at the instant of their husbands' ejaculation; or if they are uncomfortable about engaging in behaviors that feel alien or aberrant to them.[6] If anxiety about one's ability to perform adequately has an untoward effect on the male orgasm, is there any reason to believe it would not inhibit the female's as well?

In fact, the newfound concern with their orgasm is a mixed and costly blessing for many women. For some, it has indeed opened the possibility for pleasures long denied. For others, however, it is experienced as another demand in a life already too full of demands. Listen to this thirty-five-year-old woman who works part-time, takes care of a house, a husband, six children, and an aging, sick father.

> It feels like somebody's always wanting something from me. Either one of the kids is hanging on to me or pulling at me, or my father needs something. And if it's not them, then Tom's always coming after me with that gleam in his eye. Then, it's not enough if I just let him have it, because if I don't have a climax, he's not happy. I get so tired of everybody wanting something from me all the time. I sometimes think I hate sex.

While it is undoubtedly true that more women have more orgasms more often than ever before—and that most of them enjoy sex more than women in earlier generations—it is also true that there are times when a husband's wish for his wife's orgasm is experienced as oppressive and alienating—when it seems to a woman that her orgasm is more a requirement of his pleasure than her own. We may ask: How rational are these thoughts? And we may wonder: Why should it be a matter of question or criticism if, in the course of pleasuring their wives, men also pleasure themselves? When phrased that way, it should not be questioned! But if we look at the discussion around female orgasm or lack of it a little more closely, we notice that it is almost invariably tied to male pleasure. If a woman doesn't have an orgasm, it is a problem, if not for her, then because both her man's pleasure and his sense of manhood are diminished. Can anyone imagine a discussion of male impotence centering around concern for women? In fact, when we talk about the failure of men to achieve erection or orgasm, the discourse takes place in hushed, serious, regretful tones—always in the context of concern about how those men experience that failure. How many of us have ever thought, "What a shame for his woman that he can't have an erection." Any woman who has shared that experience with a man knows that her concern was largely for him, her own frustration becoming irrelevant in that moment. Any man who has experienced impotence knows that his dominant concern was for the failure of his manhood.

It is not surprising, therefore, that several of the women I talked to were preoccupied with their orgasm, not because it was so important to them, but because their husbands' sense of manhood rested on it. Holding her head, one woman said painfully . . .

> I rarely have climaxes. But if it didn't bother my husband, it wouldn't bother me. I keep trying to tell him that I know it's not his fault, that he's really a good lover. I keep telling him it's something the matter with me, not with him. But it scares me because he doesn't believe it, and I worry he might leave me for a woman who will have climaxes for him.

With these final words, she epitomizes the feelings of many women, whether orgasmic or not, at least some of the time: *Her orgasm is for him, not for her.* It is his need to validate his manhood that is the primary concern—his need, not hers. For women of the working class, who already have so little autonomy and control over their lives, this may well be experienced as the ultimate violation.

To compound the anxiety, now one orgasm is not enough. One woman, having read that some women have multiple orgasms, worried that her husband would soon find out.

> It's really important for him that I reach a climax, and I try to every time. He says it just doesn't make him feel good if I don't. But it's hard enough to do it once! What'll happen if he finds out about those women who have lots of climaxes?

These, then, are some dimensions of sexual experience in the 1970s that are buried under the sensational reports of changing sexual mores. Undoubtedly, there is a loosening of sexual constraints for both women and men; undoubtedly, more people are enjoying fuller sexual experiences than ever before. Certainly it is important that these changes are discussed publicly, that the subject of sex has come out of the closet. But that is not enough. For we must also understand that such changes are not without cost to the individuals who try to live them out, who must somehow struggle past powerful early training to a new consciousness. For women especially—women of any class—that training in repressing and inhibiting their sexuality makes this a particularly difficult struggle.

It is both sad and ironic now to hear men complain that their wives are too cautious, too inhibited, or not responsive enough in bed. Sad, because the deprivation men experience is real; ironic, because these are the costs of the sexual limitations that generations of their forebears have imposed on women. Changing such historic patterns of thought and behavior will not be easy for either men or women. For certainly, many men are still not without ambivalence about these sexual issues with reference to their women—a subtlety that is not lost on their wives. But even where men unambivalently mean what they say about wanting their wives to be freer in the marriage bed, it will take time for women to work through centuries of socially mandated denial and repression ...

> All I know is, I can't just turn on so easy. Maybe we're all paying the price now because men didn't used to want women to enjoy sex.

... and probably will require their first being freer in other beds as well.

> I was eighteen when we got married, and I was a very young eighteen. I'd never had any relations with anybody, not even my husband, before we were married. So we had a lot of problems. I guess I was kind of frigid at first. But you know, after all those years when you're holding back, it's hard to all of a sudden get turned on just because you got married.

Yes, it is "hard to all of a sudden get turned on just because you got married." And as long as women's sexuality continues to be subjected to capricious demands and treated as if regulated by an on-off switch—expected to surge forth fully and vigorously at the flick of the "on" switch and to subside quietly at the flick of the "off"—most women will continue to seek the safest path, in this case, to remain quietly someplace between "on" and "off."

NOTES

This chapter is adapted from *Worlds of Pain: Life in the Working-Class Family* (New York: Basic Books, 1976). It appears by permission of Basic Books, Inc. All rights reserved. For the purpose of this study, class was defined by both education and occupation. All the families were intact, neither husband nor wife had more than a high-school education, and the husband was employed in what is traditionally defined as a blue-collar occupation. In addition, because I was interested in studying relatively young families, the wife was under forty and at least one child under twelve was still in the home. Median age of the women was twenty-eight; of the men, thirty-one.

1. Morton Hunt, *Sexual Behavior in the 1970s* (Chicago: Playboy Press, 1974). This study, conducted for *Playboy* magazine, included a representative sample of urban and sub-urban adults, of whom 982 were men and 1,044 were women. Seventy-one percent of the sample were married (not to each other), 25 percent were never married, and 4 percent had been married.

2. For a good description of this stereotype, see Arthur B. Shostak, "Ethnic Revivalism, Blue-Collarites, and Bunker's Last Stand." In *The Rediscovery of Ethnicity,* edited by Sallie TeSelle (New York: Harper Colophon, 1973). See also Mirra Komarovsky, *Blue-Collar Marriage* (New York: Vintage Books, 1962), who, while noting that the stereotype applies to "only a small minority" of the families she studied, found that only 30 percent of the women said they were very satisfied with their sexual relations. And some of the data she presents do indeed validate the stereotype more forcefully and very much more often than among my sample where it is practically nonexistent.

3. Cf. William Simon and John Gagnon, "On Psychosexual Development." In *Handbook of Socialization Theory and Research,* edited by David A. Goslin (Chicago: Rand McNally, 1969) and John Gagnon and William Simon, *Sexual Conduct: The Social Sources of Human Sexuality* (Chicago: Aldine, 1973), whose work is a major contribution toward understanding the differences in male-female sexuality as an expression of the differential socialization patterns for women and men. These authors also point to the masculine tendency to separate love and sex and the feminine tendency to fuse them. They suggest, in fact, that the male "capacity for detached sexual activity, activity where the only sustaining motive is sexual ... may actually be the hallmark of male sexuality in our culture."

For an exploration of the ways in which social structure and personality intersect from the psychoanalytic perspective, see Nancy Chodorow, *The Reproduction of Mothering: Family Structure and Feminine Personality* (Berkeley: University of California Press, 1977), who argues that the root of the differences in male-female personality, and the concomitant differences in the development of psychosexual needs and responses, lie in the social structure of the family.

See also Ben Barker-Benfield, "The Spermatic Economy: A Nineteenth-Century View of Sexuality." In *The American Family in Social-Historical Perspective,* edited by Michael Gordon (New York: St. Martin's Press, 1973), for a portrait of nineteenth-century definitions of male and female sexuality and the fear and abhorrence with which men viewed female sexuality in that era.

4. It is for this reason that studies relying on the recollection of only one spouse for their data—as most do—risk considerable distortion. Thus, for example, when Morton Hunt reports that almost 26 percent of the married women ages twenty-five to thirty-four report having sexual intercourse between 105 and 156 times a year, we know only that this is the wife's perception, and we can assume that the recollection is filtered through her *feelings* about the frequency of the sexual encounter.

5. Again, Hunt's data, while not controlled for class, are suggestive. Using the 1948 Kinsey data as a comparative base, he reports that marital coitus has increased in frequency at every age and educational level. Comparing the Kinsey sample with his own at the fifteenth year of marriage, Hunt reports "a distinct increase in the number of wives who always or nearly always have orgasm (Kinsey: 45 percent; *Playboy:* 53 percent) and a sharp decrease in the number of wives who seldom or never do (Kinsey: 28 percent; *Playboy:* 15 percent)."

6. For a rebuke of the self-styled male "experts" on women's sexuality that is both wonderfully angry and funny as it highlights the absurdity of their advice to women, see Ellen Frankort, *Vaginal Politics* (New York: Bantam Books, 1973), 172–180. She opens this section of her book, entitled "Carnal Ignorance," by saying: "For the longest time a woman wasn't supposed to enjoy sex. Then suddenly a woman was neurotic if she didn't achieve orgasm simultaneously with her husband. Proof of a woman's health was her ability to come at the very moment the man ejaculated, in the very place he ejaculated, and at the very rate ordained for him by his physiology. If she couldn't, she went to a male psychiatrist to find out why."

Sex and Sexuality:
Women at Midlife

Sex? It's gotten better and better. For the first years of our marriage—maybe nine or ten—it was a very big problem. But it's changed and improved in lots of ways. Right now, I'm enjoying sex more than I ever did in my life before—maybe even more than I ever thought I could.

"It's gotten better and better." That's what most women say. Better than what? Where did they start from, these midlife women? Where have they gone?

To answer those and other questions, I conducted intensive, in-depth interviews with 160 women whose average age was 46.5 years. They were all women who were or had been married, who had borne and raised children, who (except for 10) had none under 13 years old left in the house, and whose class backgrounds ranged from working-class to professional upper-middle-class.[1]

It is simple enough to cite statistics on the sexual behavior of the women I met. Over half of those who were married had sexual intercourse once or twice a week; another 20 percent did so three or four times a week.[2] Close to 90 percent were currently capable of achieving orgasm, well over half doing so more than half the time. About two-thirds engaged in oral-genital sex, almost half of them often enough to consider it a standard part of their sexual repertoire.[3]

But having said those things, what do we really know about the *quality* of their sexual interaction, about its *meaning* in their lives, about its *history?* Ask midlife women about their sexual histories, and the stories come tumbling out—stories of their early sexual repression:

During the dating years, I was constantly putting on the brakes, and I just couldn't reverse on command. It took years of feeling inadequate and of hating myself, which didn't help me *or* our sex life.

stories of their painful struggle to bring to life that repressed part of the self:

> Sex was a constant source of difficulty for me as an individual and created nothing
> but conflict in my marriage. I was so closed off sexually, I really thought of myself
> as an asexual person. Getting through all that took lots of years and meant some
> terrible suffering for both of us—my husband and me. [A look of angry distaste
> on her face] God, what a waste; what an unnecessary waste.

With only a few exceptions, the memories of marital sex in the early years
brought with them an outpouring of deep feelings:

> What words can I use? They were *hard* times, *plain hard times.* It was the key issue
> in our marriage for years. It was the one that nearly wrecked us. [A combination
> of anger and bewilderment in her voice] And it wasn't anybody's fault. We were
> both incredibly ignorant. Both of us were only doing whatever was expected; you
> know, what we learned God knows when—maybe with our mother's milk. All I
> know is that for me, sex was all one big "NO."

Over and over those memories called up these women's anger about the bind
they found themselves in—a bind born of the mandate of virginity and the expectation that they would turn into sexual sirens at the pronouncement of the marriage
vows:[4]

> It was terrible at first, just terrible. He wanted me to be a virgin—that was very
> important to him before we were married—and he also wanted me to be skilled
> in bed right from the start. Imagine! It wasn't just awful, it was *impossible.* When
> I think of it now, I feel outraged because it wasn't even our fault. We were both
> just playing our parts, like puppets on a string.

What "parts" were they playing? Who was pulling the "string"? The parts, of
course, were those assigned by the culture—the stereotypical versions of sexuality with
which girls and boys of that generation grew up. These were women and men who
came to adulthood in the 1940s and 1950s. The wave of sexual liberation of the 1920s
that had brought the Victorian era to a screeching halt was past. The reaction had
set in. Two decades later, it was clear that the Victorian heritage was not gone, that
the double standard of sexual behavior had not been wiped out by the revolution of
the 1920s. It had simply changed its form. By the 1940s, it was granted that women
were capable, even desirous, of sexual pleasure. But the time, place, and manner were
carefully circumscribed—limited to only one man, only in marriage.

Thus, almost without exception, the women who came to the marriage bed
were naive, repressed, and inexperienced. Even among those who had had premarital
intercourse, it was the rare woman who found the experience enjoyable, rarer still
the woman who had orgasms in that period of her life. Indeed, most described those
experiments in illicit sex as unsatisfactory and guilt-ridden, usually acts so hasty and

rudimentary that they barely qualify as full-fledged sexual intercourse. But about that, there were no complaints. They were, after all, engaged in forbidden behaviors. Most women didn't expect to enjoy them.

After marriage, though, after sex became licit, then, it was a different story. Then, all of them—technical virgins or not—expected something more, something special, something magical to happen. They were filled with romantic fantasies that their own special prince would unlock the secrets of their bodies, their souls. They dreamed that "bells would ring," that "the earth would move," that "waves would be crashing on the shore" as they were swept away by his magical touch. And, of course, they were bitterly disappointed:

> The first time I had intercourse, I thought: Is this what I've been saving myself for? [Her expression registering the surprise she felt so long ago] *I couldn't believe it: it was such a big nothing.* I had read all those romantic novels about violins playing and bells ringing, and I absolutely believed some fantastic things would happen. My god, what a disappointment it was.

This was the "gift" of the liberated sexuality of that era—incredible fantasies and magical expectations that were bound to fail:

> I had tremendous hopes that I would flower as a sexual being after we were married. I looked to my husband to give me all the sexual pleasure I was afraid of before marriage. And when he couldn't, I was bitterly disappointed and resentful.

But the disappointment and resentment were not the women's alone, for the men shared this package of impossible expectations. Both wife and husband believed that it was *his* responsibility to open up the mysteries of sexual pleasure for her; both believed that *he* held the secret key.[5] For both, it was a distressing surprise to find that a lifetime of sexual repression exacted a price, that a woman couldn't spring into sexual responsiveness on cue. When the fantasies didn't come true, both husband and wife were caught in a bind, where each oscillated between angry blaming of the other and a deeply felt sense of personal inadequacy—often creating a vicious circle where the more the inadequacy was experienced, the more it was externalized as anger against the other:

> We came to the marriage with such high hopes. But our sexual maladjustment turned it into a nightmare of self-consciousness and resentment. It seemed as if there was no peace. I was either angry at myself or angry at him. And I think he felt pretty much the same way.

But, one might ask, were there no women who were sexually responsive right from the beginning of marriage? The answer: very few. It's true that some speak of sexual pleasure in the early years. But very rarely did that pleasure include orgasms. What was it they enjoyed then?

Some valued the sexual experience because it was the major means of communication in the new marriage—not exactly the life they had dreamed of, but better than nothing:

> I never even knew what an orgasm was then. I enjoyed sex because it was a coming together in an intimate-type way. It was the most intimate thing we ever did in those days because we didn't do much talking.

For others, there was something else as well—the satisfaction that comes mostly from giving pleasure, a quality of caring and nurturing for which women are well schooled:

> Long before I ever had an orgasm myself, I used to have a feeling of joy out of giving him joy. It didn't make a big difference if it wasn't such a great thing for me. Having someone in my arms whom I loved and to whom I was giving satisfaction was very important and gave me real pleasure.

An interesting and provocative issue this: women who take such satisfaction in giving pleasure that their own unfulfilled sexual longings become relatively unimportant. In this age, when the emphasis is so much on *taking* pleasure, we might be tempted to label such women with pejoratives—to speak of their socialization to passivity, to bemoan their tendencies toward masochism and self-denial. But that's too easy. And it leads too often to a call to arms, to a shrill and insistent demand for change, that leaves many women feeling confused and angry, inadequate or misunderstood. Worst of all, it leaves them feeling as if some prized part of themselves were being denied and invalidated—the part that's tender, giving, nurturing; the part that gets "joy out of giving him joy."

But what does this say? What of the often tragic consequences of traditional socialization practices that encourage passivity, masochism, and self-denial in women? No denying those; no denying either that the behavior I speak of here may be related to those tendencies. But let's not deny the reality and complexity of their experience when women speak of the importance of being able to give pleasure to a loved one. Let's not wipe out such giving with words of disparagement. Indeed, to do so invalidates any possibility of an authentic altruism—that kind of behavior that was glorified in the pre-Freudian age, that once was lauded as the height of virtue. It's true that the post-Freudian view that directs us to the potential pathology in such altruistic behavior is an important corrective to our earlier romantic notions about saintliness and self-abnegation. But it has been carried too far if in this era of human history we can no longer distinguish at all between the authentic desire to give and its pathological distortion: masochism.

When it comes to sex, it is this very quality of giving that is necessary to turn the sex act into a relationship. Only when two people wish to give at least as much as they wish to take does sex become a nourishing and enriching experience. Only then is the uniquely human separated from the animal.

Of course, it takes two. And until now, there too often has been only one—the woman—to do this kind of giving. The task now is not to exhort women to change or to thwart that capacity in themselves, but to encourage men to develop it more fully. No easy task, to be sure, but a necessary one if sexual relations between women and men are to fulfill their promise.

Unfortunately, in this culture, facile answers too often take the place of real struggle. Thus, we now have a whole new vocabulary of assertiveness for women and a profitable industry to match. Yet much of the rhetoric mistakes "assertiveness" for selfishness and seeks to teach women to abandon those giving parts of themselves. In fact, *real* assertiveness would mean that women would respect those gentle, tender, giving qualities enough to assert their value. *Real* assertiveness would mean that they would continue to give such care and concern in their relationships *and* would insist on getting it from their men as well. Difficult demands for women to make—made especially difficult in a culture where such values and ways of being have been consistently devalued with the label *feminine.*

These reflections aside, there was pain in the early years of marriage. And there was conflict. But most women eventually win a victory in the struggle with their repressed sexuality—a victory of nature over culture, the triumph of female sexuality over the forces that for so long have conspired to obliterate it.

As long ago as 1953, Kinsey showed that the proportion of women experiencing orgasm in marriage rises steadily through the years.[6] So it is with the women I met. "I'm enjoying sex more than I ever did in my life before, maybe even more than I ever thought I could"—common sentiments, spoken repeatedly. But it took time. For some, it was a year or two before they experienced their first orgasm; for those less fortunate, it didn't happen for a decade or more. Others commented on the dramatic change after the birth of the first child, telling not only of having their first orgasm but of experiencing spontaneous sexual feelings for the first time in their lives:[7]

> All of a sudden, I knew what it was like to feel sexual. I mean, I would get sexual feelings before that when I was stimulated, but they didn't just come by themselves. I used to wonder what people meant when they talked about being horny, but I never knew until after Lisa was born.

Unfortunately, for women who are new mothers and who must bear the burden of child care alone, increasing sexual responsiveness is not an unmitigated blessing. For it's one of life's hapless paradoxes that the physiological development of this stage of the life cycle is so poorly matched with its demands. Certainly there's joy in those early months of motherhood, but there's also exhaustion. Of course there's the wonder of a new life and a new love, but there's also anxiety. Am I a good enough mother? Will I spoil my baby by holding her now? Or will I damage him forever if I don't? Is there something wrong with me that I sometimes feel restless and discontented? How could I have been so angry yesterday—she's only an innocent child? Question upon question, born of the myths and the mandates that attach to motherhood in our society—the myth of the all-loving, all-nurturing madonna-mother; the mandates that remind her repeatedly that she alone is responsible for the healthy development of her child.[8] Preoccupied with such fears, anxious about her adequacy in this new and demanding role, the young mother finds it hard to care much about sex. In fact, for most women in this study—including those who by then were enjoying good sexual relationships—the arrival of the first child marked a significant drop in both sexual activity and sexual pleasure.

Even among those who experienced orgasm for the first time after giving birth, it usually wasn't met with pure pleasure. Rather, it was pleasure mixed with relief at finally having achieved that long-sought goal. And there was frustration and anger as well.

> It was a damned irony. Just when I couldn't have cared less, it happened. And then for years, I was too tired and too preoccupied to want it much. God, what an aggravating time that was.

In fact, from the time they're born until they leave home, the presence of children generally inhibits a woman's sexual responsiveness—a fact that is a constant source of conflict between many wives and husbands.[9] At first, the strain of a newborn infant leaves her tired and edgy much of the time. Later, other concerns about the care and welfare of children dominate her attention:

> He could be ready at any time of the day or night, no matter what was happening; and it made me very uncomfortable. You know, a child could be banging at the door, and he wouldn't be interrupted for anything. Or you could hear a kid screaming down the hall, and it wouldn't faze him at all. Well, I couldn't very well get into it under those circumstances.

These are trying times in a marriage. Whether at the breakfast table or dinner, in bed or out, young children are difficult, demanding, and often irritating companions. Even when they're at their angelic best, spontaneous interaction and communication between adults are limited just by their presence.[10] That means there's often some distance between wife and husband—distance born of the fact that their daily lives are separate while their evenings are too short, and altogether too full of distractions, to allow them to reestablish a connection quickly.[11] For most women, that spells difficulty in the sexual relationship—a consequence of the fact that for women, more than for men, sex is *part* of the total relationship, not something that stands *a*part from it.[12] Over and over, they speak of not being able "to turn on the minute the kids go to bed," of needing "some time together before jumping into bed," of not feeling "very close or sexual after we've barely talked to each other for a few days." And over and over, they also tell of the conflict these differences with their husbands create.

When children get older, they need less and demand less. But then the irritation of their seemingly unceasing demands, the constriction of their constant presence, and the worries about their physical and psychological well-being are replaced by embarrassed concern about what they might think their parents are doing behind the closed door, or what they might hear in the night:

> Just knowing that the bed could squeak or they could hear some noise makes it hard to get into sex sometimes. I feel nervous that they could walk in any time, too. We've thought about putting a lock on the door, but after twenty years of not having a lock on the bedroom door, I feel embarrassed to suddenly have one show up. What would I tell the kids? Even if they didn't ask any questions, I know what they'd be thinking, and I feel like I'd have to explain. But what would I say?

The fear of pregnancy is another important inhibitor of sexual desire and activity in women. Despite almost universal use of birth control measures, that concern remains alive for most women in their childbearing years. For some, usually those who have had the experience of an unwanted pregnancy—a child born of a birth control device that failed—concern turns to fear.

To deal with this fear, just over 15 percent of the men have had vasectomies.[13] Without exception, the result has been more relaxed and frequent sexual activity between wife and husband—the woman sometimes becoming orgasmic for the first time. When this happens, a woman credits her newfound sexual responsiveness to the freedom from fears of pregnancy:

> It made all the difference in the world not to lie there scared to death that I'd pay for this for the rest of my life. The last thing I wanted was another baby, and I never felt secure with either condoms or a diaphragm. After he had the vasectomy, I could begin enjoying sex for the first time in my whole life.

"The last thing I wanted was another baby"—no reason to doubt her words. But there's still another issue, perhaps equally important, in this complex drama between wives and husbands. Very often, a woman sees her husband's willingness to undergo vasectomy as a statement of his caring and concern for her, a statement of his commitment to something besides his own gratification and pleasure. Both together—the release from the pregnancy fears *and* the reassurance about his love and commitment that the vasectomy seems to her to imply—become powerful forces in freeing a woman to more sexual responsiveness.

In several families, there was conflict about whether or not a man would take this step. And always, for the wife, that conflict centered on both these issues, as these comments from a woman in a deteriorating marriage show:

> I can honestly say to you that from the second year of our marriage to the fifteenth, I enjoyed sex as much as he did. But no more. Not one of my children was planned. No matter what kind of birth control we used, something always happened. Five years ago, I got pregnant again for the fifth time. Fortunately, I had a miscarriage, so I didn't have to have the baby. But it turned me off sex, and ever since we have big rows over it for the first time in our lives. [Tears streaming down her face] But

dammit, he can do something about it instead of just bitching at me. He could have a vasectomy and take care of me in that way—finally. Until now, it's always been my job. Well, since it didn't work for me, it's his turn. If he cares enough about something besides himself, he'll do it. But I just don't think he does.

It should be clear by now that both life cycle and culture influence women's sexual responsiveness. At the beginning, it's youth, inexperience, and the prohibitions against female sexuality that have to be overcome. Later it's children—small ones or teenagers—and the fear of another pregnancy that impose constraints. Through all this, however, most women move steadily toward a more expansive and open sexuality—partly because some life-cycle issues are resolved, and partly in response to the changing cultural context.

Between the time these midlife women grew to sexual maturity and the time they were raising their own daughters to womanhood, profound changes in the boundaries of acceptable sexual behavior had taken place. Whether in marriage or outside of it, what for the mothers had been inconceivable for their daughters has become commonplace.[14] While a few of the most daring of the mothers had premarital sexual relations furtively, now most of their daughters are doing so openly—many living in arrangements their mothers once would have considered sinful. While most of the mothers speak with pride—albeit tinged with some sadness—about their premarital sexual naiveté, their daughters would be embarrassed to make such an admission.

I have written elsewhere about the costs to young people of this revolution in sexual behavior, of the difficulties they suffer as they struggle to cast off their parents' teachings and to change their old consciousness to match the new behavior.[15] Imagine the impact on the parental generation. Suddenly, they find themselves living in a culture that not only gives license to formerly forbidden behaviors but exalts them. Suddenly, their unmarried children become sexually active, shocking their mothers, but reminding them also of their own repressed girlhood and young womanhood, of the moments now when they dare to wonder—quietly and to themselves, to be sure—whether those old ways were indeed the best ways:

> When my daughters got old enough to have sexual relations with boys, I had to ask myself some very hard questions. Was it better the way *I* was? Did I want them to spend the first ten or twelve years of their marriage getting through the sexual hang-ups my husband and I had? I guess I was somewhat jealous of the opportunities they had even though I was upset about what they were doing and afraid for them.

Sexually, it seemed as if the culture were exploding. Wherever they turned—on film, on stage, in print, or in life—they were bombarded with what seemed like a newly liberated sexual energy, reminded of what they might be missing, told these joys could also be theirs. Simultaneously, for the first time, relatively large numbers of women were speaking and writing about female sexuality, launching a concerted attack on established myths and stereotypes. For the first time, women were speaking to and for women, insisting on defining their own experience and challenging existing interpretations of female sexuality—from the general conception of sexual inertia in women to the more specific myth of the vaginal orgasm.

But these messages of liberation bring with them also a new set of constraints, new rules for acceptable sexual behavior. Thus, despite some changes wrought by the public discussion of female sexuality by feminist writers, women still tend to see their sexual behavior in highly individualistic and personalized terms, suffering from guilt, feelings of inadequacy, and sometimes desperation, when they are not meeting whatever may be the current standards for sexual behavior. This is the paradox of the new sexual freedoms: they are not simply "freedoms" but very often new coercions—new mandates for behavior that evoke guilt and discomfort in much the same way as did the old restrictions. Indeed, in our highly conformist and goal-oriented society, these new directives for sexual behavior can be more oppressive than the old ones since, when oppression comes in the name of *freedom*, it's more mystifying, hence harder to grasp and overcome.

Thus, if some women are found to be capable of multiple orgasms, it's not just a matter of pleasure for those who can or wish to, it becomes a requirement of adequate sexual performance—the goal toward which sexual activity is directed. The pleasure a couple may have experienced before the new "discovery" too often gets lost in the determined, sometimes tortured, march toward the new goal. If she doesn't have multiple orgasms, *she* feels terrible; if he can't "make her," *he* suffers as well. From blaming themselves, they shift to blaming each other, and back again. Wherever they come to rest at any given moment, their sexual relationship suffers—all in the service of the quest for something more, something "better." Nothing wrong with the search, of course; only in the way it's conducted, only in the fact that it's alienated from internal needs and longings, dominated by the latest sexual fad. This year it's multiple orgasm, last year it was vaginal—a quest that brought needless pain and suffering to millions:

> We kept trying and trying to get me to have a vaginal orgasm. That was the Big "A"—"A" for being female, "A" for validating your husband. It was the focus of all our sex. We were no longer human beings, but guinea pigs in our own experiment.

But it wasn't, in fact, their own experiment. They were responding not to some inner mandates but to external, social ones. To some, it must seem like the ultimate paradox that, while using the language of pleasure, the recent sexual revolution has managed to do to sex what even the Puritans couldn't quite achieve: to turn it into hard work.[16] Our concern about performance and technique leaves little or no room for a playful, pleasurable, sensuous sexuality—the kind of sexual play that would lead quite naturally to a woman's orgasm. Instead, we speak with a kind of grim resolve about the techniques for "getting her ready," both women and men missing the pleasures and delights to be found in the process. The word we use to describe this part of the sexual interaction tells the story: *fore*play, the part that comes before the real thing. If we understand the social context in which language, culture, and behavior interact, this comes not as a surprise, but as another demonstration of the many contradictions in the American culture—in this case, the tension between work and pleasure that dominates public policy as well as individual life, a tension built deep into the American consciousness, part of our Puritan heritage.[17]

In this context, let's look anew at the issue of faking orgasm and its meaning to women who do it. A very small proportion of the women I met fake orgasm all or most of the time. But most have done it at some time in their married lives, and almost half still do it at least once in a while.

That's no big news. The issue claimed my attention only because most of the women who fake orgasm, even those who do it only occasionally, speak intensely about the guilt and discomfort they feel now that the phrase *faking orgasm* has become practically an epithet. They tell of reawakened fears about their sexual adequacy; they talk about feeling judged. Most of all, they plead to be understood, wanting the meaning of what they do in bed to be known before the judgments are rendered.

But who's judging? Surely not the feminist writers who have spoken out so passionately about contorted social definitions of female sexuality. Surely not those same women who have written with such compassion about the sexual conflicts women face as a consequence of those distortions. Ask the women, and they'll say they don't know who, only that they feel they're being judged and found wanting, that they feel misunderstood because there's not enough talk about what it means to them to fake orgasm, why they do it:

> It's every place you turn these days. And it makes me uncomfortable because I don't think those women who shout about how terrible it is to fake it understand what it's like and why a woman would do it.

And why do you do it?

> It's just easier sometimes, that's all. I never tell a lie about it; it just happens. [Squirming uncomfortably in her chair] Joe doesn't ask me, right? He doesn't say, "Did you or didn't you," right? So what if I just let him think I did? He needs to believe it's that way. So what if I just give him that impression?

The "so what" is that she—and others like her for whom these comments are typical—is asking those questions of herself, not of me, suggesting that she's not so sure anymore that it's really all right:

You sound as if you're asking yourself that question, not me.

> Yeah, I never did before, though. I never thought it was a problem. I've never talked about my sex life to anyone, never. But there's so much talk about things like that now, you can't help hearing and reading things. And lately, people are talking about women faking it, so I worry about it. I guess now I ask myself if it's honest or not.

[Hesitantly] And you know, I begin to think maybe there's something wrong with me that I don't have an orgasm every time.

How does it happen that way? How does it happen that she's angry at "those women who shout about how terrible it is to fake it"? How does it happen that she worries that "there's something wrong with me that I don't have an orgasm every time"? Certainly, the feminist discussion about faking orgasm has dealt with the *why*; certainly it has tried to place the behavior in the context of social expectations, not personal responsibility. Then, how does it happen that this woman, and so many like her, haven't been able to hear that message?

Perhaps women fail to hear the reassurances because their own internal anxiety about what they do is so great that it must be disowned—projected outward onto anyone who calls attention to it. Perhaps they have trouble listening because the emphasis on the social sources of their sexual behavior indeed misses something in their own experience that makes those explanations seem alien. Perhaps they don't integrate the message because there's so much noise in the social world about sexual issues that it's hard to know who's talking, hard to know what's being said—perhaps also because they have had quite enough of the changing and often contradictory cultural expectations that influence and shape their sexuality.

I came to the issue of faking orgasm with my own biases, believing that the only reason a woman fakes it is to please her partner and that, no matter what, no woman ought to deny her own experience and sexual needs in this way. But the women I met taught me anew that human behavior is never so simple, and that changing it requires understanding, not injunctions—understanding, not just of individuals, but of the social system in which they live.

It's true, of course, that one reason women fake orgasm is to please their partner. But rather than viewing that in its negative sense, let's turn the prism a bit. Then we see that the behavior is born of their caring concern for him—a gift that's born of love and the ability to give of which I spoke earlier:

It isn't as if he's not a good lover, because he is. He doesn't rush and he's not abrupt. I need a lot of attention and loving, and he gives it. So why should I make him feel like he's fallen short or he's a failure just because I don't have an orgasm every time?

But there's another reason that women fake orgasm—one that speaks more to their own needs than to their husbands'. Women's orgasms are now big business— books, films, therapies, and the like, all part of a highly profitable industry devoted to telling us how to make it happen, all selling the notion that good sex must end in orgasm. Anything else is portrayed as not quite good enough, not quite the real thing. That means that women are now under the same performance pressures that men have experienced for so long—pressures that sometimes feel incompatible with internal needs, since many women insist that it's not necessary for them to have an orgasm every time they have sexual intercourse, that sometimes they can be quite content with a loving, tender sexual experience that does not culminate in orgasm.

Whether in men or in women, such pressures ultimately generate a response. Men may become impotent. But there's no such out for women, no physiological response that makes them absolutely unable to participate in sexual intercourse. For them, faking orgasm is one way to make *in*congruent demands feel more congruent—a reasonable response to an unreasonable situation, perhaps the only way to take some of the pressure off:

> I never thought it was a big thing until now. After all, I don't have to have an orgasm every time. Sometimes I just don't need or want one, but it's important to him, so I just let him think I have it.

For some women, then, faking orgasm may be the most effective protective device available—a way of dealing with sexual mandates from a culture and a husband that are experienced, if not always consciously understood, as alien and alienating; perhaps the only way a woman has at any given moment of pleasing her man, who may be trying so hard, yet unsuccessfully, to please her.

Still, the act of faking is alienating in itself, one might argue, and ought to be dealt with in that context. Indeed, that's an important and complex issue for both women and men—one major reason that they must learn to be more open with each other about this and other sexual issues. But that alienation doesn't start with faking orgasm. Faking it is only a symptom of alienated sexuality that begins early in childhood when girls begin the process of internalizing social definitions of female sexuality that distort their experience and alienate them from the messages of their own bodies. From the beginning, it's those external cultural definitions of sexuality that dominate our consciousness, circumscribe our behavior, and define our relationship to the sexual side of our personal identity. And it's those cultural definitions and the way they are responded to that deserve our closest attention. For to allow the discussion of faking orgasm to take place outside that deeper cultural context is to burden women and men with yet more reasons for guilt and more feelings of personal inadequacy.

With all the constraints, with all the problems, there's also a liberating side to the public discussion of sex and sexuality. Whether young, middle-aged, or old, women have been listening intently, hearing the new words, daring finally to believe their own experience, to give legitimacy to the messages of their own bodies:

> God, it was like a heavy load lifted from me—from both of us—to find we were okay. But it didn't come easy. It took years of reading all this stuff that's been coming out about women's orgasms, as well as some therapy, before we began to be able to accept that whichever way I get it, it's okay.

It's true that some few still speak sadly about being unable to take advantage of a cultural climate that offers permission for more sexual freedom than they ever before dreamed of:

I wish I could be free sexually like the kids, but I can't. It just doesn't work for me. Too many years of repression, I guess, and too many lessons that I learned too well.

But for most of the midlife women I met, life-cycle changes and a culture that encourages more sexual experimentation have come together to permit the opportunity for more gratifying sexual relationships even in long-term marriages. The years of sharing the same bed means they know each other better, are more likely to know what will bring sexual pleasure, are more trusting, and, therefore, are more able to be interdependent. With the children grown, there's more privacy, more opportunity for relaxed time alone:

We're a lot freer sexually now than we ever were before. And now that it's just the two of us in the house, you can do it when you feel like it, and you can take your time—you know, just lie there together for an hour or two, or even more. It makes all the difference when you don't have to worry who's listening in one of the upstairs bedrooms.

Such changes in personal sexual behavior do not come easily, nor do they come all at once. For some, one small change has led to larger ones; for others, one has been quite enough. And most of the time, they are changes that, by current standards of sexual practice, are small indeed. But that they have come at all is testimony to women's will to struggle toward change, testimony to their capacity for growth and development in the face of repressive early training that presents formidable obstacles.

But this expanding sexuality in women is not without its paradoxical effects, not without its positive and its negative sides. For just as there is a distinct and different pattern in the work careers of women and men, so there are differences in their sexual careers and development as well.

We know that for men the passage of years means a diminution of the sexual imperative. That lessening of sexual capacity has been discussed at length, usually with expressions of regret and sadness for the lost virility of youth. But rarely do we hear about the positive impact of that fact on midlife marriage:

It's not as frequent as when we were younger (it just seemed like all the time then), but it's more meaningful and it's more enjoyable. I don't ever feel pushed into it anymore, and that's good for both of us. We don't start out with all that stuff between us—you know, his wanting it and me resisting it. Now I want it as much as he does—sometimes even more. So sex now is really very good and much more varied than it ever was. [Laughing] I guess this is one time when less is more. I mean, there's less quantity but more quality—a lot more.

Indeed, for many women, the waning of the intensity and frequency of their husband's sexual need brings an important new dimension to their own sexual experience. Until this happens, many women never have the chance to feel the full force of their own sexual rhythm, never get to experience the frequency or potency of their own sexual desires. For until this time, that rhythm, that force, was coopted by the urgency of their husband's sexual demands. For the first time, many women discover that their sexual responsiveness is cyclical, the waxing and waning of its intensity related to the menstrual cycle:

> I'd heard talk that women were supposed to be sexier around their period, but I have to tell you that I didn't know anything about it firsthand until recently. I always just thought I wasn't very sexy and that I didn't have any peaks and valleys [with a self-mocking laugh], just valleys, you know. It was kind of a wonder to me to find out about the peaks, which happened after my husband kind of slowed down.

It's not that this woman, and others like her, didn't often enjoy the sexual encounter in the earlier years. The point is simply that the initiative then usually came from the men and was related to their wishes, needs, and sexual rhythm, not to the women's. When that changes, when the men's sexual need is no longer so clamorous, women often learn for the first time about their bodies' capacity for sexual response:

> I didn't even know it then, but I never knew what it was like to feel horny. He was always there waiting and ready, and most of the time I felt as if I had to say "yes" even if I didn't feel like it. Now I *love* feeling that I'm a sexual person for the first time in my life. It's sometimes hard to believe the change.

And now the paradox. For this very shift in the urgency of male sexual response that makes life easier in so many ways also means that women again are stuck with having to quiet their own rising sexual needs. For men, there seems to be no anxiety worse than the fear that their sexual powers are waning. Thus, at the first sign of diminished sexual capacity, a woman is likely to act as if on automatic pilot to protect her man from having to confront that reality. That means she doesn't initiate a sexual encounter even at the cost of muting her own heightened sexual imperative. For her, that's not so hard. She has, after all, been trained almost from birth to repress such feelings, to deny their existence:

> There's nothing worse than to push him and have him unable to perform. If he fails, it causes more problems than it's worth. It's a shame because I feel deprived now when I never would have before. But I worry more about him than I do about myself. So I just wait for him to ask me. That's easier all around.

Perhaps she's angrier about it now than she might have been in another era and at another time in her life—angrier because now the repression is more difficult to achieve, the deprivation experienced more keenly, and the culture somewhat more permissive of her acknowledging and expressing those feelings:

I know now that this is denying oneself, that it's an enormous part of life that I've denied for a long time. It's denying feelings of self-affirmation that you need more as you get older. I can't deny those feelings so easily anymore, and sometimes I get mad that I still have to because now he can't have sex so easily anymore.

Generally, however, most women don't speak that anger very readily—and surely not to their men. In fact, a woman who experiences this sexual turnabout in a marriage is likely to tread very gingerly. She's frightened for her husband—frightened that his fear of losing his sexual potency will, in fact, become a self-fulfilling prophecy. And she's frightened for herself—frightened because she knows his sense of manhood rests on his sexual performance; frightened because she understands how dangerous to him, to her, and to their marriage is any threat to that sexual capacity:

> It's a shame men are so sensitive about their virility. But it's true. When impotence hits a man, it's a real trauma. I don't want to put him in a position of having a failure and feeling so terrible that he won't be able to make it next time. Sure, I like sex; I enjoy it. But I'm not going to die without it for a while. So I just wait.

It's true, she won't "die without it," but she will temper her sexual desire because of her concern for her husband's sense of manhood, moderate her own yearning because of his need to believe in his sexual competency. And although almost always she'll speak words of understanding, she's usually ambivalent, if not downright angry, about the situation:

> [Bursting out spontaneously] It makes me furious that just when I become a real sexual being, he cops out. [Then immediately wanting to modify the anger] Oh, that's not fair, is it? It's not his fault. Sex has always been so important to him, and I know how hard it must be not to be able to do it all the time. I guess he was what you'd call a sexual athlete until a few years ago, when that all changed. I feel very badly for him, I really do. But I guess I can't help feeling bad for myself, too. It just seems like one of life's rotten tricks.

Half a lifetime of struggling with her repressed sexuality and a woman awakens to find her husband getting ready for sleep. Indeed, one of life's ironies, "one of life's rotten tricks"—especially galling because for so many years the situation was reversed, especially so because for so long her active sexual interest was what he pleaded for, argued for. Finally, she's the one who would like to initiate sexual activity. And she can't—restrained by the fear that he'll experience it as pressure, that he won't be able to complete the act.

How often does this happen? Often enough to engage the attention and concern of about half the women I spoke with. To whom does it happen? It's hard to discern a clear pattern. But age makes a difference. The women in this study between forty-five and fifty-five—all married to men from two to ten years older than they are—spoke about the waning of their husbands' sexual capacity more often than those who were younger. But even among the forty-year-olds, it was already being felt, already a subject of concern.

It's tempting to speak only of physiological differences—of the divergent developmental paths that put the peak of male sexuality a decade or more before the female sexual peak—to explain the diminution of sexual interaction in midlife families. But there's more than biology here, more than a regrettable physiological process at work. Indeed, that's too easy an answer, too static a notion—one that fails to take into account that sexual behavior takes place in the context of a relationship, that it is an *interaction* between two people, that much of the complexity of the total relationship is expressed in the sexual interaction. Ask yourself: If it were *just* biology, how could we explain the man whose impotence or waning sexual interest is replaced by a clamoring sexuality immediately after a divorce?

In fact, where serious incompatibility of sexual desire exists, it's often related at least as much to power struggles in the marriage as to distinctly physiological issues—power struggles that, as anyone who has lived in a marriage knows, tend to get played out in bed.[18] Certainly, it was true in over one-fourth of the families I met where those power struggles were alive, dominating the sexual interaction, determining its context and frequency. In some families, they were very old; in others, they were much newer—the product of a wife's emergence as a force to be reckoned with in this era when so many women are beginning to make their presence felt in new ways.

Where the struggle has a long history, it is played out in the sexual interaction in one of two ways. Either the husband is relatively indifferent to his wife's needs, taking what he wants sexually while she simply submits, or the wife withholds—sometimes physically, by refusing to participate, more often emotionally, by becoming inorgasmic. Where the struggle is more usually manifest by a husband's failing sexual interest at exactly the time when a wife's increasing independence outside the home begins to make itself felt inside the home as well—whether in the kitchen, in the living room, or in the bedroom. She may be trying her wings on a job or at school at the same time that she's beginning to experience and assert her sexual needs and desires. After years of hearing his complaints because she doesn't initiate sexual activity, she finally does. And he turns off:

> He always wanted me to take the first step, but when I began to do it, he was always too tired or [mimicking his posture and voice] he just didn't feel like it.

How did you feel about that?

> I didn't like it, but what can you do? With a man, you can't make him, can you? You just have to wait it out.

What do you think was going on for him?

> I don't *think*, I know. I had just gotten my first job and was very excited with my life. Things were changing around here and he didn't like it.

"Things were changing around here and he didn't like it"—a common story in families, especially common as women begin to assert their needs and expect some cooperation from their husbands in getting them met. In all families, such changes in long-standing interaction patterns are difficult. In some, they are met with resistance that expresses itself in a number of overt and covert ways—not least of them in the sexual dynamic:

> When we do have sex, it's good, and I always experience orgasm now, although it's a new feeling for me to feel as if it's not often enough. There's nothing much I can do about it right now because he doesn't want me to be the aggressor. [Her eyes bright, voice tinged with a mocking anger] Oh, he doesn't say that; he has said exactly the opposite for years, in fact. But he doesn't have to say it; there are other ways to get the message across.

What do you mean? What other ways?

> I went through a period of time a year or so ago when I took him at his word. I mean, I got fairly aggressive and let him know when *I* wanted sex. It didn't take long to see how uncomfortable that made him.

If he didn't say that, how did you know he was uncomfortable?

> It was easy; he just wouldn't be interested. After the first couple of times, he'd just be too tired or too something. Whatever he was, he wasn't interested. In fact, he hasn't been terribly aggressive himself for the last few years.

"The last few years"—precisely the period when she was appointed to a municipal commission in her city of residence and enrolled in college to begin study for a bachelor's degree. When these activities come together with a new assertiveness at home, as eventually they must, the change can be overwhelming indeed, seeming to both wife and husband to threaten the stability of the marriage.

One unconscious mechanism for coping with the anxieties stirred by such a threat is to seek to reestablish the former equilibrium—which means trying to restore the relationship to the way it was. Even when that "way" is recognized by both partners as far from ideal, they generally collude in the struggle to return to the past, since it is, at least, known. And psychologically, the *un*known can be more terrifying than the known, however bad that may be.

The sexual sphere, laden as it is with so many repressed emotional and cultural burdens—guilt, shame, rigidly sex-stereotyped notions of appropriate behavior— probably is the most readily manipulable, the most easily restored to the old balance. Thus, she stops being "aggressive," and he regains the sexual initiative—not a perfect solution but a tolerable one, one that allows both to retain something: she, her outside activities; he, the feeling that he remains in control.

The issue, then, is not just sex but also power—the struggle for one affecting the other in a continuing dynamic interaction. It's true, however, that the fact that these struggles are acted out in this particular way in the sexual arena is likely to be age-related. Male impotence or sexual withholding is a more probable weapon—one not so hard on the person wielding it—at fifty than at twenty-five.

There we have it: a complex picture of a delicate and complex part of life: sex and sexuality. For women, there seems to be a disturbing disjunction between sexual development and sexual behavior. At the developmental level, women's sexuality breaks the bonds of the early repressions and gathers force and power as they move into midlife. But at the behavioral level, something else happens. There, we see that despite the development and recognition of their own internal needs and sexual rhythm, despite all the talk about the liberation of sexuality for both women and men, we still can't discuss the sexual behavior of women in marriage outside the context of their relationships with their husbands[19]—at least, not when looking at the present generation of midlife women. No matter how we turn the prism, no matter what facet of the sexual interaction we examine, women still are largely reflectors of their men's needs and wishes—responding to male initiatives and imperatives, subduing their own.

It's true that, like all peoples in subordinate positions, women have ways of striking back—covert ways that even they don't fully understand. Thus, women who are constrained from acting directly and forcefully by a lifetime of training to appropriately "feminine" behavior may become nonorgasmic or unresponsive in an unconscious attempt to assert themselves and claim autonomy. Or they may fake orgasm to protect themselves from unwelcome demands. But the price for such behavior is high indeed, since it hurts the woman who does it at least as much as it deprives the man who is the object of it.

Whether their daughters' generation will effect some fundamental change is as yet unknown. For that answer, we must wait another twenty years. They may, indeed, be successful finally in rising "up from the pedestal,"[20] in developing a surer sense of their own sexuality, in gaining the ability to assert it, and in helping their men to develop those capacities of caring, concern, the nurturance that until now have been the almost exclusive province of women. We can only hope so and wish them well. But today, the needs and desires, the frustrations and discontents, that men bring to the relationship still dictate the behavior of most midlife women, if not their desires.

NOTES

This chapter appeared as "Sex? It's Gotten Better and Better," pp. 74–103 in *Women of a Certain Age: The Midlife Search for Self* by Lillian B. Rubin. Copyright © 1979 by Lillian B. Rubin. Reprinted by permission of Harper & Row. Lillian B. Rubin, Ph.D., M.F.C., Research Sociologist, Institute for Scientific Analysis, San Francisco, California 94123. Research supported by the Behavioral Sciences Research Division, National Institute of Mental Health, Grant No. MH 28167.

1. The women were drawn into the study by the snowball method of sampling. Each respondent was asked for referrals. Subsequent interviewees were chosen on the basis of having the most distant connection—both geographically and emotionally—from the person

making the referral. Such precautions ensured that the study would not be biased by being composed of friendship networks.

2. Although just under 22 percent of the women in this study were divorced, since the sexual issues they face generally are quite different from the issues facing those who remain married, this paper deals only with women who were married or in a stable, marriagelike relationship. At the developmental level, there are, of course, no differences. But at the behavioral level, sexual issues for divorced women at midlife are likely to be felt most keenly in the unavailability of what they would consider appropriate partners.

3. For more detailed data on sexual behavior among women of this generation, see Hunt (1974) and Kinsey, Pomerantz, Martin, and Gebhard (1953).

4. Over 60 percent of the women I met were virgins when married—a figure that corresponds roughly to the Kinsey et al. (1953) data.

5. The popular marriage manuals of the day are quite explicit on the issue of male responsibility for female orgasm. See, for example, Chesser (1947), Van de Velde (1930), and also Gordon and Shankweiler (1974) for a review of recent marriage manuals.

6. Kinsey et al. (1953) showed that by the fifteenth year of marriage, only 10 percent of his sample never reached orgasm in marital coitus, and that by the end of twenty years of continuous marriage, 47 percent were having orgasm, all or most of the time. These figures comport with the findings of the present study, where close to 90 percent of the women were orgasmic, over 50 percent more than half the time.

7. For a compelling argument about the physiological reasons for the increase in orgasmic potential after childbirth, see Sherfey (1973).

8. Several recent accounts of motherhood, written by women who are also mothers, speak to the joys and pains of what Adrienne Rich (1976) calls the "institution of motherhood." All make clear that many of the problems experienced by mothers in relation to their children are related to the cultural myths around motherhood and the guilt women experience from the internalization of that package of impossible expectations (Hammer, 1975; Lazarre, 1976; McBride, 1973; Rich, 1976).

9. See Hobbs and Cole (1976) for a replication of their 1963 study, which shows that decreased sexual responsiveness in women continues to be a major problem in the transition to parenthood.

10. See Miller (1976) for a recent study showing that children tend to decrease the frequency of marital companionship; therefore, their presence generally means also a decrease in marital satisfaction.

11. Hobbs and Cole (1976) show that among the top seven problems that men and women experience in the transition to parenthood is "feeling more distant from spouse."

12. Gagnon and Simon (1973) argued that this split between sex and love, this separation of sex from the total relationship, is the hallmark of male sexuality in the American culture.

13. Westoff and Jones (1977) showed striking increases in the use of vasectomy as a means of sterilization in the years between 1965 and 1975. Among white couples continuously married for fifteen to nineteen years, the proportion of vasectomies jumped from 4.4 percent in 1965 to 19.5 percent in 1975. Among those married twenty to twenty-four years, the corresponding proportions were from 5.9 percent to 19.5 percent.

14. Hunt (1974) compared sexual behavior in the 1970s with the data from the Kinsey studies of the early 1950s to document the sweeping changes in sexual behavior across the generations. See also Rubin (1976) for data and analysis of the *meaning* of such large cultural changes in the lives of the people who are trying to live with them.

15. Rubin (1976); Chapter 8, "The Marriage Bed," in *Worlds of Pain,* pp. 134–154.

16. See Slater (1976), who also argues that our preoccupation with orgasm and the techniques for achieving it is a natural extension of the Protestant work ethic, in which nothing is to be enjoyed for its own sake except striving.

17. One can see this tension between work and pleasure played out in the public policy debates about unwed mothers, where the discussion repeatedly focuses on their alleged "licentious" and "pleasure-seeking" behavior. In reading or listening to these discussions, it is difficult to escape the conclusion that our national rage is directed not simply at their sexual behavior but at the pleasure we fancy they take in it.

18. See Rubin (1976) for an extended discussion of the ways in which power struggles are played out in a marriage at any age and at any stage of the life cycle.

19. While not wishing to deny other forms of the family—in particular, the homosexual family—I am speaking here of heterosexual familes only.

20. This felicitous phrase is borrowed from the title of Kraditor's (1968) volume of feminist writings.

Getting Younger While Getting Older: Family-Building at Midlife

One would have to be living in a cave to miss the news that the generation that brought us the sexual revolution, the antiwar movement, the counterculture, feminism, and the gay rights movement—the one that thought it would be forever young when it coined the mantra, "You can't trust anyone over thirty"—is now turning fifty. As this best educated, most literate generation in history has brought middle age out of the closet, book shelves bulge with volumes telling us that getting old isn't so bad, that women can still be "red hot mamas" and men great sexual studs.

Letty Cottin Pogrebin, looking svelte and gorgeous on the cover of her book, *Getting Over Getting Older,* assures us that, distressing though they may be, the lumps, bumps, and thinning hair of aging don't really count. In *New Passages* Gail Sheehy offers up a vision of middle age that shows us leaping from what she calls the "flourishing forties" into the "flaming fifties" and flowing from there into the "serene sixties." Even Betty Friedan has gotten into the act with a book called *The Fountain of Age* in which she insists that age is a state of mind and that the seventies and eighties are a breeze so long as we find the secret to what she calls "vital aging." And in *The Superhormone Promise,* Dr. William Regelson denies the aging process altogether, declaring that aging is "not a normal life event but a disease."

These are comforting ideas to some, I suppose. Me? I want to shout: *Oh yeah! Tell it to my brain when it has trouble getting perfectly ordinary words to my tongue. Or to my body when it huffs and puffs up a hill it climbed easily just a couple of years ago. Or to my drooping belly that no longer responds to the crunches that used to keep it in shape.*

I'm not saying that life careens downhill after fifty. I've lived long enough to know that the realization of the decades to come is never as bad as the anticipation. Not even seventy, although that, I must admit, is a serious jolt. But to talk about "the flaming fifties" and "serene sixties" so oversimplifies the modern midlife experience as to be nonsensical. There's nothing about the decade of the fifties that leads us inescapably to flaming, nor do the sixties ensure serenity. Instead, much depends on how we're connected to the social and institutional world in which our lives are embedded. That, in very important ways, is what determines our experience at any age.

Still, it's true that life after fifty isn't what it was in my mother's day. We not only look different now but have a different sense of the possibilities for living these years. Indeed, despite all the angst about graying hair, receding hairlines, expanding waistlines, sagging muscles, and failing memory, older is getting younger all the time. The buxom matron, her gray hair tinted blue, of my mother's generation has given way to a trim blonde dressed in jeans, running shoes, and a t-shirt. Newspapers and magazines feature story after story about how to beat the aging crunch. Fifty-eight-year-old Tina Turner, dressed like a teenager, appears triumphantly on the pages of the *New York Times;* the same newspaper publishes a story about "start-over dads" that celebrates, among others, the actor Tony Randall who became a first-time father at seventy-seven; in the personals columns of a San Francisco paper, an "all around nice guy" in his "early sixties" advertises for a woman "young enough to have a baby or two" because he "wants to be a dad again"; and the news of a sixty-three-year-old first-time mother leaves the world wondering what's next.

In my own life I was just three years out of graduate school when my fiftieth birthday came around, which meant that I had a very different experience as I lived that decade than did women who were living more traditional lives. It isn't a matter of good or bad, better or worse; it was just different—and complicated with costs and benefits of its own.

In 1963—the year I turned thirty-nine and decided it was time to get the college degree that my class and gender had denied me in my youth—such an experience was most unusual, since so few people, whether men or women, undertook that kind of life-changing adventure at midlife. In fact, throughout the eight years I spent on the Berkeley campus working my way through a B.A., M.A., and Ph.D., I never saw another adult—woman or man—in any of my classes. Now it's so common that most colleges have some kind of program to ease the way for returning adults.

It wasn't that women or men in the past were so content with their lives. But then there was a sense of being locked in by virtue of age and stage, and most people had a very different sensibility from the one we know today about what they thought possible or appropriate.

For me, there was enormous excitement about embarking on a career at a time when so many other women were depressed and anxious about what they would be doing with the rest of their lives. But it wasn't an unmixed blessing. For one thing, being a student on a college campus during the turmoil of the mid-1960s and early seventies anchored me in generational issues that were very far from my own. Identifying with the students, sharing their struggles, kept me connected to them in powerful ways, allowing—for brief moments—the illusion that I was one with them. But I was also twenty-plus years their senior, which meant that I could never fully be one of them. Nor did I want to be. When I turned to people who were my age mates, however—especially women who had been my friends before I became a student—I found that the bonds of common experience that formerly held those relationships together had frayed under the stress of lives that had taken such different roads.

By the time I got my Ph.D., I felt like a misfit in both places. Some parts of me and my life were connected to the twenty-eight- and thirty-year-olds with whom I had gone through my graduate program, other parts to my fifty-year-old peers. I was the quintessential marginal person, *of* each group but never fully *in* either. And I still am. The people I call my colleagues and friends today are almost universally many years younger than I am.

Now that age is no longer a predictor of the shape of a life, people commonly find themselves in a similar predicament, as any older parent of a small child will testify. The particulars of the experience may be different, but the underlying conflicts are the same. I hear it repeatedly from both men and women whose lives are out of phase with their age.

Just recently a forty-seven-year-old patient who's a highly successful professional woman came into my office saying that, after having spent the morning registering her three-year-old son in a preschool, she wasn't sure whether to laugh or cry. "I felt ancient," said this strikingly attractive woman who, to me at least, looks ten years younger than her age. "When I walked into the room and looked around, I felt like David's grandmother. Most of the other mothers were in their twenties, maybe early thirties, and they looked even younger.

"It isn't just how they look or act, it's who they are. I look at them and think, 'That was a lifetime ago.' Yet I know that in some ways I'm going to have more in common with them than with women my age who never had kids or whose kids are in college. Their kids are the ones who will be David's playmates. But I can't imagine what basis we could find for a friendship besides that; there's a gap the size of the Grand Canyon between us. I mean I've experienced so much that they don't even know about." She paused for a moment of reflection, then continued with a pained laugh, "There's not a lot more to say about it except that being there this morning was a humbling experience, especially when a couple of the other mothers came up and cooed over David and then asked if I was his grandmother."

Twenty years ago when I wrote about midlife women in a book called *Women of a Certain Age,* most people married young, had their children soon after marriage, and reached the stage we call midlife at roughly the same time that the nest was emptying. Therefore, I knew before I started that I'd be interviewing women whose children had either recently gone from the nest or were getting ready to fly away. And that's who they there—a whole cohort of women who were roughly the same age and at the same stage of life. Now, as I'm in the middle of the research for a new book on the subject, I have no idea what I'll find when I open a door.

Sure, there were some class and cultural differences then, just as there are now. Working-class women, who married in their late teens and whose children did the same, were likely to be in their late thirties or early forties when their last child left home. College-educated middle-class women, who were older when they married, generally were in their mid- to late forties when they reached that stage. But the spread was relatively narrow, and the median clustered around 46.

These small variations aside, people of a similar age were almost universally at the same life stage and facing the same marker events. The transitions of adult life—the move from single to married, for example, or the passage to parenthood, or the end of its active phase—were behind them. With few exceptions, the whole generation stood together at the psychological and chronological midpoint of their lives. Which meant also that the developmental tasks they faced, and the psychological and sociological issues that would arise from them, were very much the same.

Men and women faced different issues, of course. For men this stage of life brought them in a face-to-face confrontation with the fact that they had been at the same job or career for all or most of their adult lives; that, perhaps, they had not accomplished all they'd hoped; that their physical and sexual powers were waning; that what lay ahead was more of the same until retirement—which then was still mandatory at sixty-five in most institutions.

For women, most of whom had spent their lives in the traditional women's role in the family, it meant a major shift. After years of family work, they were suddenly unemployed—or if not *un*employed, certainly *under*employed. The job-market skills of their youth were rusty, their confidence in their ability to make their way in the world outside the home shaky. After a lifetime of being busy and useful, they suddenly faced each day asking what they would do with the rest of their lives, how they would live the years ahead now that the children were gone.

These differences between men and women notwithstanding, what's more significant for this discussion is the fact that both were brought into confrontation with the social and psychological realities of middle age at the same age and stage of the family life cycle. That's no longer true for either women or men.

The two decades since I last studied midlife have brought with them revolutionary changes in when and how women and men make choices about the various life transitions that confront them. Perhaps for the first time in history, age is no longer a predictor of life stage for a very large number of Americans. Instead, the lockstep life course trajectory of earlier generations has given way before a complicated and dramatic series of changes in the culture, the economy, and the life span.

The changing culture, coupled with new reproductive technologies, allow women to have babies well into their forties and beyond. Sperm banks provide the reproductive means for men who can't do it themselves and for women who want to do it without a man. If aging eggs are the problem, no matter. Egg donors make it possible for a fifty-year-old woman to carry a child. If that doesn't work, there are surrogates who, for a price, will carry the baby and hand it over at birth.

It's not uncommon, therefore, to find forty-five-year-old women worried about measles, mumps, and baby sitters, while fifty-year-old men gaze adoringly at a new infant—sometimes a first child, sometimes the beginning of a second family. They may be chronologically middle-aged, but their place in the social world, the issues of living that engage them, the way they feel about themselves, their lives, and their aging are very far from those that preoccupy the woman or man of the same age who has just sent a last child off to college. For the sociology and psychology of midlife, the sense of constraints and possibilities, depends on the web of relationships and responsibilities within which a life is embedded.

Which brings us to the question: How and why have such changes come to pass? Obviously, we have been witness in recent decades to a complicated and intertwined series of social, cultural, and demographic shifts that have profoundly changed our lives. But one thing is clear: Without the spectacular lengthening of the life span this century has brought none of this would be possible.

Just one hundred years ago the life expectancy at birth of the average American was forty-seven; now it's nearly eighty. Then only half of all Americans who reached the age of twenty lived to see sixty-five. As we approach the end of the century, sixty-five seems young and people over eighty are the fastest growing segment of our population. Even one hundred no longer seems just a wistful dream. Measured in evolutionary time, this near-doubling of our life span is nothing less than a demographic miracle—an astonishing, exhilarating, frightening miracle.

For all of us, then, no matter what our life situation may be, questions about how we'll live all the years ahead are inescapable. One way of dealing with those questions is in the search for renewal, for ways to renew and revitalize ourselves and our lives. We change jobs; we go back to school to train for a new career; we refuse to retire or we quit and go off to climb a mountain, real or metaphorical; we move from city to country or the other way around; we have face lifts, liposuction, and chemical peels to conceal from ourselves and the world the signs of our aging; we spend hours each week running along the city streets and lifting weights at the gym in an effort to defeat it altogether. Or most dramatic of all, we alter what has until now been the accepted path of the life course. We delay marriage and childbearing for ten, fifteen, twenty years beyond what was normal just a couple of decades ago and presto, we have found a way to fill at least some of those years.

I don't mean that people suddenly wake up one morning and say, "Hey, now that I know I'll probably live to be eighty, I don't have to get married at twenty anymore." Or that they're conscious of what motivates their changed ideas about the timing and sequencing of these life events. It's more like an unconscious process whereby the changed social circumstances give birth to new options that seem to seep into consciousness when we're not looking.

Consequently, midlife today is that oddly contradictory period when doors both open and close, when everything seems possible and nothing does. It's a time of reckoning, of celebration as we consolidate life's gains, and torment as we confront our losses, a time of decline and growth, of endings and beginnings, that often feels like both a curse and a blessing.

So, for example, a fifty-two-year-old college professor—the father of a three-year-old daughter from his current marriage and a nineteen-year-old son from an earlier one—spoke with me about his feelings about his new family: "It's like getting to do the best parts over again. The years when my first marriage worked best were when Steve was little. The sweetness he brought to the world made a difference in how my wife and I related to each other. Then it was all gone. Now with my little daughter, I get to live that sweet time over again, only this time my life is graced with a marriage that really works, too."

But as is too often the case with good news, bad news lurks just below the surface. "The only problem," he continued, his expression saddening as he spoke, "is that I worry I might not live long enough to see how she grows up. I think about that a lot. Will I be around to see her graduate from college or get married?"

In the past the markers of midlife were defined by age and life stage. People married, bore children, and came to midlife at roughly the same age. Now it's much more complicated. Take age, for example. Twenty years ago I did a study of midlife women in which the lower end of the age range was thirty-five, the upper end, fifty-four. But with people marrying and bearing children so much later while they also live healthy, vigorous lives well beyond anything we might have imagined earlier, the definition of midlife has shifted upward dramatically.

Now thirty-five seems much too young to define the beginning of middle age and sixty-five has barely seen the end of it. The same is true about old age. Yesterday sixty-five was old; today a sixty-five-year-old is as likely to be seen jogging along the city streets in sweats and running shoes as to be rocking on the front porch and watching the world go by.

We can't define midlife by life stage anymore either. Not when one forty-five-year-old woman is inching toward grandmotherhood, while her next door neighbor is clutching her pregnant belly as she chases after her two-year-old. Or when one fifty-five-year-old man is a new father, while the guy who works at the next desk has just seen his last child leave home. For common ground, whether psychological or sociological, is vitiated where the life course has taken such different turns.

I'm saying, then, that while everyone turns fifty, what that event means in a life, how it is experienced, depends heavily upon the choices a person made—or didn't make—about marriage and family when he or she was twenty-five. It isn't just that the lives of the pregnant forty-five-year-old and the grandmother are so at odds. It's that their very sense of themselves is different—the way they look at the world, the problems they see ahead, the way they deal with their own aging. So, for example, Carolyn Kendall, a forty-eight-year-old professional with two children, ages three and five, talked about the differences between her and the woman who lives next door. "I have this next door neighbor who's not much older than I am—maybe fifty—but she got married right out of college and her kids are all grown. I like her; she's a very nice person, but I just don't have much in common with her. While she was raising her kids, I was still raising hell. Now, she's free to do whatever she wants, and I'm working thirty hours a week while I try to be a good mom and a good wife, and I can hardly stay awake past nine o'clock. She's waiting for her kids to make her a grandmother, and I'm thinking about where we're going to get the money to send two kids to private school because the public schools in this city are so lousy.

"Don't get me wrong. I adore my kids, and I love being a mom. But talk to anyone my age who has little kids like this, and all you'll hear is how tired they are all the time. I sometimes think God or nature or whatever didn't mean for us to be having kids when we're so old."

Listening to Carolyn I couldn't help wondering whether she'd decide some things differently if she could rewrite the script of her life. So I asked. She looked at me thoughtfully, turning the question over in her mind, then shook her head. "I don't know, sometimes I think I would, then I realize I couldn't have done it differently. Sure I know there are some real advantages to having your children when you're younger, but I wasn't ready, and I would never have been the kind of mother I am now. If I had put my career in low gear and done a mommy track kind of thing then, I would have resented it. Now that I've done the career thing and know the ups and downs of it, it's not that important to me anymore. I've done it, so I can slow it down now and it's fine.

"Also there's something about having little kids at this age that keeps you feeling young." She stopped talking for a brief moment, then, with a rueful smile, said, "Yeah, I know, I've been in the position where someone thought I was their grandmother, and I sure didn't like that. But I'm talking about how I feel inside myself, and there it's like I can't get with the idea that I'm not far from fifty. I look at these two little creatures I just bore, and I think, *Fifty just isn't me.*

It's not so simple, however. It's true that being the mother of young children allows the illusion of youth and vigor. But her body tells a different story, as the hot flashes of menopause thrust her willy nilly into the realization of her aging. Repeatedly, women in their late forties talked of this anomaly—the disparity between the "young" lives they're living and their aging bodies. "When I think about the fact that I gave birth to a child four years ago and now I'm beginning menopause, it makes no sense at all," said forty-nine-year-old Rebecca Morgan, shaking her head in wonder. "But that's what modern technology has done for me and a lot of other women. I'm grateful for it; I would never have been able to have a child without it. But I'm very much aware that there's something peculiar about being so close to childbirth *and* menopause. It's hard to get your mind around it, isn't it? *I mean, they're separated by only four years.*

But even menopause is a different experience today. The biological changes are still with us, of course, but how they're defined culturally is light years away from what it was like for women of earlier generations. Even as late as 1970 menopause was still a quiet, if not shameful, secret—a biological event that couldn't be avoided but that nobody talked much about, not even women among themselves. Consequently, the myths around menopause—none of them kind—were legion, while real knowledge was scarce. Now there are hundreds of articles about menopause in newspapers and magazines; books about it hit the best-seller list; and in a recent TV movie based on the old serial *Cagney and Lacey,* Sharon Gless gets hot flashes while her partner Tyne Daley waves a little battery-operated fan in front of her face.

So although menopause is still with us, it's trendy now. Which makes a big difference in how the event itself is experienced. For while it's a distinctly biological phenomenon, the changed cultural norms surrounding it help to create a psychology of menopause that's quite different from the old one. When it's no longer a shameful secret, when it's no longer defined as the end of womanhood—as if we were nothing but baby machines—when we no longer believe it's the end of sexuality, women come to this biological event with a sense of freedom and confidence few women of my generation knew. As one forty-eight-year-old woman said, "No conversation with my friends ever goes by these days without at least one joke about menopause."

But what about the people who made more traditional decisions about how they'd live their first adulthood? Obviously, they're also dealing with the physical changes that aging brings, but because it fits the pattern of their lives, it doesn't seem so disjunctive to them. For them, too, work-related problems and conflicts—from child care to maternal guilt to the division of family labor—generally are in the past. With the children on their own, these families find themselves with a level of financial and social ease they could only dream about in their earlier years.

Marjorie Rathman, Carolyn Kendall's fifty-year-old neighbor, whose children are grown and no longer living at home, talks quite differently about turning fifty. "I can't exactly explain it," she said as she struggled for words, "but it was like a door opened. I did everything I was supposed to do, and now I'm young enough to be able to do anything I want. When I look at Carolyn next door, I think, *Whew, I wouldn't want to be there now.* She's always pushed and rushed, never any time for herself or to enjoy life. I don't know how she does it."

"Did you ever feel cheated about not having a career in those earlier years?" I asked Marjorie.

"Well, it's not like I gave up my work altogether. It's just that I didn't have the high-flying kind of career that women who didn't have children could have. So, sure, sometimes I had a hard time when I'd begin to think their lives looked so glamorous while I was doing diapers and going to little league and driving kids all over town. But all I can tell you is that I'm not sorry now. I'd rather be where I am than where people like Carolyn are. My life seems more in sync in every way than hers."

She paused a moment as if thinking over what she had been saying, then hastened to add, "Don't misunderstand me; I'm not criticizing how women like Carolyn live. It's a choice, and I think it's wonderful that people can make those kinds of choices now. But I think whatever way you go you have problems, and all I'm saying is I'd rather have mine than hers. At least now when I'm fifty, I feel like I have a whole life ahead of me. By the time Carolyn gets to this place, she'll be close to seventy, and there won't be that much life left."

Marjorie's husband, Warren, echoed his wife's sentiments. Having watched others around him—neighbors, workmates—who, at his age, are grappling with issues he long ago put away, he said with firm conviction, "I don't envy these fifty- and sixty-year-old guys who have little kids. Hell, they're going to be working to pay the bills right up to the day they die. Yeah, yeah, I hear all the talk about how great it is that people can do what they want when they want, but, you know, I never saw one of those guys who isn't feeling a hell of a lot of pressure. Who can blame them? They don't know whether they'll be able to work long enough to get their kids through school. How can you enjoy the kids when that's always there grating on you? On top of that the guys I know like that, they're always pooped."

When women talked about being "tired all the time," it usually meant they didn't get enough sleep. For the men, whose definition of self is so often tied to physical prowess, it was more troubling to find themselves unable to keep up with a child. "I just don't have it anymore; my back won't take it," said forty-nine-year-old Bruce Greenfield, his expression caught between sadness at the loss and anger at the realization of his limitations. "I can't do what I could do even ten years ago, but how do I tell my son I ran out of steam just when he came along. You know, it's the one thing you never think about when you keep saying later, later."

"Would you choose to do it differently if you could?" I asked.

Like so many others, he couldn't answer the question easily. After a long thoughtful pause, he sighed and said, "Yeah, I think I would. It would feel a lot different at this point if I were even ten years younger. I'd give a lot to have the kind of stamina I had then. But it wasn't in the cards then. I mean, I knew I'd get married and have kids one day, but until I met Annie, every time I was involved with a woman who brought up the subject, I was out of there. When I look at it now, I can say yeah, it would have been better to do it earlier, but then I sure wasn't ready to give up my freedom. I could do what I wanted; if I wanted to work late, there was no one to hassle me to be home and more "present," to use one of my wife's favorite words. So what do you think? I wanted it all, huh? I guess my generation thought we could have it all, too. But it never really works that way, does it?"

In many ways the men I talked to seemed less comfortable with their choices than the women. It isn't that they love and value their children and family life less, but they tend to be more resentful of the work-family conflicts that are inevitable for parents of young children. For women, those conflicts are usually resolved on the side of family; men more often come down on the side of work. Which makes for conflicts with wives that men speak of angrily.

"I don't know what she wants," complained Joe Thurman, the father of two children, aged two and six. "She wants to live this good life and wants me to cut back on work. But she's the one who wanted our second child. Don't get me wrong; I love that little guy, but somebody's got to be out there working to pay the bills now and make sure they have what they need later on, too. She says she doesn't want to work full-time anymore because she doesn't want to miss out on watching the kids grow up. That's great; I like that she's home more with them; she's a great mother and they need her. But then that means I'm it. I'm fifty-two years old; if I don't do it now, pretty soon there'll be no time left to make sure we've got those kids protected."

Repeatedly men talked about their fears for their financial future in ways that women did not. I don't mean to say that women don't also worry about how they'll educate and care for their children. But despite some important shifts in family roles, a man still expects—and generally is expected—to be the major family breadwinner. And most of the time, he is. Which means that, if he has a new baby at forty-five or fifty he's worried, not just whether he'll be around to see that child go off to college, but how long he'll have to work to make sure she or he can get there.

But many of these families would be grateful if this were all they had to worry about. For they are truly caught in the middle of the generational sandwich—women and men who, because they started so late, are raising small children at precisely the time when their parents are entering old age. So at the same time that their lives are consumed with work-family issues at home, a sick or failing parent makes a claim on their time, attention, energy, and perhaps money. For those whose parents live in distant cities, it means, as one man put it, "running back and forth across the country putting out fires." For those whose parents live nearby, there are the usual life needs— from taking them shopping to getting them to the doctor's office—that eat into time that isn't there. A set of complications for adult children that will become more and more frequent as their parents' lives are extended into their nineties and beyond.

Obviously, families that followed a more traditional trajectory also face the disruption that the needs of aging parents can set in motion. Men and women in these families talked often about the plans they had to set aside—long-awaited travel adventures, a move from city to country or from suburb to city—because a parent needed care. But for the late-starting families, the problems of failing parents are immeasurably complicated by the fact that they're already greatly overstressed by the need to feed, house, clothe, and raise small children.

For all the problems of living that confront them, however, it's not all trouble for people whose lives are not patterned on the traditional timetable. Older parents generally have a better sense of themselves and what they want. They've had years of freedom, plenty of good times, and careers that have been at least somewhat gratifying. Therefore, the constraints of parenthood don't weigh as heavily on them as on the twenty-year-old. And despite the men's worries about the financial future, at midcareer they have more resources to cope with such problems as child care and education than more traditional families had at the same stage of family life. I suspect, also, that regardless of class and social circumstances, there are far fewer cases of child abuse among older parents than among younger ones whose own unmet needs may make them less able to tolerate a small child's needs and demands. Still, these are revolutionary social changes, and as with all revolutions, this one, too, has its costs and benefits. Some people celebrate these changes, believing that life is richer now. Some mourn the past, finding today's world more difficult to manage. In fact, comparing better or worse, harder or easier, makes little sense, partly because such comparisons nearly always rest on memories of the past that are better than the reality ever was. It's somewhat like the idealization of the dead, where even some pretty monstrous characters get whitewashed in the minds of those left behind.

The fact is that today women are tired because they have too much to do; yesterday they were depressed because they didn't have enough to keep them busy. In the past men worried about dying at fifty; now they're concerned about what they'll do with their lives for thirty years beyond that marker event. We may think of our increased life span as a gift, a burden, or some combination of the two. But there's no doubt that it offers options for living that were impossible before—options that are driven by a set of social, culture, and demographic shifts that won't go away because we wish it were so.

As we reflect on these transformations, there's not much doubt that life has become more complicated—or at least differently so—as new possibilities have brought with them new ways of being along with a variety of new problems. For when you turn the sociology of aging on its head, as we have in these last two decades, there are inescapable social and psychological consequences. Our task now, it seems to me, is not to waste our time in nostalgia for a past that never was but to figure out how we as a society will live with the new possibilities that are open to us in the most fruitful way.

REFERENCES

Friedan, Betty. 1993. *The Fountain of Age.* New York: Simon and Schuster.

Matthews, T. J., and S. J. Ventura. 1997. "Birth and Fertility Rates by Educational Attainment: United States, 1994." *Monthly Vital Statistics Report* 45, no. 10, supp. Hyattsville, MD: National Center for Health Statistics.

Pogrebin, Letty Cottin. 1996. *Getting Over Getting Older: An Intimate Journey.* Boston: Little, Brown.

Regelson, William. 1997. *The Superhormone Promise: Nature's Antidote to Aging.* New York: Pocket Books.

Rubin, Lillian B. 1979. *Women of a Certain age: The Midlife Search for Self.* New York: Harper and Row.

Sheehy, Gail. 1995. *New Passages: Mapping Your Life Course across Time.* New York: Random House.

U.S. Bureau of the Census. 1996. *Statistical Abstracts of the United States.* Washington, DC: Government Printing Office.

Ventura, S. J., J. A. Martin, T. J. Matthews, and S. C. Clarke. 1996. "Advance Report of Final Natality Statistics, 1994." *Monthly Vital Statistics Report* 44, no. 2, supp. Hyattsville, MD: National Center for Health Statistics.

Out of the Closet

I sometimes think the story of aging in our time is a tale of "yes, buts ..." Yes, the fact that we live longer, healthier lives is something to celebrate, but it's not without its costs, both public and private. Yes, the definition of *old* has been pushed back, but no matter where we place it, our social attitudes and our private angst about getting old largely remain intact.

If a public conversation on aging is to have any value, we need to talk about how much has changed and how little, about the social and psychological meanings of living so long and how they interact with each other in a society that, at best, is ambivalent about its old. We need to think aloud about the impact of our increasingly long life span on those who follow us; about the pleasures, the pains, and the many sorrows this stage of life brings; about the gift our expanded life span has bestowed upon us and the significant costs that accompany it.

But instead of complexity, we get oversimple tales about the wonders of the "new old age," along with treatises on "age power"[1] and tips on how to make these "the power years."[2] I sometimes think old age is two different countries. There's the real old age for those of us who live there and know its conflicts and contradictions. Then there's the old age of those who write about it, most of them middle-aged women and men who live a long way from my country and are so frightened of coming to it that they grasp at half truths and offer them up as if they were the whole story.

Until recently, aging and old age lived largely in the social closet. But with 78 million baby boomers—that huge cohort that shaped everything it touched as it swept through society, the one that thought it would be forever young when it coined the mantra "You can't trust anyone over thirty"—now turning sixty, silence is no longer possible.

As this best educated, most literate, and largest generation in history moves toward old age, concerns about our long life span have come center stage. Economists worry about the impact of our increasingly aging population on the nation's productivity; politicians wring their public hands about how the old will soon bankrupt what's left of our social welfare system; and some of the younger generations, many of whom don't believe they'll ever be old, complain that there will be nothing left for them. Occasionally, too, we read about the abuse of the old—a nursing home where residents are seriously mistreated, a famous family in which a 53-year-old son accuses his 82-year-old father of abusing his 104-year-old mother[3]—and we're appropriately horrified.

But while the wealthy and prominent make headlines, the one to three million older Americans who are abused by their caregivers go largely unnoticed.[4] For like the homeless, those who are already old are mostly not in our social sights, except maybe when they do something to call attention to themselves, like make demands on the public treasury for such things as insurance to cover prescription drugs. We have an epithet for them then: "greedy geezers," coined a decade or so ago by then senator Alan K. Simpson. Or when they walk irritatingly slowly as they board the bus or the subway. We're impatient, wishing they'd get out of our busy way, out of sight, and we look away, repelled, loathe to see what could be our future.

In his highly regarded treatise, *Aging and Old Age,* Richard Posner considers "the factors that from a rational-choice perspective are likely to influence the treatment the elderly will receive from society." It makes "biological sense," he writes, that while we're "genetically programmed" to protect the young, we're not similarly wired toward protection of the old. "Inclusive fitness is unlikely to be promoted by the devotion of huge resources to the survival of persons who, by reason of advanced age, are not reproductively or otherwise productive, either actually or (like children) potentially."[5]

Strip away the awkward language and what you have is a cold calculus that we're not worth the cost, whatever that may be. Small wonder we so fiercely resist the idea of being old. Who wants to be invisible? Or to have so little social value? Or to be criticized as greedy when all you've asked for is something citizens of every other Western democracy take for granted?

Both Friedan and Posner published their work on aging in the early 1990s when it was already clear that we were witnessing a demographic revolution in the making. By 2007, it had arrived. Over 36 million Americans—12 percent of the total population—presently are over sixty-five. In the single year between 2003 and 2004, 351,000 people arrived at the cusp of old age. This before the first of the baby boomers begin to reach that milestone. After that the numbers skyrocket. The Census Bureau projects that by 2050, 86.7 million people, roughly 21 percent of the projected population at that time, will be sixty-five or older. That's an increase of 147 percent over the present number. Compare that to the population as a whole, which will have increased by only 49 percent over the same period.[6]

Given the drama of these demographics and their implication for the future of our society and the people who live in it, it's no surprise that age is on our collective mind big time these days. Predictions vary depending on the mind-set of the predictors on whether they see the glass as half full or half empty. The pessimists see disaster as they warn of the crises that lie in wait: The financial burdens on the social system will prove unsupportable. Medicare and Social Security will go broke.

The economy will falter as the nonproductive old outnumber the productive young. The burden on families will be intolerable as sixty-five-year-olds find themselves the caregivers for their eighty-five-year-old parents at the same time that they're worrying about their future and how they'll support their own old age.

Those who see a half-full glass tell us the worries are overblown. Sure, they say, the social institutions designed to ease the old age of earlier generations, whether health care, housing, or Social Security, are not adequate to deal with the huge aging population that looms ahead. But with the political will and sensible planning, old programs can morph into new ones that will meet the realities of our continually expanding life span.

True, the optimists grant, many sixty-five-year-olds are caring for eighty-five-year-old parents, but 60 percent of those over eighty-five continue to live independently. They agree, too, that the ratio of those over sixty-five to what we now call "the working-age population" will nearly double in the next fifty years. But, the optimists remind the pessimists, the working-age population is already being redefined upward, as witness the legislation outlawing age discrimination, the disappearance of mandatory age-based retirement in government and industry, and the increase in the age at which Americans can claim Social Security benefits. With the promise of an aging population that is heartier, healthier, and better educated than ever before, it's reasonable to assume, the optimists insist, that increasing numbers will remain in the work force.

Maybe, maybe not, the pessimists reply. Ask the 40 percent of sixty-five-year-olds who are taking care of their aged parents and you'll hear another tune. In fact, even those whose parents live independently find themselves preoccupied with their welfare, worrying about a future they know is coming, wondering how they'll manage when it does. What's more, the idea of being on the job until eighty and beyond may appeal to a Supreme Court justice or a world-famous television journalist, but is that what the average person, whose job is neither so important nor so glamorous, wants to do with these newfound years?

The arguments continue, but they're more form than content. No matter which side of the optimist/pessimist divide they fall on, everyone agrees that something new is emerging, something we might call the next life stage, the one that never existed before, the one for which we have no name and no template. We're living longer but doing it better, getting older but staying younger, and no one quite knows what to do about it—not even whether it's a blessing or a curse.

While the experts talk, those of us who are old are busy living the reality of aging in a society that worships youth and pitches it, packages it, and sells it so relentlessly that the anti-aging industry is the hottest growth ticket in town. Think that's hyperbole? Plug the term "anti-aging" into Google and you'll come up with over three million hits.

From the scientists tucked away in their labs who, with the aid of federal dollars, search for the key to yet a longer life, to the 17,000 physicians and scientists who are members of the recently spawned American Academy of Anti-Aging Medicine whose Website boasts that "aging is not inevitable" but "a treatable medical disease,"[7] to the plastic surgeons who exist to serve our illusion that if we don't *look* old, we won't *be* or *feel* old, to the multibillion-dollar cosmetics industry whose creams and potions promise to wipe out our wrinkles and massage away our cellulite, to the fashion designers who have turned yesterday's size ten into today's size six so that 40-year-old women can delude themselves into believing they still wear the same size they wore in college,[8] to the media pundits who have recently taken to assuring us that sixty really isn't sixty anymore—the old and those who soon will be counted among them are big business, at least insofar as anti-aging products and services are concerned.

And if that isn't enough, the *New York Times* features a front-page article about the latest boon to the American entrepreneurial spirit:[9] a growing array of "brain health" programs on Internet sites, in "brain gyms," workshops, and fitness camps; an increasingly robust business in "brain healthy" food; and not least a Nintendo video game that, the instructions say, will "give your prefrontal cortex a workout." Speaking with the *Times* reporter, a spokeswoman for the American Society on Aging exclaims, "This is going to be one of the hottest topics in the next five years—it's going to be huge." Will any of it help you remember where you left your glasses, why you walked into your bedroom, or the storyline in the film you saw a few days ago? "That's the challenge," she adds. "How much science is there behind this?"

In a searing article published in the *New England Journal of Medicine*, Kate Scannell, a practicing geriatrician, decries the denial of aging that dominates our culture and argues that our refusal to accept the fact that "old age isn't just a state of mind but also a state of the body" has created a "compelling mythic structure" that not only obscures reality but is a great disservice to all of us, not just the old.[10]

"We are regularly consumed with commercial messages that promote an experience of aging that is far more possible on billboards than in the three-dimensional lives of most elderly people," Dr. Scannell writes, as she tells the story of a seventy-six-year-old woman who came to see her complaining that she could no longer do her usual advanced set of yoga poses without discomfort. When Dr. Scannell explained to her that "losing elasticity and flexibility with aging was a natural and regularly observed human phenomenon," the patient refused to accept the idea and insisted instead that the doctor do something. "'Well, just because that happens doesn't mean that it's healthy or inevitable, right?' she demanded. 'It's a physical process, so there must be a supplement or hormone or something physical I can take to counteract it.'"

"Our culture's compulsive spinning of old age into gold," Dr. Scannell concludes, "can inflict psychospiritual harm when it lures people into expecting a perpetually gilded existence, with an infomercial alchemist available at every rough and turbulent bend in the road to provide correctives that keep our lives shiny." And, I might add, it hinders the development of badly needed social policies that would benefit the growing ranks of the aged. If, after all, getting old is something we can avoid, then it's not social policy that's needed to ease the problems of old age, it's personal responsibility.

In the last week alone I've read two articles, heard one radio program, and watched a TV show all proclaiming that sixty is the new forty and eighty the new sixty. Any minute I'm expecting someone out there to be redefining one hundred as advanced middle age.

Granted, given that the subject occupies my mind these days, I'm more likely than most to be tuned to it and notice every mention. But apparently it's hard for anyone to miss. An eighty-year-old friend whose body is showing serious signs of age reported with a bitter laugh that her son called one day to cheer her up with the news that he'd been watching television and heard some self-proclaimed expert talking about "the new old age."

"Can you believe it?" my friend asked. "My 56-year-old son who should know better just by looking at me these days called to tell me that 80 is the new 60. And I think he believes it." She paused for a moment, sighed, then, "I was so irritated I wanted to hang up on him, then I thought, well, I guess he really needs to believe for him it will be different."

Where do these people live? I wonder. *On what planet?* It's certainly true that despite all the angst about graying hair, receding hairlines, expanding waistlines, sagging muscles, and failing memory, older is getting younger all the time. But sixty as the new forty?

Tell it to the fifty-five-year-old I had dinner with last night who complained that he'd had to stop running because his knees have given out.

Tell it to my friend who was looking forward to celebrating her sixtieth birthday until she got "a wakeup call" (her words, not mine) when the pain in her back was diagnosed as a degenerative disease.

Tell it to the sixty-three-year-old who, when she heard the phrase, said bitterly, "Yeah, well two good friends died recently, and that didn't happen when I was forty."

Tell it to the fifty-nine-year-old who told me how startled he was when, during a conversation about aging, his dinner companion reassured him that they needn't worry about coming up on sixty. "I couldn't believe this intelligent woman really thinks that sixty is the new forty," he exclaimed. "I'd never heard it said before, and I thought she was kidding. I actually laughed, but she was really serious. I mean, sure, I know that sixty isn't what it used to be. I still have plenty of energy—well, maybe not as much as I used to have, but it's still plenty, and I can work as hard as I ever did. But it sure as hell isn't forty. At forty I didn't have the pain that's with me most of the time now. And if my body didn't remind me that I'm closing in on sixty, the mirror does. When I see my weathered-looking face with all its wrinkles and sags, I don't have any illusion that sixty is anything but sixty. It's different now, probably better than ever before, but still sixty."

Never mind reality; it doesn't sell. Instead we get fantasy talk about sixty as the new forty and glossy tributes to the blessings of aging. "Age has given me what I've been looking for my entire life—it gave me *me,*" exclaims the writer Anne Lamott. "It provided the time and experience and failures and triumphs and friends who helped me step into the shape that had been waiting for me all my life."

Would she give it up for thinner thighs or a flatter belly? On her bad days, perhaps, but mostly her answer is: "Are you crazy?"

Sounds great, no? Who can argue with the experience of growing into a self you like and respect? Who would say it isn't one of the gifts of getting older? But she was forty-nine when she wrote those words, middle-aged by today's definition, and coming to terms with oneself is what that life stage is all about. As I write today, a forty-nine-year-old can expect to inhabit this middle stage for the next fifteen or twenty years and, if she's lucky, healthy, and open to the experience, these can be vital, growing years.

But then comes "the new old age" when Ms. Lamott and her peers will confront the next twenty or thirty years and giving up thinner thighs is the least of their worries. "Every one of my friends loves being older," she enthuses. "My Aunt Gertrude is eighty-five and leaves us behind in the dust when we hike." Maybe so, but I wonder how Aunt Gertrude feels when she goes home alone to nurse her sore muscles, eat her solitary dinner, and count up the losses that lie next to the pleasure of the hike.

It's time for something more, something besides our fantasies and denials, something besides the one-sided media representations about all the ways of being old that are supposedly open to us now: the seventy-six-year-old who runs the Boston marathon in respectable time, the eighty-five-year-old who plays a mean game of tennis every day, the former president who parachutes from a plane to celebrate his eightieth birthday, the eighty-one-year-old who climbs El Capitan in Yosemite, the ninety-two-year-old who still has an eye for the women and the wherewithal to do something about it, the eighty-two-year-old who sells her first painting.

I know these possibilities. I am the eighty-two-year-old who sold that painting. And I know the complex of feeling and fear that drives people to such adventures in their old age, the deep-seated need for something to give meaning to a life, the illusion that if we climb one more mountain we can control not just life but death as well.

Like Aunt Gertrude, I love it when I can match or best a younger companion in the outdoors, or when I see some fifty-year-old huffing and puffing on his treadmill at the gym when I haven't broken a real sweat. But these are transient moments of triumph that live next to the more permanent realizations about the diminishing self that old age brings.

This isn't to say that the heroic feats of the old don't deserve celebration, that they aren't useful in offering up an image of what may be possible. But while we applaud, it's well to remember that it's the rare person at any age, let alone old age, who has the will or the wherewithal—whether internal resources or financial freedom—to even think about climbing mountains and jumping from planes.

What's more, when the media turn their attention to other excitements and our fifteen minutes of fame has passed, we're left alone to contemplate the reality that, no matter how inspiring the accomplishment, no matter how much notice it gets, having achieved the goal, we still face the question that haunts all of us who are confronting a very long old age: "Now what?"

Yes, "Now what?" That's the big question no one is asking. What if those scientists working in their labs actually find the key to the fountain of youth? What if we could live to 125? How will we live those years? What will we do with them? What will sustain us—emotionally, economically, physically, spiritually? Who will we become? These, not just whether the old will break the Social Security bank, are the central questions about aging in our time.

NOTES

1. Ken Dychtwald, *Age Power: How the 21st Century Will Be Ruled by the New Old* (New York: Tarcher/Putnam, 2000).

2. Ken Dychtwald and Daniel J. Kaldec, *The Power Years: A User's Guide to the Rest of Your Life* (Hoboken, NJ: John Wiley & Sons, 2005).

3. James Barron and Anemona Hartocollis, "As Mrs. Astor Slips, the Grandson Blames the Son," *New York Times,* July 27, 2006.

4. M. S. Lachs and K. Pillemer, "Elder Abuse," *Lancet* 364, no. 9441 (October 2, 2004): 1263–1272.

5. Richard Posner, *Aging and Old Age* (Chicago: University of Chicago Press, 1995), 202–203.

6. U.S. Census Bureau, "Older Americans Month Celebrated in May," *Facts for Features* CB05-FF/07-2 (April 25, 2005).

7. Anti-aging has become such big business that, in just a few years, the academy's membership has grown from a few hundred physicians to the 17,000 they now claim. And they are not alone. Dr. Allen Mintz, chief medical officer and CEO of the Cenegenics Medical Institute, claims to have developed a protocol that guarantees a new kind of aging. For $1,000 a month or more, doctors associated with the Institute provide treatment that includes the injection of performance-enhancing drugs, some of them illegal except under clearly specified conditions, like testosterone, human growth hormone, and dehydroepi-androsterone (DHEA)—all substances that can get athletes banned from their sport.

8. Stanley Tucci's character in the 2006 film *The Devil Wears Prada* strips away the young assistant's pride in her size six with an acid-tongued reminder that "six is the old four-teen." Vanity sizing of women's clothes isn't just a throw-away line in a film. While American women are getting heavier—on average weighing about 155 pounds and five feet four inches—sizes continue to dip, so much so that Banana Republic now offers size 00 (probably formerly size 2 or 4), and other designers have introduced a size called "subzero."

9. Pam Belluck, "As Minds Age, What's Next? Brain Calisthenics," *New York Times,* December 27, 2006.

10. Kate Scannell, "An Aging Un-American," *New England Journal of Medicine* 355, no. 14 (October 5, 2006): 1415–1417.

PART IV
POLITICAL
PERSPECTIVES

Why Don't They Listen to Us?

While the intensity of political polarization that grips the nation today is relatively new, America has been drifting to the right for decades.[1] Since the assassination of John F. Kennedy in 1963, only three Democrats have occupied the White House and, of those, Bill Clinton alone survived for more than a single term. Although poll data show that most voters think the Democrats are better on such central issues as the economy, jobs, health care, and education, they continue to return Republicans to power. Republicans now occupy the governors' mansions in twenty-eight states and own both the House and Senate, where leadership has been increasingly drawn from the radical right.

With the untimely death of Senator Paul Wellstone, we lost the most consistently progressive voice in either house of the United States Congress. If our ideas and our politics have been in the service of those less advantaged, as we believe so passionately, why have we had such a hard time making ourselves heard in ways that count? How did our voice (the voice of economic opportunity, the voice of heart that speaks of justice and equity in education, jobs, health care, taxation) find so little resonance with the very Americans for whom we claim to speak?

In his intriguing book, *What's the Matter with Kansas?* (New York: Metropolitan Books, 2004), Thomas Frank argues that culture now trumps economics in the political sphere and offers as explanation yet another, if more sophisticated, version of false consciousness. "People getting their fundamental interests wrong is what American political life is all about," he writes on the very first page of his book. "This species of derangement is the bedrock of our civic order; it is the foundation on which all else rests" (p. 1). American politics is, he insists, "a panorama of madness and delusion worthy of Hieronymous Bosch: of sturdy blue-collar patriots reciting the Pledge while they strangle their own life chances; of small farmers proudly voting themselves off the land; of devoted family men carefully seeing to it that their children will never be able to afford college or proper health care, of working-class guys in Midwestern cities cheering as they deliver up a landslide for a candidate whose policies will end their way of life" (p. 10).

This is heady, angry stuff, words that make me want to cheer and weep at the same time. And in his description of the facts, he's right. But there's a kind of contempt underlying the passion of Frank's words, a dismissive shrug, an "it's-hard-to-believe-anyone-could-be-that-blind-and-stupid" dimension that fails to give any credibility or rationality to the behavior he so accurately describes, as if it comes out of some kind of conservative and/or media smoke and mirrors rather than anything in personal experience.

Let me be clear: I don't take a backseat to anyone in my anger at the right, especially the radical religious right and its neocon partners. Their ideological inflexibility, the way they manipulate the facts to fit their preconceptions and sell their falsehoods to the American public, is both outrageous and frightening. But my concern here is to examine the political behavior of the millions of other Americans—those working-class and lower-middle-class women and men who are not driven by ideological rigor, who are not convinced that they speak the word of God, yet who listen appreciatively to the Rush Limbaughs, Sean Hannitys, and Bill O'Reillys as they rail against us as "liberal elites" who have lost touch with the people, and who went to the polls in our recent presidential election and voted accordingly. Why do they subscribe to a politics that in Thomas Frank's words, "strangles their own life chances"?

True, the right has had more money and is better organized than we are. True, they spent the last few decades setting up right-wing think tanks whose sole purpose was to turn out millions of words in support of their ideology, while we assumed we would prevail because we stood for the economic interests of the little guy against the rich and privileged. True, they see black and white, while we see a world shaded in grays, which is a much harder sell, especially when people are feeling a need for certainty in what has become a very uncertain world. True, also, there are larger geopolitical forces that operate without regard to anything we do or don't do.

These are, indeed, formidable barriers to communicating with those whom progressives think of as their natural constituency. But none of it explains how blue-collar, working-class America, traditionally a Democratic stronghold, transmuted into Richard Nixon's "silent majority" and from there into "Reagan Democrats," setting the stage for the Republican Party and its corporate constituency to dominate the political arena in the coming decades. Why, in the face of exploding deficits, a war that has become increasingly unpopular, a three-year recession, millions of jobs lost and not replaced, a public education system that's a national disgrace, prescription drugs made by American manufacturers that cost half or less in neighboring Canada, and a health care system that's the most expensive in the world yet fails to provide the most elementary care for tens of millions of Americans, why—when we're on the people's side of all these issues—don't they listen to us?

But, one might ask, who is the "we" of whom I speak? It's a legitimate question, one I've asked myself as well, since there is no easily identifiable left, no progressive group that can claim to speak for the variety of people and positions that lay title to the left side of the political spectrum, no "we" that speaks with the kind of authoritative and unified voice we hear from the conservative right. Not since the heyday of the American Communist Party whose adherents spoke with the kind of on-message discipline we now see among right wing conservatives has any group or organization on the left been able to enforce that kind of control. Even the antiwar movement, the closest thing we have to a movement capable of mobilizing tens of thousands of people to action, is an amalgam of individuals and groups whose politics range from liberal Democrats to the various shades of the fractious left.

Nevertheless, there is a more or less unified sensibility among these people and groups who form the "we" I refer to. They are dominantly well-educated urban folk who find common ground on political issues—most importantly on the war, but on economic and social policy issues like social security, Medicare, Medicaid, poverty, gun control, civil liberties, and civil rights, as well as on the lifestyle and cultural issues that have roiled American politics so deeply: abortion, gay rights, the role of religion in public life, divorce, family values, stem cell research, the very meaning of life itself, to name a few. And while the academy may not be the hotbed of left politics the right portrays it to be, liberal and progressive social scientists from universities around the country have increasingly sought to become public intellectuals, part of the march of pundits across our television screens and the pages of our daily newspapers, in the service of defending against the right's onslaught in the culture wars.

Yet our voices rarely rise above a whisper in the public consciousness. Why have we had such a hard time making ourselves heard?

The question inevitably takes us back to the history and unfinished business of the last several decades, to the enormous upheavals in the social-cultural makeup of the nation that started with the Civil Rights Movement in the late 1950s, was followed by the various liberation movements of the sixties and seventies—sexual, feminist, gay—and culminated in a cultural revolution that challenged nearly every aspect of established American life, including the way we looked, dressed, and behaved in public. Blacks, who before had been consigned to the back of the bus, were suddenly in contention for white jobs, especially white working-class jobs. Women's traditional roles, whether in the family or in the larger world, gave way before the intense scrutiny and protest of the feminist movement, while men looked on in bewilderment and anger. The codes that had for so long guided sexual behavior, at least the public face of it, fell before the onslaught. Homosexuals, alien others reviled as queers and faggots, turned out to be our own children, who leaped out of the closet demanding acceptance. All of it leavened, if not sparked, by a massive disillusion with a government that, using various tactics ranging from dissimulation to outright deception, continued to escalate the war in Vietnam, which, even with the sacrifice of nearly 60,000 American lives, we couldn't win.

For those who saw the events in a positive frame, these were at best liberation movements, at worst eruptions of youthful exuberance, with perhaps a touch of excess. For the others—the silent majority of the Nixon era, the blue-collar Republicans of the Reagan years, and not least, the growing number of evangelical Protestants—these changes were at best disconcerting and somewhat alarming, at worst shocking violations of the moral order, of the laws of God and nature, the twentieth-century version of Sodom and Gomorrah.

It was the perfect political moment for the conservatives, who since the defeat of Barry Goldwater in 1964 had felt victimized by the "liberal media" and isolated from the political mainstream, to step in as the voice of the people, the voice that echoed their anxieties about the pace of change and called for a return to God, morality, and family values. The airwaves bloomed with a host of personalities dedicated to getting the message out, men like Rush Limbaugh who gave voice to white male rage about women's changing roles by railing about "feminazis"; and women like Laura Schlesinger, the physiologist turned talk show therapist, who lamented the abdication of character in modern life, talked about God's laws as if they had been handed down to her personally, and advised the troubled souls foolish enough to call to shape up and stop whining.

As the movement grew, it gave birth to a stable of pundits and policy analysts who write for such periodicals as *Commentary, Policy Review, The American Spectator,* and *The Weekly Standard* and make the rounds of the cable news networks and Sunday morning talk shows. At the same time, conservative money poured into organizations such as the American Enterprise Institute, the Heritage Foundation, and the Project for the New American Century, think tanks that supported a group of right-wing writers whose job was to stir the anger and fear people felt into a stew that would boil over and scorch what they called the "liberal elite," each generation becoming more vitriolic until we now have Ann Coulter, who accuses liberals of treason. Before long they had framed the debate, and the initiative was theirs. (See George Lakoff, "Framing the Dems," *American Prospect* 14, no. 8 [September 1, 2003].)

The intensity of the right's reaction, the wholesale condemnation, the moral certainty with which it was expressed, predictably led to a counterreaction on the left, although interestingly, apart from Michael Moore and Al Franken, there haven't been nearly as many easily identifiable national personalities. As the attacks from the right escalated, liberals and progressives found themselves on the defensive, and their positions, too, hardened. Pretty soon both sides had drawn a politically correct line behind which they hunkered down—a wall that, while not made of bricks and mortar, would soon separate us as completely as the Berlin wall did the two Germanys.

I say "both sides" because it's true. But here I'm not concerned with them; I want to talk about us, about how we promulgated and enforced a politically correct line on a series of key social-cultural issues that played into right-wing charges that we were out of touch and helped to consolidate our virtual isolation from America's lower-middle and working class.

Enforced! I can almost hear the astonishment as some readers ask derisively, "Who are the enforcers? Have progressives jailed anyone for being politically incorrect?" No, of course not. But if there were no pressure to remain silent, how do we explain the many times we sat at meetings wanting to dissent but didn't for fear of being politically incorrect? Or the times we wished for a fuller, more nuanced discussion of the subject at hand but stilled our thoughts because we knew they would be unacceptable, that our commitment to the cause would be questioned?

It's possible to dismiss the idea of coercion in voluntary associations only if we don't take seriously the human need to feel a part of a community, especially in difficult and contentious times. When we feel under siege, as we have increasingly in recent years, there's an impulse to pull together, to tighten bonds, to take comfort and affirmation in the presence of others like ourselves. This is "our community"—colleagues, friends, comrades with whom we share a world that frames our lives. To speak out against the "party line" is to set ourselves up as an outsider and risk being excluded. Or if not wholly excluded, sent to the periphery, someone who suddenly becomes the "other," not out perhaps, but not quite in.

Unfortunately, our silence creates emotional and intellectual conflicts that can be costly both personally and politically, as I found out a decade ago when I published *Families on the Fault Line* (New York: HarperCollins, 1994), a book about working-class families. Some readers of an early draft of that work criticized my use of the word *black* (the designation almost all the people I spoke with used to identify themselves) instead of *African American,* which was then the politically correct term. Others questioned the fact that I referred to *illegals* (the word used by every Latino I spoke with) instead of the newly minted *undocumented workers.* And still others told me I should "push the delete button" on my computer before going public with my doubts about the efficacy of bilingual programs, even though these were also the concerns voiced by many of the Latino and Asian families I interviewed.

I struggled with these criticisms, fought silently with my critics and myself, and finally decided to write about the intellectual and emotional dilemmas they posed. In the final version of the book, therefore, I recounted the criticism and mused aloud about the constraints of needing to be politically correct (p. xii). What obligation, I asked myself, do I have to honor my respondents' definition of self and their opinions on some of the red flag issues of the day? What responsibility to the political subtleties of the time? To my own political convictions? How do I write what my research told me was a true picture of the lives I wanted to portray and not give aid and comfort to right-wing bigots?

I leave it to others to decide how successfully I answered those questions. What I know is that going public about the problems raised by the need to be politically correct didn't endear me to my critics and left wounds that didn't heal easily.

A caveat here: I understand the impulse to keep our differences to ourselves and to vet the work we put into the public arena for fear that our words will be distorted to serve the agenda of the right. But I also know that, no matter how carefully we say our piece, we cannot protect ourselves or control the way our ideas are used—or abused. I learned that lesson firsthand when I published *The Transcendent Child* (New York: Basic Books, 1996), a book that examines how and why, despite living in families where poverty, neglect, and abuse were commonplace, some children manage to become functional adults while others, often in the same family, do not. The theory I developed to answer the question sets forth a complex of psychological qualities and social conditions that make it possible for some people to transcend a problem-filled past and develop flourishing adult lives. Not a word to cast blame on those who don't, not a syllable to suggest that their plight is due to their own failing, or because they're stupid, lazy, or unwilling to pull themselves up by their bootstraps. Yet within weeks of publication, I became the darling of right-wing radio talk shows whose hosts insisted that this was my message, even shouting me down when I argued that it was not.

These real concerns notwithstanding, the consolidation of power by the political right in these recent years has convinced me that by insisting on political correctness, we not only have played a part in impoverishing the national discourse but, in doing so, we helped to marginalize ourselves politically and lost what should have been our natural constituency. Our belief that we had to hold the line lest it crumble completely, our fear that in granting any legitimacy at all to the pervasive cultural anxiety of the time we would give fuel to the enemy, led us to take positions on many issues that damaged our credibility with a considerable portion of the American public.

Let's go back, for example, to the 1960s and 1970s when the sexual, gender, and cultural revolutions were roiling the American society. In each of these struggles, there was both hope and danger. The Pill and the sexual revolution that followed promised important breakthroughs in women's ability to express their sexuality more freely and openly. But as with all revolutions, there were excesses and unintended consequences, among them the shift downward to younger and younger ages, until some among us were defending the right of fourteen-year-olds to be sexually active while most remained silent.

I'm not suggesting that we should have joined the right in arguing against sex education in the schools in favor of an "abstinence only" position. Even if I believed in it, common sense tells me it wouldn't have worked in the highly sexualized society in which our teenagers live. But surely we could have spoken up publicly and agreed with thoughtful and frightened parents that most fourteen-year-olds are too immature, too prone to give way to peer pressure to make an informed consent decision about sex. Never mind the argument that fourteen-year-olds in Samoa or some other island paradise manage their sexuality quite well. American kids generally do not, as witness the number of unwanted pregnancies, as well as the many stories I've heard from teenage girls about the role of peer pressure in their "decision" to become sexually active (*Erotic Wars: What Happened to the Sexual Revolution?*).

Move up a couple of decades to the 1980s when "crime in the streets" was the biggest issue in American politics. While the right argued for more police, for tougher sentences, for trying juveniles as adults, we insisted that racism and overheated media coverage were at the core of the furor, that the perception of crime didn't match the reality and, with as much fanfare as we could muster, presented statistics to prove the point. It struck me even then that we were mistaken to try to reorder perceptions with facts, partly because we failed to take account of the psychological reality that experience overwhelms statistics no matter how compelling the numbers may be, but also because the perception of crime wasn't totally illusory.

Not that there wasn't truth in our side of the argument; it just wasn't the whole truth. I believe unequivocally that racist assumptions are built into the American psyche but, in this case, they were fueled by the fact that a disproportionate number of street crimes were committed by young African Americans. The media were often irresponsible and always sensationalist in reporting crime, but they didn't make it up. Crime *was* on the rise; the streets in urban communities *had* become more dangerous; and, while most people were never themselves mugged, it was enough to know someone who had been—whether a personal acquaintance or a victim encountered on the eleven o'clock news—to create the kind of fear for personal safety that was so prominent during those years.

Back then there was a saying that "a conservative is a liberal who got mugged on his way to the subway." When I first heard it, I was outraged by those flip words; now it seems to me that they weren't entirely wrong. So today I wonder if a conservative isn't a working-class guy who heard the "liberal elite" (as the right has effectively labeled us) tell him he had nothing to fear when experience told him otherwise—not just on crime but on a whole slew of issues that have turned the nation into a cultural and political battlefield.

Take the family values debate. While the events of these last decades left most Americans worried about their families and longing for a return to what felt like a less tumultuous past, feminist writers told them it was all nostalgia, that the families they remembered never existed. We weren't totally wrong, but anyone who lived through those earlier times, as I did, knows also that we weren't wholly right.

Yes, the image some now hold of the family of the fifties is part fantasy, but the reality was also a time of relative quiet in family life. Yes, if the families the right celebrates had been so perfect, they wouldn't have given birth to the revolutionaries of the sixties, who among other causes, wanted to smash the family as they knew it. Nor would the divorce rate have soared as soon as women became more economically self-sufficient. Yes, in those allegedly halcyon days many women awakened every day with what Betty Friedan so aptly labeled the "problem that has no name," but those same women also found a certain amount of gratification and safety in their families. And even those who were actively discontent (and I was among them) didn't recognize their families as the oppressively hierarchical patriarchal institution feminist scholars were describing. Yes, there was much to celebrate as feminists led the way in opening the doors of the occupational world and women gratefully flooded through. But there were also legitimate questions about what happens to children when both parents work full-time, which we preferred not to talk about. Yes, most Americans agreed that divorce was a reasonable option when it became too hard for wives and husbands to live together no matter what the reasons, but that didn't mean they were ready to crush the institution of marriage itself. I have no brief for those writers who bemoan divorce and warn us that our children will be damaged forever, but our refusal to see and discuss the pitfalls in divorce for everyone in the family, fathers included, was another of those politically correct blind spots that distanced us from people we wanted to reach.

Even on abortion, that most contentious issue of all in the culture wars,[2] we missed opportunities to build alliances. Not with the hard-core right-to-lifers, to be sure, but with the majority of women and men who might agree on a woman's right to choose, but not a child's. Our reasons for standing against legislation that required a parent to be notified before granting an abortion to a teenager (some parents would force a decision on an unwilling child, others would be abusive) weren't all wrong. But they weren't all right, either. It is, after all, in the nature of the parent-child relationship that parents impose decisions about things large and small on their sometimes unwilling children. True, the abortion decision is larger than most, and a girl forced to continue a pregnancy faces consequences that will affect not only the rest of her life but the life of the child she will bear. Nevertheless, our refusal to acknowledge the real dilemmas inherent in how and when to draw the line between parental authority and responsibility and an adolescent child's rights left us more isolated than we should have been on abortion, especially when most Americans at the time favored our side of the abortion debate.

Whether on welfare, race, or identity politics, we kept silent when we might have built bridges. We resisted talking about the role of Aid to Families with Dependent Children (AFDC) in the rising rate of illegitimacy in the African American community and called those who did racist. I don't say this as an advocate for the Clinton welfare reform program, which has its own serious deficiencies: not enough effective job-training programs, no adequate child care to allow a mother to work in peace even if she finds a job, and perhaps worst of all, no guarantee that she will keep the health care her family was entitled to under the Medicaid program for the poor once she has a job. My argument is simply that our opposition to the reform of AFDC, even after it became clear that its unintended consequences had created a whole new set of social problems, left us with little influence either with policy makers or the general public in the debate about how to change it.

On race, too, we failed to speak out at crucial moments and to face up to self-evident truths. For decades the left has argued that the antisocial behavior of significant numbers of African American youth (dropping out of school, getting pregnant, gang behavior, drugs) is a direct result of the painful realities under which they live and the hopelessness and helplessness their plight generates. Once again, we're not wrong, but we're not wholly right either.

No doubt the prospects of African American youth have been seriously affected by massive neglect of our public school systems, very high levels of unemployment, crushing poverty, police practices that criminalize behavior that's treated like a boyish prank in white suburbs, and a long history of prejudice and discrimination. But as William Julius Wilson, a Harvard scholar who can't by any stretch be called an apologist for the right's view on race, argues, there are also behavioral causes of black poverty—decisions and choices that are not the inevitable result of social constraints but of an amalgam of culture and personal behavior that is destructive to both the individual and the community. To believe otherwise is to strip an entire population of any agency and to treat them as if they were as helpless to influence the direction of their lives as leaves tossed about in a hurricane. Well meaning, perhaps, but ultimately condescending.

As was the huge flap that arose recently, mostly among whites, when Bill Cosby scolded black parents for their failure to parent and young people for their illiteracy and irresponsibility. The white liberal press, mainstream and Internet, huffed and puffed, white readers wrote letters of protest, and Barbara Ehrenreich published a stinging rebuke ("The New Cosby Kids," *New York Times,* July 8, 2004). A few weeks later, Barack Obama used his platform as keynote speaker at the Democratic convention to say much the same, albeit in language kinder and gentler than Cosby used. "[The] government alone can't teach kids to learn ..."

Obama said, "parents have to parent . . . children can't achieve unless we raise their expectations and eradicate the slander that says a black youth with a book is acting white." To which Harvard professor Henry Louis Gates, Jr., himself an African American, virtually shouted "Amen" while noting also that black Democratic delegates were "galvanized" by Obama's words. "Not just because they agreed, but because it was a home truth they'd seldom heard a politician say out loud" (*New York Times,* "Breaking the Silence," August 1, 2004).

As racial and identity politics became increasingly strident, we were right on economic issues but tone deaf to the cultural and emotional sources of white working-class fear and anger. They objected to what they saw as minority privilege, and we called them racist, which was probably true but did nothing to facilitate an alliance with them. I'm not saying that we should have backed away from our support of affirmative action, minority scholarships, and other attempts to level the playing field. And perhaps their rage and fear were so great that no bridge was possible. We'll never know because we couldn't hear their *cri de coeur.* Instead, we spoke from our own privileged position and tried to silence their resentment by reminding them that they were the beneficiaries of a long history of white privilege.

Certainly, if we consider privilege from the long view of history, whites of all classes have been (and still are) privileged when compared to African Americans and other people of color. But tell that to the white working-class people I studied, men and women who were struggling to pay the rent and put food on the table, and you'll get an earful about what that "privilege" feels like to them.

A decade ago I wrote about the emerging movement of European American clubs and warned that in these groups we could see "the outlines of things to come" (*Families on the Fault Line,* p. 191). The clubs themselves faded away but the consciousness of self as other, an idea that had been alien to whites of any class until identity politics came to dominate political life, took root and evolved into what we see today: America's white working and lower-middle class claiming for itself the status of another aggrieved group, only this time the largest in the land. And unlike earlier working-class movements of discontent, it isn't the bosses or the corporations or even the government that are the target of their anger, it's us, "the liberal elite."

This, then, is the political reality we face today—a reality that, as I've been arguing, we had a hand in creating. History, however, is useful only if we can take its lessons forward to a different future. But these aren't easy truths to take in, especially for a generation that cut its political teeth on the slogan of the 1960s: *If you're not part of the solution, you're part of the problem.*

Friends and colleagues who read earlier drafts of this article generally agreed that the insistence on being politically correct had hobbled discourse on the left and too often kept them silent. Yet they didn't see themselves as an active part of the problem. Instead, each one said something akin to "Yes, but not me." In silence, however, there is complicity, and each of us who failed to speak, or who complained *sotto voce* to some trusted friend, has been part of the problem.

It's time to break the silence.

There's much to do in the coming years to build a set of institutions that can begin to compete with the highly organized, enormously well-funded network of newspapers, periodicals, think tanks, publishing houses, and TV and radio stations the right already has in place. But no institutions will save us until we find the way to reframe the debate so that it's on our terms, not theirs. That means opening up discussion among ourselves to debate and develop positions and strategies that, while honoring our own beliefs and values, enable us to build bridges across which we can speak to those who now see us as an alien other.

It's not enough to speak in another voice, however. We must learn to listen as well, to develop a third ear so that we can hear beneath their rage the anguish it's covering up. Only then will we find our way into the hearts and minds of those Americans who have been seduced and exploited by the radical right into "strangling their own life chances." Only then will we be able to stop asking, "Why don't they listen to us?"

NOTES

1. This was written several months before the 2004 election. With the forces of the right now firmly in control of the federal government, it's more important than ever for liberals and progressives to take stock. I hope this article will provide the basis for one of the many thoughtful discussions that are now examining where we have been and where we can go from here.

2. Same-sex marriage has recently joined abortion at the top of the list.

What Am I Going to Do with the Rest of My Life?

In 1979, I published a book that had in it a chapter titled "What Am I Going to Do with the Rest of My Life?"[1] Then, I was writing about women who at forty found themselves facing a frighteningly empty future. As one woman put it: "Pretty much the whole of adult life was supposed to be around helping your husband and raising the children. I mean, I never thought about what happens to the rest of life. He doesn't need your help any more and the children are raised. Now what?"

Much has changed in the intervening decades. Then, most forty-year-old women had devoted themselves to being wife and mother, only to awaken to the realization that they no longer knew who they were beyond the confines of those roles. Now, the same women have most likely been in the labor force for years and, as a result, have some broader, less elusive sense of self. Now, instead of bearing her first child at nineteen or twenty, a woman is likely to be twenty-six, and for a significant subsection of the population, much older, maybe even forty.

In the mid-twentieth century, when American life expectancy hovered around sixty-five, questions about the "rest of life" presumed something like twenty more years, and it was mainly women who asked the question. Men knew what the rest of their lives would bring. If they were lucky enough to live that long, they'd work until retirement, then die shortly thereafter. Now, a man who reaches the age of sixty-five can expect to live into his early eighties, a woman even later.[2]

In fact, people over eighty-five now represent the fastest growing segment of our population. As we live longer, healthier lives, the question, "Now what?" comes later, for some at sixty, for others not until seventy or more. But no matter how delayed, the question will arise with the same inevitability that death itself arrives on our doorstep. Only now it isn't just women who ask the questions, it is men as well—men whose sense of identity is threatened as they contemplate years without connection to those institutions and activities that structured their daily lives and gave them meaning.

It makes no difference what our station is, whether high or low, we will all stand at the abyss as, by the very nature of living so long, we are forced to look into a future we cannot know and confront the combination of hope and fear that accompanies that reality. "I wouldn't know what else to do,"said Mike Wallace, the renowned television journalist, when, at eighty-eight, he was asked when he might leave the show at which he'd worked since 1968.[3] When, a short time later, he suddenly announced his retirement without explanation, his former producer, Don Hewitt, speaking partly from his own experience, explained, "You get to a certain age ... and you're not as gung-ho as you thought you were going to be. But you hang on to *who you were* [italics added] because you don't know any better." To *who you were,* not *what you do,* because, as is so often the case, what you do becomes who you are.

This is uncharted territory, a stage of life not seen before in human history. Where before twenty-five years on the job bought a gold watch, a retirement party, and not much time left to enjoy it, now you're wondering what you'll do, who you'll be, for the next twenty or thirty years. But it isn't only old age that's affected by a life that, like the Energizer bunny, just keeps going and going. This single demographic fact ricochets around the society like a shot fired in an echo chamber, undergirding the most important social and cultural changes of our time and revolutionizing the private sphere as well as the public one.

Throughout history the very concepts of childhood, adolescence, adulthood, and old age, and the cultural norms that accompany these stages of life, have been shaped, at least in part, by the length of the life span. When, in the seventeenth century, forty was advanced old age, there was little thought to the special needs of childhood, and the idea of adolescence didn't exist.

In our own time, we have seen extraordinary changes in the meaning of each of these life stages. Children, once valued as necessary contributors to the family economy, now are the cosseted, protected food for what Diane Ehrensaft calls "expectable parental narcissism,"[4] a phenomenon that has become "expectable" only in the last few decades. True, the worst excesses of these child rearing patterns are seen among upper middle-class families. But working-class parents, too, are more involved in their children's lives—more protective, more concerned about what they see, hear, and do, about their safety, their culture, their values, their future—than ever before.

Adolescence, once defined as a haven for children between thirteen and eighteen, continues to expand into the twenties and beyond. As the new economy has mandated more advanced training and skills, college now serves the function that high school once did. Consequently, about one-quarter of our young people have at least some college, which means that someone is paying the bill, whether through grants, loans, or parental beneficence. And that, in turn, means that post-teeners, who would have been working and self-supporting before, remain in a dependent, adolescent state for many more years.

As the boundaries of adolescence advance, the definition of adulthood changes as well. Until recently, marriage was the entry point into adulthood, a milestone people sought. That's no longer so. When people are living to eighty and beyond, the definition of adulthood becomes fluid and choices that were unavailable, even unthinkable, before suddenly come into view. There's no longer any social necessity to marry off people by their teens to ensure that they'll live long enough to launch the next generation. Nor is there any psychological imperative to rush into marriage when the years stretch so far ahead and when, at the same time, the privileges of adulthood that once went with marriage alone are now readily available to singles as well.

I don't mean that people consciously think these things. Rather it's axiomatic that cultures change in response to changing social conditions. The demographic reality of an era is inevitably reflected in the development—often without conscious plan—of new social norms and roles. As the content of socialization changes in the external world, the psychology of our internal world shifts as well. Suddenly, new and unseen possibilities about work, family, identity become visible and acceptable. If you can't get a decent job at a living wage, why not retain your identification with the youth culture as long as you can? If working for the rest of your life means doing the same thing for sixty years, maybe beginning later is a better idea anyway. If you're going to live to eighty, what's the rush about growing up, getting married, having children?

As the leading edge of the baby boomers—that huge cohort that has shaped everything it touched as it has swept through society—turns sixty this year, concerns about our increasingly aging population have come center stage. Predictions vary depending on the mind set of the predictor, on whether she/he sees the glass as half full or half empty.

The pessimists see disaster as they warn of the crises that lie in wait: The financial burdens on the social system will prove unsupportable. Medicare and Social Security will go broke. The economy will falter as the nonproductive old outnumber the productive young. The burden on families will be intolerable as sixty-five-year-olds find themselves the care givers for their eighty-five-year-old parents.[5]

Those who see a half-full glass tell us the worries are overblown. Sure, they say, the social institutions designed to ease the old age of earlier generations, whether health care, housing, or Social Security, are not adequate to deal with the huge aging population that looms ahead. But with the political will and sensible planning, the old programs will morph into new ones that will meet the realities of our continually expanding life span.

True, the optimists say, many sixty-five-year-olds are burdened with the care of their eighty-five-year-old parents, but sixty percent of people over eighty continue to live independently. Yes, between 1990 and 2050 the ratio of those over sixty-five to what we now call "the working-age population" will nearly double. But the working-age population is already being redefined upward, as witness the legislation outlawing age discrimination and the disappearance of mandatory age-based retirement in government and industry. With the promise of an aging population that is heartier, healthier, and better educated than ever before, it's reasonable to assume that increasing numbers will remain in the work force.

Maybe, maybe not, the pessimist might reply. Ask the 40 percent who are taking care of their aged parents, and you'll hear another tune. Indeed, even those whose parents live independently find themselves preoccupied with their welfare, calling more often, worrying about a future they know is coming. What's more, the idea of being on the job until eighty and beyond may appeal to a Supreme Court Justice or a world-famous television journalist, but is that what the average person, whose job is neither so important nor so glamorous, wants to do with these newfound years?

The answer is complicated. It's true that many of those who remain in the work force beyond what was once the accepted retirement age do so out of choice. These generally are the professionals, men and women who find satisfaction in their work and whose identity is tied to it. Many more, however, stay in the work force or return to it after retirement out of need, sometimes economic, sometimes psychological, often a combination of both.

The economic side is straightforward: Most pensions, when they exist, aren't adequate to support their needs; most people don't have enough savings to pick up the slack. Psychologically, it's more complicated. During their working years, most people look forward to retirement with fantasies about all the things they couldn't do when they were working, whether playing golf, remodeling the kitchen, or spending more time with the grandchildren. Then reality hits.

"Okay, so I pick my grandchildren up from school two days a week, but what about the rest of the time?" asked a seventy-four-year-old woman. "Sure, I keep busy, but that's just what it is—keeping busy. It doesn't have a lot of meaning, if you know what I mean."

"If I played golf every day, there'd still be too many days in the week," said one seventy-six-year-old. "I mean, I love it but … ," his words trailing off as if he were searching for a way to avoid the thought he didn't want to speak.

The pleasures they'd looked forward to are indeed pleasurable, but not quite enough to still the restlessness that sets in, the sense that there must be something more, or to quiet the question that asks so insistently: Now what?

Go to any mall in America that houses stores like Home Depot, Wal-Mart, Target, and all the other shops that eagerly hire older workers because they're so reliable, and you'll find formerly retired women and men on the floor, usually doing jobs well below their capacity. Talk to them, as I have, ask them why they're working, and nearly always the answer is some version of what this seventy-one-year-old former salesman said: "I'd been retired awhile, and I just couldn't take it any more. I woke up one morning and thought, 'What the hell am I doing with my life? Christ, if this is life, what's being dead like?'" Then, he added with an ironic smile, "The extra cash doesn't hurt either."

Whether optimist or pessimist, however, all agree that something new is emerging, something we might call the next life stage, the one that never existed before, the one for which we have no name and no template. For those who see a half-empty glass, the problems dominate the conversation. For those who see it half full, this "new old age" promises limitless options and opens possibilities earlier generations couldn't even dream about.

Maybe it takes someone who is already well into old age to know that both are true and that neither describe the complex social and psychological reality of this new stage of life.

Four decades ago most studies of old age posited something called "disengagement theory," whose basic assumption was that healthy aging required people to disengage from meaningful life activities. As people lived longer, healthier lives, it became clear that there was more than disengagement to these years, and the theory came under questioning. But as is true in many parts of American life, whether social or scientific, the new heedlessly sweeps out the old. Disengagement theory was discarded in favor of one that foresees a life of endless engagement—a new view of aging that's as one-sided as the old one was. For like everything else about old age (about life itself, in fact), it's not all or nothing, not disengagement or engagement, but both forces working inside us all the time. The pull of disengagement that feels like preparation for what is inevitably our future, a subtle pulling away, an inwardness that wants solitude and keeps us from entering the social world as fully as before. The push toward engagement that seeks to give meaning to the present while delaying the future, the wish to be seen, to be heard, to be counted, to be needed.

But instead of complexity, we get oversimple treatises about the wonders of the "new old age." It makes me think old age is two different countries. There's the real old age for those of us who live there and know its conflicts and contradictions. Then there's the old age of those who write about it, usually middle-aged women and men who, like a child who's afraid of the dark and keeps telling herself there's nothing to fear, draw rosy pictures as they try to convince themselves that no unknown monsters await them.

In a droll, smart essay, Anne Lamott writes eloquently about the blessings of aging. "Age has given me what I've been looking for my entire life—it gave me me. It provided the time and experience and failures and triumphs and friends who helped me step into the shape that had been waiting for me all my life." Would she give it up for thinner thighs or a flatter belly? On her bad days, perhaps, but mostly her answer is: "Are you crazy?"

Sounds great, no? Who can argue with the experience of growing into a self you like and respect? Who would say it isn't one of the gifts of getting older? But she was forty-nine when she wrote those words, middle-aged by today's definition, and coming to terms with oneself is what that life stage is all about. As I write today, a forty-nine-year-old can expect to inhabit this middle stage for the next twenty years or so and, if she's lucky, healthy, and open to the experience, these can be vital, growing years.

Sure, there will be losses in those middle years: The body sags, it hurts in places we didn't know we had, memory slips, friends die. But there will also be gains. At work, they have the satisfaction of a job well done whatever their status is at closing time. At home, their children are grown, probably married or partnered, and have their own children. They revel in grand parenthood, the pure pleasure of loving a child, of watching her grow, of seeing their own future, the continuity of their line for at least another generation in that child.

But then comes "the new old age" when they confront the next twenty years and giving up thinner thighs is the least of their worries. "Every one of my friends loves being older," Ms. Lamott enthuses. "My Aunt Gertrude is eighty-five and leaves us behind in the dust when we hike." Maybe so, but I wonder how Aunt Gertrude feels when she goes home alone to nurse her sore muscles, eat her solitary dinner, and count up her losses.

I love it when I can match or best a younger companion in the outdoors, when at the gym I look across at some fifty-year-old huffing and puffing on his treadmill and I haven't broken a real sweat. But these are transient moments of triumph that live next to the more permanent realizations about the diminishing self that old age brings.

The media give us endless stories about the new ways of being old that are now open to us—about the seventy-five-year-old who runs the Boston marathon in respectable time, the eighty-five-year-old who plays a mean game of tennis every day, the ninety-one-year-old who climbs El Capitan in Yosemite, another nonagenarian who still has an eye for the women and the wherewithal to do something about it, the eighty-two-year-old who sells her first painting.

I know these possibilities. I am, in fact, the eighty-two-year-old who sold that painting. But I also know the complex of feeling and fear that drives people to such adventures in their old age: the deep-seated need for something to give meaning to a life, the illusion that if we climb one more mountain we can control not just life but death as well. And I know, too, that while these are inspiring feats, worthy of note, having achieved the goal, we face yet again the question, "Now what?"

For most of us, even those who are healthy and active, our extended old age will most likely feel like some combination of blessing and curse. Certainly there are moments when we enjoy what feels like the "warm autumn" celebrated in a *New York Times Magazine* article entitled, "The Age Boom."[6] There's something to be said for being freed of responsibility, for waking up each day to the knowledge that you're not obliged to perform, for feeling you've earned the right to pick and choose what you'll do and whom you'll do it with, for having the time to read the novels you've hungered for but couldn't get to before, for having the emotional leisure to reflect on your life and the world around you in more depth than was possible when the demands of daily life kept you busy.

But these newfound freedoms come with a price. Ask anyone who is living this new life stage and you'll hear also about the times when it feels like a cold and lonely winter. For along with the gift of time comes the realization that time itself is now finite, that we hold the end always in our sights. It's a show stopper. A fifty-ish friend tells me he'd like us to join him and his family on a trip two years hence, and all I can think is: *If I'm here in two years.*

How do you plan for a future when you don't know when time will stop? That's true for all of us, of course, but for the old it has an immediacy that can't be denied. "There is not time to become anything else," laments Doris Grumbach. "There is barely enough time to finish being what it is you are."[7]

The limits of time, for me at least, are once again both a blessing and a curse. A blessing when I experience the relief that it will soon be over, that I can give up the struggle to make meaning of these years and just go to sleep, even that permanent sleep we call death. A curse because then I remember that when I die, I'll never again hear my daughter's "Hi, Mom" on the phone, never see my adorable four-year-old great-grandson grow up, never laugh or cry with a friend again, never see another sunset, never read another book, never write another line, never paint another picture, never wander through the galleries of the Met, never taste another hot fudge sundae. *Never:* a cold and lonely word.

It's not just the realization that we're close to the end that makes this time so difficult. For the pleasure in our newfound freedom to "just be" comes with the understanding that it's possible only because we've become superfluous, because we've lost our place in the world, because our presence is no longer needed, and that in addition to being unnecessary—or perhaps because of it—we've also become invisible, just another one of the old people, featureless and indistinguishable from one another, who take up space on the bus.

Invisible. "You know what I miss most as I get older? asked Mary Cantwell in a conversation with novelist Jean Rhys. "That look of anticipation in a man's eyes when he first meets you."

"Yes," sighed Ms. Rhys, then well over eighty and not far from death, "I miss it still."[8]

It's not just that we're no longer seen as desirable sexual partners. Rather invisibility follows us into many corners of life where we used to count, whether on the job or in the social world. "I'm a lot smarter today than I was thirty years ago, and I'm better at my job now than I was then," said a sixty-five-year-old executive who lost his job to one of those corporate mergers we know so well these days. "But these yo-yo kids who are in charge don't even see me and what I can do; they only see my age, and that's the end of it." A plight common enough to warrant a *New Yorker* cartoon featuring a cigar-smoking, bewildered-looking seventy-ish man looking out the window of the office he's about to leave for good and saying ruefully, "I think I've acquired some wisdom over the years, but there doesn't seem to be much demand for it."

How can it be otherwise in a society that idolizes youth, that has little reverence for its own history, that moves so quickly that yesterday's knowledge has already been rendered obsolete? In such a social setting, whatever wisdom about life we who are old have gathered seems like ancient history, not ... What's that word that has dominated our lives for the last several decades? Ah yes, "relevance." We're not relevant.

Until now we who are old were tethered to society through a series of institutions—school, work, family, church, community—that structured our lives, defined our place in the world, and gave shape to our identity. We had goals then, destinations to which we looked forward, things to accomplish, from raising the children to climbing the professional ladder, that gave life its meaning. But as Freud noted a long time ago, a strange thing happens with success. Instead of entering into that subjective state of grace we expected success to bring, we often become unsettled, feeling adrift, as if something has gone out of life.

Freud thought such feelings were a response to the guilt we experience over our good fortune. Perhaps so, but it surely isn't that simple. For this is one of those times when winning and losing are opposite sides of the same coin. We finally achieve a long-sought goal and instead of the unambiguous joy of winning, we feel something else, an emptiness where the goal lived, a sadness that suggests loss. After organizing our lives around the pursuit of a goal—raising the children, writing a book, getting tenure, a big promotion, winning the gold, actually or metaphorically—we find that it's not the destination that has given life its meaning and continuity but the journey itself.

This is the dilemma of the new old age. The journey continues, but to what end? If we discover ourselves at midlife, old age—yes, even the new old age—is when we lose what we found, when the vigorous, vital, growing, passionate self is replaced by something new. You look in the mirror and see a face that looks like you but isn't you. At least not the "you" you hold in memory. It's somewhat like running into an acquaintance you haven't seen in years, knowing that you knew her once, that there's still something familiar there, but not being able to place her in time, space, and memory.

The face falls, the body rebels—physical changes that are mirrored in the psychological shifts that age demands. It's the two together that are so hard to bear. The self we sought and fought for through our earlier years, the one we finally grew into, the one that defined us to ourselves and the world outside isn't exactly gone; it's turned into a pale shadow of what we once were. As a friend, age seventy-five, wrote me awhile ago, "I hate it when my body won't do today what was so easy yesterday. But I think the thing that troubles me most about my age is that the old passions have faded. Not just sexual passions but the passions for living as well, for walking the beach, for—I don't know what—for all the things I used to get passionate about— politics, eating, traveling, socializing, even friends. Only music remains. It's like there's someone else inhabiting my internal world, and I miss the old me terribly."

He's not living a life of the walking dead. He remains an active man, going to the gym every day, writing and publishing his work as he has for years, and, despite his lament, still taking pleasure in his family, his friends, his beloved dog. But the spark with which he once used to engage this life, that small, fiery light that was so much a part of him, is missing.

Yes, I know about the seventy-ish woman who put an ad in the *New York Times* seeking partners with whom to explore her sexuality. I've read all those articles and books about women who blossom, sexually and otherwise, in old age. I just don't know whom these writers are talking about. Not that such women don't exist. But to cast them as representative of women in old age (even in late middle age) is a travesty, the fantasy of those who have bought the cant that old age is *only* a state of mind, people who need to believe that they'll never be old and never die, and who want to impose those beliefs on the rest of us as a way of abating their own anxieties.

As for me, I read my friend's words, listen to him when we speak on the phone, feel his despair, and know that he speaks to my heart as well. But I know also that this is only one side, that in another part of me (him, too) I really don't want to engage the world in the same old way, that it's a blessing to be less driven, to be able to slow down, to be more contemplative, to bank the fires a bit. As Bill Moyers put it so eloquently in an article announcing his retirement two years ago, "You feel an irresistible urge to slow down, take your foot off the accelerator, touch it to the brake—gently, but surely—and start negotiating yourself out of the fast lane."[9]

Yes, I say to myself, I know just what he means. But again, there are shades of gray, as, judging by his continuing public presence, I suspect Mr. Moyers has discovered. I took myself out of the fast lane nearly three years ago and have no wish to go back. But that doesn't mean I don't still miss it. Not the speeding along, but the person who drove the car. She was the self I lived with for so long and knew so well. There's a hole inside me where she used to live, a hole I can't help probing, my mind wandering to it as if impelled by some unknown force as I mourn her loss.

I think of those lines from Tennyson's "Ulysses": *How dull it is to pause, to make an end / to rust unburnished, not to shine in use.* I know one doesn't have to rust unburnished, but it sometimes feels like that. Then I go to my studio, take brush to canvas, and watch a miracle in the making, a miracle I could never have known without the gift of time this new old age has brought.

As I stand before the easel feeling something very like joy, I grasp more fully than ever the duality of this time of life, the reality of both the pains and the pleasures, even while recognizing that the pain outweighs the pleasure too much of the time. But that's just the point. It's *some* of the time, not *all* of it.

Those of us who now live in this new old age are moving through unmapped terrain, searching for a path where few have gone before. No small task, but one well worth the doing, not just for ourselves but as part of the legacy we will bequeath to our children. We may not always like it, but what choice do we have? As an eighty-three-year-old friend who just wrote her first novel remarked, "There aren't a lot of options. We either sit on the railroad platform and watch enviously as the trains streak by, or climb aboard a dilapidated one that chugs along slowly, knowing that it could stop at any moment. But at least we're traveling."

NOTES

1. *Women of a Certain Age: The Midlife Search for Self* (New York: Harper & Row, 1979).

2. Race, class, and ethnicity play a part in determining life expectancy, with those in the white middle class being the most privileged in this as well as other aspects of their lives.

3. *New York Times,* March 15, 2006, 39–43.

4. *Spoiling Childhood* (New York: Guilford Press, 1999).

5. In an article entitled "As Parents Age, Baby Boomers and Business Struggle to Cope," Jane Gross reports that nationwide over 20 million people are dealing with ailing parents (*New York Times,* March 25, 2006).

6. Jack Rosenthal, March 9, 1997, 39–43.

7. *Extra Innings: A Memoir* (New York: Norton, 1995).

8. *New York Times Magazine* (March 9, 1997).

9. "Farewell to the Sixties" (*AlterNet,* March 17, 2004).

Race and Gender in Politics

Race and gender—hot topics, even without the recent primary election that pitted a black man against a white woman. With it, they're incendiary. But even a brief look at the historical record tells us how much the past is parent to the present. The conflicting claims of race and gender, the arguments about who has been this society's greatest victim, whose issues are most immediately in need of redress, have been going on for a long time, most notably dating back to the post–Civil War era when the suffragettes confronted the question: Do they support passage of the Fifteenth Amendment to the United States Constitution that would give black men the right to vote while leaving women out?

In language that reflected the heat of the issue, Elizabeth Cady Stanton, who had been a strong and consistent voice for the abolition of slavery, told her followers that it was "a serious question whether we had better stand aside and see 'Sambo' walk into the kingdom first." Further, she argued, women voters of "wealth, education, and refinement" were needed to counteract the effect of former slaves whose "pauperism, ignorance, and degradation" could prove a danger to the American political system.

A century later, when President Lyndon Johnson expanded an earlier affirmative action order to include women as well as men of color, women and blacks once again found themselves in competition for the jobs that were newly open to them. And now again, we've seen race and gender cross swords in the most passionately contested political primary campaign in history. For those of us for whom the causes of gender and racial equality are inextricably linked, it has meant difficult and often painful choices. No matter who won, we lost something.

Yet even as I write those words, a "yes, but …" springs to mind as I recall some of the struggles of the early years—what we felt then, how it looks now. I remember the outrage when the famous Virginia Slims cigarette ad appeared in the late 1960s. It featured a smiling—and of course beautiful—young woman smoking a cigarette and a tag line reading, "You've come a long way, baby."

Never mind that we who had been struggling for gender equality didn't think the right to kill ourselves with cigarette smoke was great progress; we weren't in the mood to celebrate because we didn't think we'd come nearly far enough. Now, looking back, I can see that there was a certain truth to the line. We *had* come a long way from where we started, just as the civil rights struggle brought important, if not fully realized, gains for black Americans. And it's even more true now than it was then.

It was only a little more than forty years ago—well within the living memory of many of us—that the United States Supreme Court declared the statutes banning mixed-race marriage (laws that had been on the books since 1661) unconstitutional. In that same decade, federal law, for the first time in history, prohibited discrimination in employment based on race and sex.

The gains in the courts and the legislatures notwithstanding, racism and sexism were rampant. Civil rights workers were murdered, black Americans were still being denied the right to vote (still are in some places), a married woman couldn't get a credit card in her own name, and even for the young male revolutionaries of the time, equality and justice didn't mean the women with whom they worked, studied, and slept. In one of the most shameful incidents of the time, women were jeered off the stage at the national convention of SDS with catcalls designed to keep them in their place, which, for the men, was on their backs, at the coffee machines, or ironing their shirts.

Four decades later, we witnessed the extraordinary, exhilarating—and yes, sometimes aggravating—spectacle of a black man and a white woman competing to carry the Democratic Party banner into the next presidential election. Yes, I know, four decades is a long time to wait, and for Hillary Clinton's supporters who dreamed of a woman in the White House next year, it has been maddening to find that the wait will be even longer.

We'll argue into eternity about just how much misogyny played a part in Clinton's defeat—how much the irrational hatred she generates in some quarters is related to sexism, how much to what I think of as "Hillaryism," and how much the product of an early misguided campaign strategy that leaned so heavily on the past. At the very moment when Americans—their economic, social, and cultural nerves rubbed raw by a half century of identity politics and nearly eight years of a failed and divisive administration—were yearning for a different future, the Clinton campaign kept asking them to look back.

Into that longing for something new, something that would bring back some sense of hope, of unity, something that would call to us to end the angry divisiveness and forge another way, stepped Barack Obama—a young, charismatic, biracial, post–baby boomer newcomer who spoke the language of change and sang a song that told us we were all one, and that together we could reach the mountaintop. In offering a vision of a people united by a shared identity and the common bonds that are our heritage, he mesmerized a nation.

However differently others may see and analyze the trajectory of these two campaigns, it seems undeniable that the role of race and gender in politics today is a far cry from the simple and brutal sexism and racism we knew in the past. So it's worth stepping back from the fray and widening the lens to ask: What impact have these two difficult and contentious areas of our social life had in this political season?

The answer, I think, is a lot and a little. Clinton's gender both helped and hindered her, just as race played a role in Obama's campaign for good and ill. It was gender that brought to Clinton large numbers of women who might well have been Obama supporters in a contest against a man. Race led equal numbers of blacks and many whites to Obama who surely would have been Clinton supporters against almost any white man. And it was both gender and race—the historic nature of this election and these candidates—that fostered the media attention (some might say "frenzy") that helped give both candidacies such immediacy.

This simple calculation is itself a big statement about how far we've come on the issues of race and gender. Certainly, gender and racial stereotypes are still with us and create real problems for those who would try to climb past the barriers put before them. But it also may not be too far off to suggest, as Geraldine Ferraro did rather clumsily about Barack Obama, that neither he nor Hillary Clinton would have been contenders if it weren't for their race and gender.

Would the progressive politics of John Edwards have gotten so little attention from Democrats if he hadn't been up against a white woman and a black man? We can blame the media for turning them into superstars and drowning out other voices, but that could only happen because of the electrifying reality that one of these two was the likely candidate of the Democratic Party.

It takes nothing from Obama's or Clinton's talents, or their qualifications to wear the mantle of the presidency well, to suggest that it wasn't just a contest between two people that drove worldwide interest in this election and brought to the polls the largest number of voters in the history of American primary campaigns. It was race and gender as embodied in these two particular people that generated the excitement. For they represented something new in American politics, something earlier generations never believed could happen—if, that is, they ever even thought about it—and they are, therefore, symbols who stand for something much larger than themselves.

Clinton and her supporters complained that the media were tougher on her than on Obama because the overt expression of sexism is more socially acceptable than racism—a charge that has some merit. The silence was deafening when someone from a right-wing, Clinton-hating organization asked John McCain, "How do we beat the bitch?" and he answered, "Excellent question!" It's safe to say that he wouldn't have dared reply so cavalierly to a similar question about Obama that used the "n-word." Indeed, it's likely that no matter what the questioner's feelings about the possibility of a black man as president, he wouldn't have spoken them with such ease and assurance that he would give no offense.

Such sexist episodes and comments are infuriating, and there's no excusing them. But it's also true that gender cut both ways in this election. Clinton herself brought gender front and center into her campaign, and neither she nor her staff or surrogates were shy about playing the gender card, whether in presenting herself as the gutsy, take-no-prisoners trailblazer fighting the cause of all women against great odds, or as a victim with complaints about sexist bias, whether in the media, on the debate stage, or about "the boys" who were "piling it on." We can argue about whether her complaints were valid, were pumped up to suit the politics of the moment, or both. But there's not much doubt that together these images served to stir the passions and outrage that brought women to her side.

In contrast, from the beginning Obama, mindful of the racial tensions awaiting a black man reaching for the presidency, emphasized his biracial background and quite consciously presented himself as a person who transcends racial categories. And it seemed momentarily possible that he could pull it off, that America was ready to make peace with its agonizing racial history. His race was rarely mentioned openly in the national media, not even after his surprise win in Iowa—one of the whitest states in the union.

But the subtext of race lay just below the surface, waiting to explode. As he piled up victory after victory, scurrilous racist sniping appeared all over the Web, the Clintons vented their anxiety about the unexpected threat he posed with subtle and not-so-subtle racial references, and a video of words taken from various sermons given by Obama's pastor, Jeremiah Wright, burst on the scene.

Suddenly, white racial anxieties rose from the ashes of hope. Never mind his white mother and grandparents; never mind his charismatic appeal or his own more complex biracial sense of identity. Barack Obama became a black man who tapped responses ranging from wariness to outright racial hostility—an effect that holds steady months later, with polls showing that somewhere around 20 percent of whites say that his skin color makes a difference in whether they can vote for him. And as it became increasingly clear that Obama would be the nominee, campaign staffers and surrogates began to report a rising rate of ugly racist incidents in the field, the word *assassination* was spoken aloud, and what was background became foreground as many Americans, white and black, found themselves living with the fear that a white bullet would stop him.

But the influence of race and racial definitions isn't limited to white sensibilities. In a book entitled *Shadows of Race and Class,* the author, Ray Franklin, argues that the respectable, educated, black middle class is forever "shadowed" by the dominant images of the behavior and stereotypes that define the black poor and underclass. That shadow, Franklin argues, follows blacks wherever they go as they're caught between their own black identity and their anxieties not to be seen as "them," those "others" who cast a shadow of discomfort, if not actual shame.

It's in this shadow, I believe, that we find some deeper understanding of Barack Obama's public presentation of self. For it's not only white racism that accounts for some of the difficulty he has had with white working-class voters, but his own internalized "shadow," his anxieties, not about who he is but about how he will be seen. After a lifetime of creating a public presence and identity that defy the stereotypic images of black men, he's caught between competing demands—the internal need to maintain the distance between himself and the shadow, and the political need to present himself as "everyman." The bind, then, is this: If he sticks with that public persona, as he has, he's characterized as an elitist, one who can't relate to ordinary people. If he softens the image, leaves behind his contained manner (some call it uptight or arrogant, but would it look like that if he were white?), and exchanges his $2,000 suit, crisp white shirt, and perfectly knotted tie for a more casual look, he risks becoming a reminder of those other black men, those guys who speak black English and before whom women clutch their purses more tightly to their sides.

This isn't just a problem for American blacks. It's the cost of wearing a stigmatized identity. The educated German Jews who immigrated in the mid-nineteenth century and assimilated fully into American culture found themselves shadowed and shamed by the presence later of the alien culture and behavior of large and visible numbers of Jewish immigrants from eastern Europe. For it's nearly inevitable that, when those of different race, ethnic, or religious backgrounds are stereotyped, it's the most visible that defines the entire group. So, if young black men commit crimes, or the 9/11 terrorists were Muslim, all blacks and all Muslims are tarred with the brush.

The same is true for women. None of us is wholly free from the shadows of the stereotypical images that have defined women for so long. It's at least partly why Hillary Clinton has such a hard time finding the balance between intellect and emotion, between the tough, hard-hitting fighter and the compassionate woman. She's stuck with women's classic double bind that, despite the gains of the last few decades, remains very much alive. If she fights like a man for what she wants, she's too fueled by raw ambition; if she doesn't, she's not strong enough to be commander in chief.

This, then, is one snapshot of our times and the complications and contradictions that infuse the issues of race and gender in politics today. Others may interpret it differently, but one thing is certain: Barack Obama and Hillary Clinton are the living embodiment of our success in conquering some of the worst aspects of gender and racial bias, while their campaigns—the fears, the biases, the anger, the prejudices they have evoked—remind us of what has yet to be done. Each side has some legitimate complaints, but together they have blazed a trail that will make it easier for those who will surely come after them.

Credits

"Sociological Research: The Subjective Dimension," *Symbolic Interaction* 4, no. 1 (Spring 1981). Copyright © JAI Press Inc. Reprinted by permission of the University of California Press.

"Family Values and the Invisible Working Class," from *Audacious Democracy: Labor, Intellectuals, and the Social Reconstruction of America,* edited by Steven Fraser and Joshua B. Freeman. Copyright © 1997 by Houghton Mifflin Company. Reprinted by permission of Houghton Mifflin Harcourt Publishing Company. All rights reserved.

"*Worlds of Pain* Revisited: 1972 to 1992," in *Worlds of Pain: Life in the Working-Class Family* (New York: BasicBooks, 1992). Copyright © 1992 Lillian Breslow Rubin. Reprinted by permission of BasicBooks, a member of Perseus Books Group.

"Is This a White Country, or What?" in *Families on the Fault Line: America's Working Class Speaks about the Family, the Economy, Race, and Ethnicity* (New York: Harper-Collins, 1994). Copyright © 1994 Lillian Breslow Rubin. Reprinted by permission of HarperCollins, Inc.

"The Approach-Avoidance Dance: Men, Women, and Intimacy," in *Intimate Strangers: Men and Women Together* (New York: Harper Perennial, 1983). Copyright © 1983 Lillian Breslow Rubin. Reprinted by permission of HarperCollins.

"Blue-Collar Marriage and the Sexual Revolution," in *Family in Transition: Rethinking Marriage, Sexuality, Childrearing, and Family Organization,* 6th ed., edited by Arlene S. Skolnick and Jerome H. Skolnick (Glenview, IL: Scott Foresman, 1989). Copyright © 1989 Lillian Breslow Rubin. Reprinted by permission of Scott Foresman.

"Sex and Sexuality: Women at Midlife," in *Women of a Certain Age: The Midlife Search for Self* (New York: Harper and Row). Copyright © 1979 Lillian Breslow Rubin. Reprinted with permission of Harper and Row.

"Out of the Closet," in *60 on Up: The Truth about Aging in America* (Boston: Beacon, 2007). Copyright © 2007 Lillian Breslow Rubin. Reprinted by permission of Beacon Press, Boston.

About the Editors

Michael S. Kimmel is Professor of Sociology at the State University of New York–Stony Brook. He recently coedited *The Jessie Bernard Reader* (Paradigm 2008).

Amy E. Traver is Assistant Professor of Sociology, Department of Social Sciences, City University of New York, Queensborough.